ᗪamned Deceptions

DAMNED
DECEPTIONS
The Cults In Light of Contract Law

Dennis Knotts

Strategic Book Publishing and Rights Co.

Strategic Book Publishing and Rights Co., LLC
USA | Singapore
www.sbpra.net

For information about special discounts for bulk purchases, please
contact Strategic Book Publishing and Rights Co. Special Sales, at
bookorder@sbpra.net.

ISBN: 978-1-948858-44-1

Book Design: Suzanne Kelly

Cover Design: Ronald G. Patterson

DEDICATION

To Pastor Harold Anderson, PhD. To Pastor Jack Clark.
And to Dave Melhuish for allowing me to teach our
School of Ministry sessions on the Cults.
Those sessions led to this book.
Thank you.

And a special thank you to the Late Dr. Walter Martin
who introduced me to Apologetics through
his class on the Cults so many years ago.
I pray you are enjoying your rewards in Heaven.

"And for this cause God shall send them strong delusion,
that they should believe a lie:
That they all might be damned who believed not the truth..."

(II Thessalonians 2:11–12)

TABLE OF CONTENTS

AUTHOR'S NOTE

All Scripture used in this book is what I call The *King James Version [simplified]*. You will not find this version on any website or in any bookstore. It is the original King James Version ordered published by King James. However, some people do not understand the King James Version of the Bible.

I could have chosen a Modern Translation Version to help you understand, but there are issues being raised by scholars even today that some Modern Translations have used different sources than the King James sources. In one case, a source was deliberately edited by the author because he did not believe that Jesus was divine; and so whole sections, teachings and events were intentionally omitted. These omissions have been proven to have been in the older, reliable translations. Therefore, given the great care and number of scholars who worked, checked and then double-checked the translations among themselves, the original King James Bible is probably our best, most accurate and most-tested translation available.

And so I used the original King James Bible, and being an English major I was able to change "*thees*" and "*thous*" into "*you*" without any real effort or great skill. Where a word had a different meaning at the time of King James, I have used the original meaning of the word and placed it inside of [brackets] so you know of the change. This way we have used the most correct translation, and I have made it easier to read.

No doctrines have been changed in this process.

The original teachings and meanings have been preserved.

A PRESENTATION OF CREDENTIALS

Allow me to take a moment to present my credentials. You would think that when dealing with a topic such as this, I would need to be an attorney with my own law practice. I am not. I am a lowly claims adjuster. More specific, I am a workers' compensation claims adjuster—or I was until I retired. I know; it's like being a publican or tax collector. We are not a popular profession, but it is the profession God placed me in for this very reason.

Given the topic, you will find that my occupation is a perfect training ground to become proficient in this area.

I have spent forty years in the insurance claims area as a claims adjuster. My initial training was with a multi-line/multi-state insurance company. Here the training and focus was on the insurance policy. An insurance policy is a contract; and, therefore, it falls under contract law. To put it simply, if it is not in the contract, then it is not covered.

One of the hardest parts of my job had to deal with that harsh reality. People had lost things of value. They were suffering. They needed help; but the harsh laws of contract law make it very clear that you do not do the *moral thing*. You do not do the *right thing*. As a claims adjuster we were mandated to do the *legal thing*. We had no authority to do anything else—no matter how much we wanted to. I struggled with this reality every day. The legal things were simple: if the kind of loss sustained was not listed in the insurance policy; then it was not covered.

When I began to actually handle claims, I moved over to workers' compensation claims. Most of my career was single line/single state coverage—specifically, California Workers' Compensation Insurance. Here all policies were identical throughout the state no matter which insurance company you worked for. Therefore, coverage was standard throughout the state. This forced me to study California Labor Codes as the California Labor Code made the decision as to whether or not something was covered. Again, if it was not covered by the Labor Code, then it was not covered.

Let me share a stage of my career, and how this prepared me to write this book. I entered the workers' compensation claims adjusting industry in the early 1980's. At that time, it was difficult to get good training to do my job. My training program was actually: "There's your desk" and "There's your files." All the training I had in contract law was no longer applicable to workers' compensation because for the work comp industry, every insurance company was required to offer identical insurance policies.

The real information about how and when to provide benefits now depended on a government standard called the California Labor Code. This book told us when something was covered and when it was not covered. This book told us what to pay and when to pay benefits. You needed to know the California Labor Code in order to do your job.

Big insurance companies did not offer training in workers' compensation because it differed from state to state. So national insurance companies had no training in how to calculate benefits or when to pay bills. Again, all that was in the California Labor Code, and it only applied to California. There was one agency, the Insurance Education Association, that offered five classes and a certificate in handling workers' compensation claims. At that time, that was all that was available.

When I had a question about a case, my supervisor would tell me to call this attorney, and then he would hand me a business card. I would call the attorney and he would say, "That's a good question. Send me the file, and I'll look into it."

If I had a medical question the supervisor would say, "Call this doctor." And then he would hand me a business card. I would call the doctor, and he would say, "That's a good question. Send the patient over to me to examine, and I'll get back to you."

If I had other questions, I was given other business cards of investigators and other services. I was sending everything out to others. They would call and tell me what to do. They were making all of my decisions for me, and I still had no idea what I was supposed to do. I was nothing more than a glorified clerk for these professionals. The entire workers' compensation industry at that time was on *"cruise control."*

I signed up for my first class with the Insurance Education Association [IEA]. It was basic work comp. I came back from the first class more confused than ever. I asked my supervisor, "What's this Labor Code they keep talking about?"

"We've got one around here somewhere." We searched for a few weeks and found the only copy in the office—again, this was a multi-million-dollar nationwide company. It was on the bookcase of a liability adjuster who had no idea what it was. It was several years old, but the supervisor told me, "That's okay. They don't change that much."

I started reading the Labor Code, and I had questions. When I asked my attorneys these questions, they said I was wrong. *"That can't be right."* When I presented one of the Regulations to my supervisor, he took away the Labor Code. I could not be trusted with it. I was told to do what my attorneys and doctors told me to do.

Five years later, and working for a different company, I saved up enough money to buy my own Labor Code. Insurance companies did not provide them to adjusters back then. Now it was mine. I read it. I highlighted codes and regulations. I made notes. I did research and tabbed my book. I would call my attorneys, and they would tell me I was wrong. This time, I would argue back and quote Labor Codes. *"It can't say that."*

I had stumbled onto one of the great secrets of our industry. No one was reading the Labor Code. No one knew what to do. Everyone had *"always done it like that"* and so no one wanted to question authority or make changes. You just did what everyone else did, and no one knew why we did it.

This was a sad time for the workers' compensation industry in California. I cannot tell you how many times I was in the courtrooms as settlements were negotiated. People's lives were determined not by the facts of the case or what the law said. Settlement were based upon who owed who a favor, or whose turn was it to win this time. Bogus reports on both sides were generated, and then they split the difference. Facts no longer had any weight or meaning in the system. Truth was not just ignored, it was no longer allowed.

Another three years later and not only am I supervising claims in another company, and had my own Labor Code and set of case laws to review; everyone in my office had their own Labor Code. Also, I was now teaching classes for the Insurance Education Association. I refused to use the textbooks they recommended, and insisted everyone have their own Labor Code as their textbook. We went through the Labor Code. We read it for ourselves. We took it apart and put it back together.

What was so rewarding was having so many of my students coming back to class and saying, "*I read that Labor Code to my attorney and he never heard of it.*" Or "*I read that Labor Code to the other side, and he had no idea that was in the Labor Code.*" My students started learning Labor Code. They cited Labor Codes, and they were throwing the industry into sheer chaos because my students knew how the system was supposed to work. They had the Labor Code to prove it. We took back the industry and held our attorneys, investigators and doctors accountable. We made the decisions on the files and not them; and we knew why we made the decision that we did. Facts and truth mattered once more.

One night as I was teaching Labor Codes, one of my students asked me how I analyzed Labor Codes and figured out what they meant. As I was explaining my thought process to him, it hit me that I was doing to the Labor Codes exactly what I would do with Bible verses. That was a life-changing moment in my life and in my career. God had sent me into workers' compensation to teach me how to read and analyze Labor Codes so I would also read and analyze Bible passages. For those who saw the original *Karate Kid* movie, workers' compensation was my "*Wax on; wax off*" lesson from God.

Now during my forty years of experience I was always at the right place at the right time. God seemed to take control of my career to put me where I needed to be. Most of my career, I still handled claims or supervised claims except for a few breaks where I served as Corporate Trainer or as an Expert Witness. The last seventeen of my years in the business, I worked for a public entity, and served as their Special Investigation Unit. This means I worked to uncover and report fraud.

As a Special Investigation Unit, I performed the work of a detective, but without the gun and badge. It fell to me to investigate various cases where adjusters felt that there was fraud. They would report it to me—or I would become aware of certain questionable activities—and I would need to go through the case, document by document, to see if there was any evidence suggesting fraud. I would compare their actions to various laws and codes to see if they had broken any of them. If I felt there was a need, I would hire outside investigators to obtain more information, or I would hire attorneys to take depositions to explore the case further.

If I felt that there was sufficient evidence, I would prepare the paperwork and file the case with the District Attorney and the Department of Insurance Fraud Bureau. A number of the cases I was involved with did make the news. One was even the topic of CBS's show: "Whistleblower."

I need to make it clear that I was not the only one reporting the fraud. If it was employee fraud where people claimed they were injured and disabled when they were not, then I was the sole source for the case. But when you deal with vendor fraud [doctors, providers and attorneys] then my employer was one of many insurance companies filing their cases and building a much larger case throughout the state. Each insurance company had a Special Investigation Unit, and we all brought different pieces of the puzzle to the table. We all worked together. Many of the frauds were too massive or complicated for any single person to figure it all out or prove the fraud and abuse involved. This has always been a team effort.

As an Expert Witness and Special Investigation Unit, I have given depositions, testified before Grand Juries, and testified before juries and judges in actual court proceedings. I have done this both in civil court and in criminal court.

I spend over thirty years teaching claims handling, fraud investigation and Labor Codes to employers, claims adjusters, attorneys, doctors and even an occasional judge sat in a few of my classes.

Over the years, my various employers also used me as a legal analyst. Whenever a Bill was introduced into the State Legislature or it was signed by the Governor, it fell to me to study the proposed Bill/signed Law, and determine what it was actually saying, and what procedures we would need to put into place. I would then teach workshops in house and for the industry on how to best implement the changes in the law.

In the latter half of my career, I was responsible for attending public hearings on proposed Regulations—and in some cases proposed Legislation—relating to the workers' compensation industry in California.

In addition to all of the above, when I first entered the workers' compensation industry, claims adjusters went before the Workers' Compensation Appeals Board [WCAB] to defend the company's position on claims decisions. The WCAB is the court of law for the workers' compensation system. In my later years, even though insurance carriers used attorneys to represent them, I was the company's lien specialist; so I would go to hearings and trials in order to direct our attorneys, and help them prepare and present our cases before the WCAB.

This taught me how to prepare a case for trial and how to appeal a case if it were necessary. So, while not an attorney, within the workers' compensation system I was able to perform many of the functions of an attorney. The workers' compensation system is unique in that the claims adjuster is allowed to represent the employer/carrier before the WCAB.

All of the above prepared me for this and several other manuscripts I am preparing.

It was in the mid-1990's that I found myself between jobs; so God sat me down and had me write a manuscript entitled, *Contract Written in Blood.* In this manuscript, I took my years of claims handling and investigator experience, and went through the entire Bible. I did a legal analysis of the Bible to see what it said, what the claims were that it was making, was there evidence supporting these claims; and if it were ever submitted to a court, would these claims hold up.

God brought me to this conclusion: the Bible is a legally-binding contract between God and mankind. He also brought me to the conclusion that Christianity [and Judaism] are not traditional religions. They are, in reality, legal systems. This means that they are not a collection of personal beliefs. Even though belief and faith are key components to both systems, their foundation is contractual law. The contract takes priority over the beliefs. In other words, it does matter what you believe. Just like purchasing an insurance policy, you might believe that you are covered for something; but if the contract does not provide coverage; then you are not covered.

Upon my retirement, I was asked to teach in our Church's School of Ministry. Specifically, I was asked to fill in for the pastor on the topic of the Cults. I did a seven-week session dealing with the Jehovah's Witnesses and the Church of Jesus Christ of Latter-Day Saints [the Mormons]. Are there other Cults out there? Of course, but these two seem to be the ones that many people have to deal with.

I had the opportunity back in my college days to take a class on the Cults that was taught by the late Dr. Walter Martin. He wrote the textbook that colleges were using for their classes on the Cults: *The Kingdom of the Cults.* Our classes were recorded and became several cassette tape sets on dealing with the Cults.

Dr. Martin took the approach when teaching the Cults of asking the question: "Who is Jesus?" I agree that this is the most important question when dealing with any discussion of the Bible and the Christian faith. However, as I taught this session, God pulled up my training in claims handling and fraud investigating to supplement my point of view relating to the Cults.

Most recently, God has placed it on my heart to go back over these classes and present them as a book that will guide people to identify various Cults and how to test Cults to see if they are "*of God*." I will be applying Dr. Martin's focus on Cults, and I want to give him credit where credit is due. He did lay the foundation upon which I am building.

There is another source for my presentation. My daughter heard a speaker in chapel at college many years ago talking on the topic of the *Mathematics of the Cults*. The presentation was made by Watchman Fellowship Inc. out of Arlington Texas. In this presentation, there was a discussion of what I call *The Mathematics of the Cults*. There is also a blog by Brent Cunningham that discusses this very concept. I am not sure which is the original source for this very creative and accurate definition of a Cult, but I will note both of them so you are aware this is not just a topic presented by one author.

So let's get the preliminaries out of the way, so we can jump in and take a look at the Cults in light of contract law.

Dennis Knotts, WCCP

August 17, 2019

AUTHOR'S COMMENTS

Let me begin by setting the stage for this legal argument. I am a believer. I believe that Jesus Christ is not only the only begotten Son of God; but He is God the Son. I believe that He was born of a virgin and entered the human race. In other words, He became one of us. I believe He lived a sinless life, and that He physically died upon a Roman cross in such a way that it complied with the Law of Moses. He made Himself a sacrifice for sin—the sins of the entire world past, present and future. I believe His body was dead and in a tomb for three days. I believe that He physically rose from that tomb three days later in the same physical body He had died in. It was transformed into the kind of body waiting for us when we go to Heaven. I believe that, even now, Jesus is in Heaven and before the Father pleading our case before Him.

I believe the Bible is God's Word—message—to the human race. It is how He has revealed Himself to us, and where He explains what He is doing for us. I believe the Bible is inspired by God as it was written. Finally, I believe that salvation is the free gift of God. It is ours for the asking. We will never be worthy of it. We will never earn it. We will never deserve it. And so God made it a free gift, or none of us would ever be saved.

You now know a little bit about my beliefs. I also believe in the spirit realm. This is where God, angels, Satan and demons operate. I believe because this is taught in the Bible, and in my own research, I have found enough proof for me to accept what the Bible is saying about this. There is a war taking place in the spirit realm between the forces of God and the forces of Satan. Many times this plays out in our all-too-physical world.

In writing and researching this book, there have been many spiritual battles trying to force me to lose faith and to give up.

There have been struggles to believe that this book might make a difference. When I started this manuscript, I hoped that it would fall into hands of those in the Cults and it would open their eyes.

It is important to know the audience you are writing for. However, with further research I had to face the reality that the Cults have gone to great lengths to continue to deceive their members, and to keep them away from books like this. They will not accept it as a gift. They will not read it. They will not believe it. So why do I continue to write it?

It is one of the harsh realities of dealing with Cults. We would all like some guaranteed verse that we can recite to Jehovah's Witnesses and Mormons who come to our doorstep that would cause the scales to fall from their eyes, make their minds grasp and comprehend, so that they would see the True Jesus, and accept Him as their Savior.

I have been part of these doorstep confrontations—not that I have ever been a member of a Cult—but I have cast my pearls before them, and seen their eyes glaze over. They cannot see because they lack the Holy Spirit to guide them.

Let me share the reality of dealing with a member of the Cults. This is how they will discover the truth. It will not come from a single one-time doorstep encounter. The person sharing must make a greater commitment than that. It will come from a friend or a relative who spends a lot of time with them. You do not use the Gospel as a scattergun to hit as much as you can with a single burst. You are a gardener—nothing more. You plant a seed here. You water a seed there. You pull out a weed. You give it light and love. Slowly, the right question will form in their minds. The Holy Spirit will guide them and they will ask a question that does not make sense to them. Then—and only then—does the house of cards begin to collapse.

So I may have written this for people trapped in the Cults, but only indirectly. I have written this book for you—believers like myself. But you are believers who have friends and/or family living in the deception. I pray you will take this book, and God will let you transform this book into the seeds that need to be planted. That it would transform into the water and sunlight that seed needs. That it will empower you to pull the weeds that are keeping the seed from bursting through into the light of the Gospel.

You are my audience; and so I entrust this information into your hands to minister with those who are lost but who think that they are found. Hopefully some of these legal arguments will help you to guide your friend or family member to ask the question that opens their eyes. Each person is different; and so each question will be different. Pray as you use it. Use it with love. And use it with patience because only God can bring a seed to life. Let God use you and this work for His honor and His glory.

ASK THE HARD QUESTIONS

It is a reality that you will never learn if you do not ask the hard questions. As I've mentioned, I was a claims adjuster. There was an entire class on how to take a statement. When we began training people to be claims adjusters or investigators, we would prepare a template that would provide the questions we needed to ask in order to get the information we needed to make our decisions.

Now people would come to me and ask to have their investigation company added to our panel so that we would hire them to do investigations and take statements. I would always ask for copies of their prior investigations. If that investigation gave me all the information I would need to make the right decision on my case, I would consider them. However, if they did not ask all the questions, I could not use them. They could not provide the information I needed. They did not do the job I hired them to do.

There would also be a warning sign if someone said something in their statement that was important; and rather than expanding the investigation and asking more questions about that comment, they moved on to the next question. That told me they were just reading the list of questions, and were not listening to the answers.

The key is that you want to find the truth. The truth will always win out—it will prove itself. There should never be a problem with asking questions and continuing to ask questions until you get to the truth, unless the person who is answering the questions does not want you to discover the truth. Someone who will not answer questions is normally someone trying to hide things.

As I did this manuscript, I did my research. I read what the founders and leaders had to say about these religions. I checked into their teachings. Before beginning any investigation, you need to do your research. You need to know what they are saying. You need to test the information they are giving you. Is it reliable? Does it make sense? Does it contradict other information? This manuscript is an investigation—the kind of investigation I would be required to conduct before I denied a claim or committed the company to making a payment. I had to be sure before my company would be sure. If I was not convinced, then there is no way that I could convince anyone else.

Now there will be those who read this and say, "But this is an issue of faith! You never question faith." I would disagree. It is an issue of faith only so far as you believe what someone is saying. It is an issue of faith only when you come to that point where there are no more answers available. In that case, you must review the information and answers that you have, to see if it is enough to convince you or allow you to make a decision. Nothing is—or should—be blind faith.

The Bible and Christianity do require faith, but the Bible and Christianity provide evidence and proof. They do answer questions. There are things you can investigate and research. When Paul was at the city of Berea and he presented his teachings, he noted that the Bereans would listen to him, but then they would go back and check the Scriptures to see if what he was saying was true. Acts 17:11:

"These were more noble than those in Thessalonica, in that they received the word with all readiness of mind, and searched the scriptures daily, whether those things were so."

Asking questions is good. Asking questions is allowed. If someone tries to discourage questions, that is the person I would no longer trust.

So in this manuscript, I keep asking. As an investigator, I had to keep asking until I uncovered the truth. There were other adjusters who would ask questions just until they got the information that they wanted. Then they would make their decision, and they would normally make the wrong decision.

There is an actual case that became case law. This case went to trial before the WCAB. The worker was driving a truck, and was injured. The employer claimed the worker was an Independent Contractor and, therefore, not an employee. If the driver were not an employee; then that worker would not be entitled to benefits. The adjuster asked a couple of questions, looked at a couple of documents; and never completed the investigation. Nothing was confirmed or verified. He got enough information to agree with the employer's opinion, and then denied the claim.

When the case went to trial, the employee's attorney continued the investigation with his client on the witness stand. He asked the questions the adjuster should have asked. He presented the evidence that the adjuster ignored. The claims adjuster's decision went down in flames, and the judge ruled that the worker was an employee and entitled to benefits.

You do not investigate until you hear what you want to hear. You investigate until there are no more questions, or no more answers, and then you review all the evidence from all sources.

Most of this manuscript will be questions. It will be me following the logic of someone's statements. I am not special. I am not above average intelligence. But I do ask questions. Sometimes I have to ask the hard questions. But if you keep asking and keep searching, the truth will be revealed. And this has always been the end result of any investigation I conducted. I wanted to know the truth, no matter who was telling it to me.

In this case, since we are dealing with your eternal destiny, I would hope that you will want to ask questions, too. I hope that my questions will prompt you to ask questions of your own. I hope my answers will give you insight, but do not stop with just my investigation. Conduct your own investigation. But if you conduct your own investigation, be ready to ask the hard questions—especially questions you are afraid to hear the answer to. That is how you find the truth. You find the truth only when you refuse to accept anything less.

It's your eternity…make sure you know the truth while you still have time to change your decision.

PRELUDE

WHY THIS TITLE FOR THIS BOOK?

It all began with a phone call asking me to fill in for our pastor. We had a School of Ministry, and we were about to begin the session on the Cults. It started as filling in the first evening. Then it was extended to the second class night. Finally, they said, "Can you teach the entire session?"

It was supposed to be just six weeks, but there was so much information I had to extend it to seven weeks. Instead of covering several Cults, we ended up focusing on the Jehovah's Witnesses and the Church of Jesus Christ of Latter-Day Saints [Mormons]. Even with seven sessions, there was so much more that needed to be said—hence this book.

My approach for the class was to focus on the Bible as a legally-binding contract between God and mankind. It was a new and different approach. When I felt led to write this book, I thought I would use a title that told you what I was going to do. I used the working title of *The Cults in Light of Contract Law*. My consultant—my wife—told me the title was boring. So I tried to think of something to catch them off-guard, and more as a comeback than an actual recommendation. I was in what my daughter calls a "*snarky*" mood, and so I said, "How about *Damned Deceptions?*"

To my surprise, my wife liked it. Then I was hard-pressed to find another title that she liked as much.

So why, *Damned Deceptions*? I suspect the publishers won't like that title. I really wanted to use the description of deceptions. This is exactly what the Cults are. People are being deceived. Jesus warned of this. Matthew 24:4:

"And Jesus answered and said unto them, 'Take heed that no man deceive you.'"

So I knew "*deception*" had to be in the title. But why "*Damned Deceptions*"? Because the more I thought about it, the more I realized that these deceptions will result in people being damned to Hell for all eternity.

I hate to be that blunt. I would rather talk about the love of God. But having been in insurance and claims adjusting, you have to be blunt. You have to tell the truth. You are not doing anyone any favors by letting them think that they might be covered when the contract says that they are not. This is the reality I am talking about here. We are talking about where a person will spend eternity; and so I do not want there to be any ambiguity here. This is not my decision. This is God's decision as to where you will spend eternity. I am just the messenger in this case.

As a claims adjuster, I used to struggle with passing on bad news. I hate to give bad decisions. But I came to learn that I was not the one making that decision. The Law or the contract was making that decision; and I was just letting the person know. The same is true here. I am not the one making the decision. God is making the decision, and He had the Bible written to tell us what that decision will be. So in this case, I am just the messenger, not the person making the decision.

So many people twist God's decision around. "So, if I do not accept Jesus as my Savior, God's going to send me to Hell?" No, that is not the message. As someone who has read my share of contracts and laws for over forty years, that is not a true and accurate reading of the Law. That statement is someone twisting the message in such a way so that you want to feel justified in rejecting it. They misrepresented the facts in order to persuade you to reject Jesus. They do not want you to make a completely objective decision regarding your eternity. It's all part of the deception. That very question is designed to lead you into deception.

When we do an analysis of the Bible in light of contract law we will see that the following is the actual truth of the matter, and a better reflection of the facts making up that truth: "You are going to Hell. I am going to Hell. We are all going to Hell." That is the truth. That is the reality we are dealing with. Remove God completely from the picture. Remove Jesus from the picture. Let's suggest that Jesus was never born into our world and that He never died for our sins. What is the reality of our world minus Jesus Christ? Each one of us will die, and each one of us will spend eternity in Hell. God is not sending us there. We send ourselves there by our actions.

Each person born into this world carries the sin nature in them, and that will send each and every one of us to Hell. You are not going to Hell because God is mad at you for rejecting Jesus and He is taking it out on you. God does not need a reason to send us to Hell. You have already provided it. God has written this contract as a way of giving us an option to avoid Hell as our eternal destiny. The message is this. "You are going to Hell. This is how you can avoid it."

So it dawned upon me that these deceptions are the worst deceptions possible. They convince people that there is another way to Heaven. There is another way to avoid Hell. These people have been deceived into thinking that they have found the way into Heaven that everyone else has missed. They believe that everyone else is wrong, and that they alone are right. And so they do not consider that they are still going to Hell. They do not consider what the Bible has to say. They do not know that they are going to Hell. They do not know that they need to be saved. Therefore, they refuse to listen as to what they must do in order to be saved. Dr. Martin has noted that people who are deceived do not know that they have been deceived. They do not know that they are deceived, and so they continue in their deception.

"If what you believed about God and the Bible is wrong, wouldn't you like to know the truth?" But Satan has convinced people that Christianity is just a religion and a set of beliefs. No one can prove a religion wrong since it deals with the afterlife. And so no one wants to hear your opinion.

As our next chapter will outline, Christianity is not a religion. It is a legal system. The terms of the contract are carefully laid out and documented. There is physical evidence to support the legal requirements. But those trapped within the Cults have been told that they are right and everyone else is wrong. Therefore, they will not listen or consider the evidence.

Because of their refusal to reconsider their position, these deceptions result in their being damned to Hell for all eternity. This is the result of these deceptions—people are damned and going to Hell. But they have been deceived into thinking that they are saved—that they are one of the elite people who are truly saved, and the rest of us are all still lost.

So there is a serious need to do a detailed analysis of God's contract and of these Cult's doctrines to see which one holds up to the scrutiny, and what each of these doctrines is actually saying when you follow the logic.

We will look at the contract God has given us and then we will explore the teaching of the Cults. I will use the Bible as a legal document God has written, and we will use legal theory and common sense to find the truth. As I am discussing a legal document, then I will occasionally make reference to how this would play out in a court of law. This may make the reality of the claims easier to understand. If Christianity and Cults were to stand before the same judge, which would have the greater chance of being accepted into evidence? These are truths that you cannot afford to be wrong about. You cannot let yourself be deceived into thinking you already have found the way when you have not. You should demand your Plan of Salvation meet the same legal standards and credibility that you would demand if you were on trial for your life.

If you think you have already found the way; then the danger is that you stop looking. You stop asking. You stop considering. These are things that we will be doing throughout this book. We will consider. We will ask questions. And we will not stop until we have found what evidence and logic tells us is the truth.

The Latter Day Church founder—Brigham Young—encourages us to pick up the Bible and examine their teaching by it.

Paul gives believers a very important piece of advice. What I find interesting is that the Jehovah's Witnesses use this same reference and piece of advice. If we are all looking for the truth, then the truth will be the same for all parties, so long as all parties use the same evidence, ask the same questions, and do not stop until everything has been tested and investigated fully.

This is what a trial does. It forces all parties to consider the same evidence. It forces all parties to use the same laws. And this should force all parties to come to the same conclusion. It is a very structured investigation seeking to uncover the truth.

This is how a court of law works. All evidence is submitted. All evidence is tested. That evidence that lacks credibility or was not properly obtained is removed from the decision. What we have left is evidence that is credible, and which was properly obtained. The concept is that anyone can look at this evidence and come to the same conclusion. The judge is an objective third-party with no "*dog in the race*." He/she is looking at the evidence, comparing it to the law; and this is what that decision should be. If all of this was done correctly, each judge in each appeal should come to the same conclusion.

Here is an important point about litigation. If you appeal a judge's decision, you do not get to litigate the case all over again. There is no new evidence [or it is very rare]. What you are arguing is whether the judge followed procedure in accepting and identifying evidence; and given the facts of the case, did the judge make the correct decision—the decision mandated by law. You identify the facts of the case—the truth. Those facts dictate the decision the judge must make. The law tells the judge which decision to make. No one, not even a judge, is above the law. We must all make decisions based upon the law. When dealing with God, the Bible is the Law. No one—not even Jehovah's Witnesses or Latter Day Saints—is free to ignore that law and make decision contrary to the law.

Paul's advice is important because he challenges us to never stop thinking about what we believe. Never stop and think that you have it right. I have spent fifty years checking and rechecking what I believe against what the Bible teaches. Have my beliefs changed? No, but each time I bring it back and put it to the test, my understanding of why I believe what I believe does. I am more convinced. I have a better understanding of what I believe and why. My doubts are resolved. But I still come back and review my belief systems with the Bible—what it actually says and not what people tell me it says. I do not accept second-hand information. I always test it for myself.

The danger of deception is that those who are deceived do not know that they are deceived. They do not know how to test their beliefs for themselves. Unless we follow Paul's advice, each and every one of us can be deceived into believing something that is not true. Here is Paul's advice. I Corinthians 13:5:

"Examine yourselves, whether you are in the faith; prove your own selves. Know you not your own selves, how that Jesus Christ is in you, except you be reprobates?"

What is Paul saying here? He is telling us to make sure. A relative began to doubt whether he/she was saved. The solution was easy: go back and ask Jesus to save you. *Do overs* are allowed where God and salvation is concerned. Here is the proper application of this verse: "Are you saved? Make sure that you are."

This applies not just to Latter Day Saints and Jehovah's Witnesses. This is not exclusive to just Cults. If you are a Baptist, are you saved? If you are a Catholic, are you saved? Are you a Methodist, a Lutheran, an Episcopalian, a Non-Denominational, a Calvary Chapelite…are you saved?

Stop for a second. Make sure that you were not deceived into thinking you are saved when you were not. I was. I went forward in a Southern Baptist Church when I was eight years old, and said I wanted to be saved. They had me fill out a card, meet the Church and be baptized; but I was not saved. I had never personally asked Jesus to forgive my sins or to be my Savior. It was not until I graduated high school that someone pointed that out to me, and I made sure that I was saved.

Here is what you do; pray this prayer and mean it:

"Jesus, I am a sinner. I have broken your Law, and I am sorry. I accept your offer of salvation. Please forgive me. Please make me one of Your own. Write my name in Your Book of

Life, and fill me with your Holy Spirit. Let me come to live with you in Heaven when I die. Thank you. Amen."

The basic prayer is even simpler than that; but I just wanted to make sure that you covered all the variations. It can all be boiled down to: "Forgive me. Save me." But I figured if you wanted to make sure that you were saved, then pray that prayer to God and mean it. He promises that you will be saved.

Now write down the date and time in your Bible. If you ever have any doubts in the future, go to your Bible and check the date. On that date, at that time, God saved you. Now you know. Now you have proof. Now you are saved.

If you don't remember praying that prayer or something like it, and meaning it as you prayed; you may not be saved. You do not have to be in a Cult to be deceived. All it takes is someone not knowing how to lead you in a prayer for salvation. That happened in the Southern Baptist Church with me. It can happen in a Catholic Church. It can happen at Calvary Chapel. It can happen anywhere with any denomination. If you don't remember such a prayer in your life, stop right now and pray it and mean it. You have just examined yourselves as Paul instructed. You are now saved. The Bible even guarantees it. John 6:37:

"All whom the Father gives me shall come to me; and he who comes to me I will in no wise cast out."

Add in Romans 10:13:

"For whosoever shall call upon the name of the Lord shall be saved."

Do not trust yourselves. Since each one of us is capable of being deceived, take this opportunity to test your own beliefs and compare them to what the contract is saying. Make sure that you personally test your beliefs to make sure that they are true. Again, the most terrifying concept about deception is that those who are deceived do not know that they have been deceived.

CHAPTER ONE

THE BIBLE AS A LEGAL DOCUMENT

Let me take a moment to discuss contracts—specifically insurance policies, as this is where I have most of my experience. A contract is an agreement—normally in writing. This agreement may be between two or more parties. There is always the First Party. This is the party making the agreement with others. This is the party that has written the contract and controls the contract. Then there are the other parties. These are the people seeking to benefit from this contract and entering into the agreement.

There is a reality that the courts hold the party who wrote the contract to a higher standard. They could make the contract as clear and as binding as they choose to. Therefore, any ambiguity or flaws in the contract go against the one writing the contract. The person writing the contract can make the contract say anything they want it to say, and the party signing the contract chooses to enter into the agreement, or not, based upon what they believe the contract is offering. If the First Party intentionally or accidentally uses language that led the person signing the contract to believe something else, then the courts will rule in favor of the person signing the contract, not the person who wrote the contract.

When I was first in the insurance industry, we were dealing with a debt that had been created by fraud. I wrote a letter to the company, and I made it clear as to what the debt truly was, and what we felt we actually owed. I was very blunt. I cited the Laws of California, and how if they cashed the check we were sending; then they were accepting our terms and were entering into a contract with us concerning the true value of the debt.

My wife kept telling me to be more polite. She thought I was being harsh. She wanted me to tone down the letter. I told her that I was writing a contract and I had to be as clear as I could be—even if it offended the other party. They had to know what they were agreeing to. There could not be any ambiguity in the wording. The company cashed our check, and we paid the debt. A year later, they called us into their office and wanted more money. I produced a copy of the letter, and they laughed at it. I simply told them that the next phone call they should make should be to their attorney, and to make sure that the attorney understood contract law, and what a breech of contract would cost them. They never called us back after that, and the debt was canceled.

Know the contract you are agreeing to. Read it over before you sign it. Make sure that you understand it. That is good advice no matter who is offering you the contract. In this case, God is the one who is offering the contract. Read it over. Ask your questions. Make sure you know what you are agreeing to before you sign the contract—even if it is one offered by God.

The next point of the contract is that it must establish jurisdiction. Contract law falls under the jurisdiction of the civil court, not the family court or the criminal court. When I litigated certain issues on workers' compensation cases, our jurisdiction was the Workers' Compensation Appeals Board [WCAB]. Any issues relating to on-the-job injuries were tried in that legal arena. However, if there was a dispute over the insurance policy itself, that moved the case over to civil court. This is because contracts and agreements [promises] are a civil issue and deals with how we interact with each other. There are rules to ensure that we *"play nice"* with each other—that we act in a civil manner. So any contract where one party promises something to others falls under the civil court jurisdiction.

The term *"jurisdiction"* is actually made up of two Latin terms. *"Juris"* refers to the law. *"Diction"* refers to speaking. So *"jurisdiction"* is a fancy legal term identifying who has the authority to speak on what a law is telling us to do. In other words, who has the right to make the decision?

You can go to many people and ask for many opinions, but that is all they will be—an opinion. It will not be a verdict or decision until the person making it has the legal authority to rule on this matter—they have the authority to enforce their decision.

As an example, let me discuss a case I was involved in many years ago. It was a workers' compensation case. That meant a Workers' Compensation Judge had to hear the case and make a decision. The case settled and benefits were awarded to the employee and his attorney. After the case was complete, a lien appeared on the case that was not present during the case. A lien is a bill that someone asks the judge to order us to pay. It was filed after-the-fact. That, in itself, should make the lien invalid. You must present your lien before the case is settled—while the judge still has the jurisdiction to enforce it.

The lien was what we call a *Cost of Living Lien*. Someone claimed that they were entitled to the employee's settlement money to pay their costs for food, clothing and housing. Normally a landlord will stop eviction proceedings, and give the employee time to get their settlement to pay for back rent. The landlord would then file a Cost of Living Lien with the WCAB to ensure that they were paid the money the employee owed them.

In this case, the lien was the same amount as the employee's entire settlement. If the lien had been filed timely and accepted by the WCAB, we would have withheld payment to the employee, and with the court's permission, paid the entire settlement to this lien holder instead of the injured worker. Since the lien was filed after the case was closed and the settlement was paid to the employee, there was no money left to pay the lien holder; and if the lien were valid, the employer would now have to pay the costs out of its own pocket. Now you understand how the law works in this case.

When we received the lien, my attorney told us to go ahead and pay the lien without challenging it. I looked at the lien and I knew two things from my own investigation. The first is that the lien was not filed at the time they said it was. We personally went through the entire case file at the WCAB before the judge received our settlement documents. The judge ordered us to do so. We were required to take the WCAB file and review each page, and list each and every lien that was in the WCAB file. Both my attorney and I did, which is how I knew that lien was not there at the time of settlement.

The judge also went through every page in the WCAB file before approving the settlement, and the judge listed every lien in the file at that time on his settlement document before he signed it. Each and every lien on that case was documented by my attorney and I and the WCAB Judge before the settlement was signed or approved. This lien was not there. The lien had a receipt date prior to our settlement, and so someone backdated the lien and submitted it after-the-fact. [Again, I deal with fraud. I notice these things.]

The other thing I knew was that it was filed by the employee's wife. It seems that the employee had packed up everything he had, taken the settlement money, and went off for a long vacation with his girl friend…he just forgot to take his wife. She wanted the same money he had received. There were just several legal problems. First, she was not an employee of our insured. She could not be covered under workers' compensation. Second, she had not been injured—except for a broken heart. Third, her lien had not been filed in a timely manner, and she could not prove that she was entitled to the money. There was no legal obligation for our insured to pay her; and, as a claims adjuster, I can only issue payments for which my insured is legally obligated to pay. There was no legal obligation.

As I noted, my attorney told me to just pay the lien, but I refused. There was no legal basis. The settlement was set aside. We had a trial, and the wife came and testified before the judge.

Now let me add some information here. During the trial, we asked if they were legally separated. They were not. We asked if she had filed for separation with the Marriage and Family Court. She had not. We asked if there were any court orders awarding her alimony or other compensation. There were not. This is why she had filed the lien with the WCAB. [Someone who worked at the WCAB had suggested this to her, and had backdated the lien for her.]

Now this specific court had a reputation for ignoring the law and doing what it wanted. The judge felt she was entitled to something for staying with her husband all during his injury and his case, and he awarded her lien. We were ordered to pay the settlement a second time, this time to her. This would double the cost of the claim and have a negative impact on our insured.

I did not believe that the judge had the authority to give her money that we did not owe. So I instructed my attorney to file an appeal.

My attorney refused to file. [Yes, he was that kind of attorney.] And so I filed the appeal myself. As a claims adjuster, I could legally do that for the first level of appeal. My argument was simple. It was a question of jurisdiction. The Workers' Compensation Judge was acting as a Marriage and Family Court Judge to award her some kind of alimony for her husband's infidelity.

A Workers' Compensation judge can only rule on issues related to on-the-job injuries. He cannot make a ruling that properly belongs to the Marriage and Family Court. The judge would have to be sworn in and given legal authority by the state to hear Marriage and Family cases before he could issue awards and orders. He was not. He was a Workers' Compensation Judge and nothing more. [Sorry, your honor.] I filed my appeal and my attorneys were freaking out. They warned me I would lose the appeal, and this judge would not forgive or forget me. I stuck to my guns.

I understand from sources that the Appeals Board called the judge when they got my appeal and asked the Workers' Compensation Judge one question: "Do you really want to do this?" His response was to cancel his original order and deny the lien.

Now I have tried to keep this concept simple for those who have no dealings with the legal system. However, I need to stress; the law controls all aspects of decisions and actions. Let me simplify the role of a judge for you. The role of the judge is to determine what evidence can be trusted. Once all the evidence that can be trusted has been identified, the judge determines the facts of the case—what actually happened. Then the judge must examine the laws relating to this problem. The law will tell the judge what kind of decision to make. Yes, even the judges are controlled by the law. A judge cannot make a decision that is contrary to the law. If a judge does that, even a judge will be called upon to defend that decision using the law. If the law does not support such a decision, the judge's decision is overturned. Once the facts of the case are established, the law—not the judge—determines what the decision will be.

There are many harsh realities of the legal system. This is just one of them. Those who have the legal authority can issue decisions, awards and orders. The rest of us cannot. All are required to obey the law, even if someone does not want to - even if that person feels that it is not fair. The law is not about what is fair—it should be. The law is not about what is moral—it should be. The law is what our lawmakers made it to be—legal. Nothing more, and nothing less. This is why you must be very careful about which laws you allow lawmakers to pass. Once they are laws, they will then control you.

The law forces everyone—including God—to act according to the law, and not based upon our own desires, feelings or opinions. I was forced to do a lot of things in my job that I did not want to do, but I had to do them because of the contract, and because of the laws. The actions I took were legal. That is what the law required.

Fortunately, God made a law that is fair; it is moral. He gave that Law to Moses. Once the law was handed down, it applies to everyone—even God. God, as the supreme judge—must obey the Law and do what it says to do. God does not want to send anyone to Hell, but the Law will force Him to do this if we do not accept His alternative.

Why is that Law so harsh? Take a quick look at the Garden of Eden, and then look at our world today. That is what sin does to paradise. It corrupts and destroys paradise. God has prepared an eternal paradise, but to preserve it as perfect, He cannot allow sin in. It must be removed. It must be dealt with. Its power must be broken. No matter how much God loves us, He cannot allow any of us into Paradise while there is still sin in our lives or while sin still has power over us. It would corrupt Heaven forever.

So God judges sin. He even judged it when it was found in Jesus as He hung on the cross. God bars sin from ever getting into Heaven. Either you remove the sin, or you can't come in. If you have never sinned, you're in. But none of us has "*never sinned.*" All of us have sinned in some way. It might be small. It might be great; but a single sin can infect. A single sin can corrupt. Not a single sin can be allowed in.

The Law is now in place. It applies to God the Father. It applies to Jesus the Son. It applies to each one of us. If there is sin, we are barred from Heaven.

Unfortunately, once we have been infected, we cannot be allowed into Heaven. We are infected with sin at birth. Even if we never committed a single sin in our lives, we have the sin nature. We might have avoided giving into that sin nature for ten years, twenty years, sixty years. But can we resist the sin nature for a thousand years? A hundred thousand years? A million years? We won't; at some point, we would give in and sin would then be in Heaven. Sin would have power to corrupt Heaven. So both sin and the sin nature must be removed.

God put into place a legal system. He created a contract that resolves this problem forever to all who enter into the contract with Him. It is part of the Law He handed down. The same Law that keeps sin out allows for our sins to be forgiven. But it requires Jesus. He is the one appointed by the courts to pay the price of sin and break its power forever. Anything else—anyone else—will not be able to remove sin and set us free. It has to be Jesus, or we are not set free of our sins. We are not delivered from our sin nature. If we trust anyone else, there will be sin in us and we will be barred forever.

So, hopefully, you have a little better understanding of how and why God does what He does. He loves us, but He cannot allow even a single sin in. For the sake of Heaven and all those who come to live there, He cannot make an exception—no matter how much He wants to. No Sin Allowed! That's the Law. But God does love us. He does want us to be with Him for all eternity. And so He created a legal alternative to remove the sin from us forever. He sent Jesus to die for our sins. Jesus has the power to remove both the sin and the sin nature from us so we can enter Heaven and live with Him. All we have to do is ask. However, we reject His offer at our own risk.

***

So back to this concept of jurisdiction…you cannot make a decision and have that decision enforced unless you are legally empowered to make the decision. I will be stressing this later on in the book, so I want you to properly understand the concept of jurisdiction. As we look into the Bible as a legally-binding contract, we will see that the first thing God does with this contract is to establish His jurisdiction. If He has the jurisdiction, then He has the legal right to set standards for His Creation, and to hold them accountable for breaking those standards. He also has the right to create this contract, and He is the only one who has the legal right to alter or change this contract.

This concept is central to this entire book. No one, other than God, can change or alter the contract God is offering to the human race. If anyone else alters or changes the contract, those alterations and changes will not be honored. It would be like you changing the terms of your car insurance policy after an accident, and expecting your insurance company to honor your changes. They will not. Let me repeat this in all capital letters to drive the point home. ANY ALTERATIONS OR CHANGES TO THE CONTRACT WILL NOT BE HONORED! I hope I have made my point. And you now know where this book is going to eventually lead.

God opens the Bible with a statement that establishes jurisdiction. Genesis 1:1:

"In the beginning God created the heavens and the earth."

We see this kind of statement when you are dealing with issues of intellectual property or copyright issues. The person claiming to own the intellectual property must prove that they own the intellectual property. For copyright laws the person obtains the copyright by being the creator of the work. The author must submit testimony and proof that he/she wrote the book.

It is as if God is in the courtroom, sitting on the witness stand, and making His opening statement under oath. With the opening statement of the Bible, God is establishing His legal authority over the Creation by claiming to be the Creator— the sole Creator. As such, He holds the copyright on the earth and the universe. That is His opening statement. "I made the universe out of nothing. I made the earth out of nothing."

Now this is interesting because God is establishing His ownership or authority over something very specific. God made the earth and the universe [heavens]. He does not mention how He made the heavens in any detail. He just made them. He made them out of nothing. He owns them. He has legal authority over them. But He is not making a claim for the heavens at this time.

Now He does make an important declaration in the Hebrew language in this verse. The Hebrew word "*Bara*" is used for "*created*." "*Bara*" literally means "*to make out of nothing or to call forth out of nothing*." There was nothing there when God started. God made the heavens and the earth out of nothing. This is important because if God took existing material, and made the heavens and the earth out of it; then God would have to share ownership of the heavens and the earth with whoever provided the materials God used. Therefore, God makes it clear. "No one else was involved in this. I made everything out of nothing." [Let me just note here, that this is the correct translation of the word, "*bara*". Later in the book, Joseph Smith will suggest a different meaning for the word, "*bara*." He is wrong.]

At this point, God offers no other testimony relating to the creation of the heavens. He does, however, give a detailed description of how He made the earth. This tells us that God's focus in going to be on the earth. Out of all the universe, God is dealing specifically with the earth in His testimony. Ownership of the earth is essential to any legal claim He is going to make over the human race.

In a copyright case, the author will establish his ownership of the work by providing testimony concerning how he/she made the work in question. If I were in court trying to establish my copyright over one of my books, I would testify as to how I came up with the idea, and when and why I wrote it. Was there any research I did to prepare for writing the book? If I had early drafts of the book, these would help prove that I wrote it. If there were people who were with me when I wrote it, I would call upon then to testify to establish when and how I wrote the manuscript. The more information and details I provide, the stronger my argument; and the greater chance my copyright will be upheld, and I will be recognized as the creator of the work.

God went through six days of Creation. He initiated and completed several stages of Creation. There was at least one complete Creation per day. It started at the beginning of the day and it was completed at the end of the day. God was establishing His ownership or authority over the earth one day at a time. He was not establishing ownership over the sun, moon and stars. Why? He did make them. He was laying the foundation for the legal point He needed to make. He had to establish that He created man and woman. This is His closing statement in Chapter One of Genesis. He made man and woman. He made them male and female. He opened Chapter Two with His testimony concerning how He made man and woman, and in what order.

God made Adam out of material that was part of the earth. Therefore, God had to prove that He made the earth by Himself out of nothing. He owned the earth. He owned the materials He used to make man. God made man. God owned man. God used materials that were part of man to make woman. Because He owned man and the materials he used to make woman, God owned woman as well.

As the Creator, as the owner of the copyright for Adam and Eve, God has the legal authority to do whatever He wants with

His Creation. Let's assume that I had written a manuscript. I may have shared the story with friends. I become depressed, and hate how the manuscript turned out. I want to burn it. I want to change it and kill the hero of the story. My friends love the story the way I originally wrote it. They want to protect the story. They file a lawsuit in civil court. I submit evidence that I wrote the book. I am the sole author. I do not have to share the copyright with anyone else. The courts agree with me. I go home, put the manuscript in the fireplace, and light the fire. No one can stop me. They cannot call the police to stop me. I have established that I am the author. I own the copyright. I can do whatever I want with my creation no matter what anyone else says or thinks.

God has established His claim to the human race. In order to get to this claim He had to do several things. First of all, God had to make the universe and everything in it. He had to make it out of nothing. This is what the opening statement declared: "In the beginning God created the heavens and the earth."

So God begins with His opening statement: "I made everything out of nothing." This is why He mentions the heavens in His opening statement but does not go into detail concerning the heavens. God went into more detail about how He created the earth because the focus of His ownership and copyright will be made from things [dust] that existed before God made man. As God is describing how He made man, He made man out of the dust of the ground. (Of course, God had already created the dust.) Then God made woman out of man. (Again, God had already made man.) God is establishing His authority over both man and woman as their Creator.

Just as a contract [or insurance contract (policy)] establishes which state, country or court has jurisdiction over the contract and has the legal authority to enforce the contract if there is ever any issue, so God begins His contract by establishing His jurisdiction and legal authority over mankind.

What does God do once He has established His authority as the Creator? He sets rules for His Creation: "Do not eat of the fruit of the Tree of Knowledge."

11

So before God could set restrictions on the human race, God needed to have authority over it. He established His authority by documenting how He created mankind and all Creation.

As an analogy, consider your children. As the parent—the person who created the child—you have authority to set restrictions and rules for your children. If your child violates those rules or restrictions, as the parent [Creator], you have the right to enforce the rule or restriction. You have the legal authority to punish your children in order to enforce your rules.

Now if your neighbor down the street decides he does not like rock music. And he declares that no one can play rock music, he has exceeded his legal authority. He can enforce this rule in his own home or in his own car. He can enforce his rule with regards to his children. But if he comes down to your house, breaks into the house and beats your children for listening to rock music in their own home, he is a criminal. He is a tyrant. As such, you have the right—even the obligation—to stop him, report him and resist him.

This is key to our worldview. Many people do not consider where the arguments they are making lead, but in a court of law this is a valid defense. If you believe in Evolution over Creation, this is not just a matter of opinion. By choosing Evolution and rejecting Creation, we are declaring that God did not make us. Evolution declares that we made ourselves. Since God is not our Creator, God has no legal authority over us. Since God has no legal authority over us; then God cannot make rules or laws concerning us. We are free to break these rules and laws whenever we like. If God tries to enforce these rules or laws on us, then He has become a tyrant—a dictator. As such, we have an obligation to rebel against Him and drive Him out of our world, and keep Him out of our world.

That is where the argument of Creation versus Evolution leads to if you follow the logic of the argument. It changes the core beliefs of our world. God becomes the enemy that must be resisted and defeated. We now have a moral obligation to do so.

This is why it is so vital to God's contract with mankind that He establishes His legal authority over us. It follows that He now has the legal authority to set laws and restrictions for our race. If we break or violate these laws or restrictions, God has the legal authority to punish us in order to enforce them. It also gives God the legal authority to create and offer a contract with mankind.

So the next step after Creation is the setting of rules and restrictions. God made it easy. There was only one: "Do not eat the fruit of the Tree of Knowledge." God gave us permission to do anything and everything else. The only limit was on eating this forbidden fruit.

Now during this time, there was no problem. There was no need. God provided for all the needs of mankind free of charge. He asked for nothing in return. There was no need for a contract. Therefore, there was no contract in place. Life went on in the Garden for Adam and Eve. And then Satan—through the serpent—got involved. He questions God's law. He questioned the results of the transgression. "You shall not die." He then told the very first lie: "You shall become as God." [This is the same lie that the Latter Day Church is repeating even now: "As God is, you may become."]

"If you break God's Law, and you eat the forbidden fruit, you shall become like God." This is an important point that I will be discussing later in this manuscript.

When Adam and Eve ate the forbidden fruit, two things happened. The first is that they now knew good from evil. They understood right from wrong. They were now like God in that one point, but only in that one point. Moreover, with the knowledge of right and wrong came the burden of always doing what was right and never doing what was wrong. If you want to be like God, then you bear the same burden of God, and must always be perfect. Instead of one rule, there were now thousands of them. And we are legally responsible to uphold each and every one of them.

They also came to understand what God had warned about. Romans 6:23 puts it this way:

"The wages of sin [singular] is death…"

With the eating of the forbidden fruit, Adam and Eve broke the Law of God. They had committed a sin. Sin now existed in the world. God had warned that in the day that they ate of the forbidden fruit they would surely die. With the introduction of sin into the world, death followed. Adam and Eve began to die physically. It was a long and slow death that took hundreds of years to finalize. But they did die spiritually when they ate the forbidden fruit. They would then die physically many years later; but the process began the day that they ate the forbidden fruit.

Some people teach that there was a hierarchy in the Garden. Adam and Eve were a three-fold being. There was spirit. There was mind. And there was body. These same people also teach that by putting appetites above the needs of the spirit, Adam and Eve inverted this hierarchy; and they were now body [physical needs], mental and spirit [last]. Adam and Eve would now forever be ruled by their physical needs/appetites.

The Law had been given: do not eat the fruit. The Law had been broken. The end result of this is that the action created both sin and death. There was now a need for some action on the part of God to prevent the end result of sin: death. Therefore, there was now a need for a contract. How do we deal with sin and death? Genesis 3:15:

"And I will put [hostility] between you [Satan] and the woman, and between your seed [sin and death] and her seed; it shall bruise your head, and you shall bruise His heel."

God is speaking to Satan through the serpent here. God will put enmity between Satan and the woman. Enmity is defined in the Hebrew as "*hostility*" or "*hatred*." There is now going to be a conflict. The end result of this conflict will culminate where the seed of the serpent [sin and death] will wound the Seed of the Woman.

Now this is the first contract. It was a verbal contract. Notice an important point in the passages where God is judging Adam and Eve. God did not curse Adam. God cursed the ground for Adam's sake. The curse that should have fallen to Adam for his sin was transferred to the ground [Adam came out of the ground]. The ground would bear the curse and bring forth thorns and weeds.

When Jesus stood before the crowd and Pilate declared, "Behold the man!" Jesus was bearing the curse that belonged to Adam. He wore a crown of thorns on His brow. Thorns were the curse God transferred to the ground rather than cursing Adam directly. God did not curse Eve. The only one whom God cursed was the serpent.

Next, God was speaking of the Seed of the Woman. A woman produces the egg. Man produces the seed [sperm]. It is the Seed of Abraham. It is the seed of Isaac. It is the seed of Jacob. It is always the male seed. This is the first reference to the Virgin Birth. Now I will discuss this in more detail when discussing the birth of Jesus in a later chapter. However, let me just give a brief discussion here.

When I approach the Bible, I approach it the same way I was trained to analyze and interpret laws. Every word, every phrase and every provision must be understood and accounted for. For this reason, I force myself to read the actual passage. I pay attention to the words. I have to define each word and all of its possible meanings. Unfortunately, people have read or heard passages so many times, they "*fill in the blanks*" in their mind and never realize exactly what the passage is saying. Such is the case here.

If you go to Luke 1:35, where this prophecy is fulfilled, it is vague enough to let everyone interpret the description of how a virgin can become pregnant so it does not shock or offend them. They define terms and descriptions within their own comfort zone. Luke's account tells you what God did, but it does not describe how God did it in any detail. Most people believe that the Holy Spirit did something, but they do not stop to think, "What did the Holy Spirit actually do?" Some think, "God worked a miracle." Yes, He did; but what was the actual miracle that He worked?

This is why I use the prophecy of Genesis 3:15. It makes it very clear that this woman will produce her own seed. People will automatically redefine "*seed*" in their minds so it becomes "*egg*." "*Seeds*" are produced by the man. "*Eggs*" are produced by the woman. They cannot comprehend how a woman can have a male's genetic material inside of her and still be a virgin—outside of artificial insemination. So, without realizing it, they have mentally altered the original prophecy. "Yes, a woman will produce an egg, and it will somehow become pregnant."

That is not what the prophecy says. It specifically refers to the "*seed*" of the woman. It does not say, "*The egg of the woman.*" The woman producing an egg is natural and normal. It is not a miracle in terms of being out of the ordinary for a woman to produce an egg within her.

Now I am aware that "*seed*" in the Hebrew can have other meanings. So can the word "*virgin*" in Isaiah. If you choose to use these other meanings, then you remove the prophecy of the virgin birth. Both prophecies can refer to any woman giving birth with nothing miraculous about it. The translators did not lightly choose the words that they did when looking at multiple options. There were two committees and they checked and double-checked each other's work. They chose these meanings for a reason. With regards to "*seed*" in every other case where it was used in Scripture, it is referring to the result of the male's genetic material. We would need to answer the question, "Why should it be different when it is used here?" There is no reason for choosing one of the other meanings in the Hebrew in this case.

There is a rule we use in interpreting and applying laws. It is very simple: "we give the words their usual and ordinary meaning." In every day usage, what does this word mean? That is how we should treat the Bible as well. If the Bible intends a different meaning, the Bible will define the term for us. Otherwise, if that's what it says; then that is what it means.

When the translators chose this as the translation in every other translation and use, then it must be used that way here. It predicts the virgin birth. It sets the Messiah apart from every other person born into the human race. So this is why I am going with the definition of "*seed*" as the male's sperm [genetic material].

God is predicting a miracle. He is predicting something that should never happen on its own. A woman will produce a "*seed*"

16

of her own. That is a seed [sperm], not egg. Basic Biology 101, they are not the same thing. This should never happen on its own. That is why this is a miracle.

The woman will become pregnant because her body will produce both an egg and a sperm out of her own genetic material. They will join in her womb producing an embryo. That is what God and the Holy Spirit will cause in Mary's womb. God will cause the miracle to happen. The Holy Spirit will cause this to happen; but what is happening according to Genesis 3:15 is that Mary's body is given the ability to produce a "*seed*" [sperm] in her womb out of her own genetic material. You must look at the original prophecy, take it apart word by word, understand each word, phrase and provision; and then put it back together.

This is the first prophecy of the Virgin Birth. God intentionally used the word "*seed*" here and not "*egg*." This means a woman is going to produce a seed in her body, and that seed is going to merge with her egg. In plain, easy to understand terms, a woman's body is going to produce a sperm from her own genetic material. That sperm will join with her egg. Everything will be her own genetic material. No one will be adding anything of any genetic or physical material to her. Her womb will become a self-contained reproductive system.

God declares that there will be a seed produced by a woman. A woman will literally cause herself to become pregnant with her own genetic material. That is what this prophecy is saying. A woman will produce a child without the aid of any man. In other words, God was speaking of a Virgin Birth. The first term of this contract deals with a virgin giving birth to a child without the aid of any man.

This male will be wounded by sin and by death; but it will not be fatal. The wound inflicted by this male born of a virgin will be a head wound for sin and death. It will be a serious wound—more serious than the wound inflicted on the Seed.

Now notice something. This information was provided by direct revelation. God told Adam and Eve exactly how this coming contract would work. It would be related to a man who was born of a virgin. This man would break the power of sin and death over the human race. But how would that work? Genesis 3:21:

"Unto Adam also and to his wife did the Lord God make coats of skins, and clothed them."

Although most people miss this passage and its implications, this is the first animal sacrifice. God performed it. God gave Adam and Eve a visual example of how this male born of a virgin would break the power of sin and death.

When Adam and Eve sinned, by eating the forbidden fruit, the first thing that happened was that their eyes were opened, and they became aware that they were naked. Therefore, nakedness is a picture of sin. God covered the sin—the nakedness—by killing innocent animals, and using the skins of these animals to cover the nakedness—the picture of sin. In other words, an innocent must die in the place of the guilty to remove sin.

So here, God provides a visual representation of the contract. A male born of a virgin will break the power of sin by being innocent and yet dying in the place of the guilty. His blood will be shed, and He will die to break the power of sin and death.

***

God is silent for several generations until He calls to Abram who is living in Ur of the Chaldees. God selects Abram as the line through which this man born of a virgin will be born into. Genesis 2:2–3:

"'And I will make of you a great nation, and I will bless you, and make your name great; and you shall be a blessing:

And I will bless those who bless you, and curse him who curses you: and in you shall all families of the earth be blessed.'"

This is the calling of Abram, who will eventually be called Abraham. Through Abram shall all the families of the earth be blessed. Now it just makes sense that if God is going to send this man born of a virgin through Abram's line that God reveals to Abram the Big Picture. What did Abraham know about this male who was to born of a virgin who would break the power of sin and death?

***

To answer this, I am going to offer a quick view of an old and detailed study. This study suggests that when God named the stars, He gave them names that would tell the birth, life, death and return of Jesus Christ. In other words, if you know the names of these stars and their meaning, you can tell the Gospel using only the stars and constellations.

When I first heard this claim, I was at a Home Bible Study. I told the teacher that it sounded like someone had tried to "spiritualize" the Zodiac. At that time, a lot of people were taking secular things, and trying to make them sound Christian. He handed me a book from his library, The Gospel in the Stars by Duane Edward Spencer, and challenged me, "See for yourself." I accepted his challenge, and for the first few pages, I could see how someone was trying to make this sound Christian. I felt justified in my original assessment. But page after page, and chapter after chapter evidence was presented and continued to build to the point that there was no way someone was twisting the names and meaning of names of the stars, and there was no way this message could have been placed in the heavens by accident. I was convinced.

Now this was not a new thing. I did further research on my own. The first person to investigate and research this topic was Frances Rolleston. His book, *Mazzaroth or Constellations*, was published in 1862. Rolleston was a linguistic expert who was versed in several ancient languages from the Middle East. He did the physical work and research of collecting the works of various astronomers from Albumaze the Arab Astronomer and other experts up to the research of Caliphs of Grenada whose work was completed in 850 AD. He also collected and organized the Tables of star charts attributed to Ulugh Beigh. He was considered the Tartan Prince, and an astronomer whose work was completed in 1450 AD.

Another scholar took Rolleston's work and continued it. This was Dr. Joseph A. Seiss of Philadelphia. He produced the book, *The Gospel in the Stars* in America in 1882.

The next scholar to take up the torch and continue this research and study was Ethelbert William Bullinger [E. W. Bullinger]. He wrote his book, *The Witness of the Stars* in 1893. He cited the work of Frances Rolleston and Dr. Joseph Seiss. [All of these works are available on Amazon in various formats. I invite you to conduct your own research.]

These three works were considered the final word on this study, and we do not see much information added since Bullinger. However, there was the book I was given by the Home Bible Study teacher. It was written by Duane Edward Spencer. His book is also named *The Gospel in the Stars* and was printed in 1972–79 years after Bullinger's work. His book is out of print at this time. [You might find it at ABEbooks.com.]

We are seeing that this topic is coming to the public's attention once more, and several other authors are publishing their versions of this study. These authors are up-dating the language and writing style from that used in the 1800's. There is Ken Fleming who published his discussion of this topic in 1981, under the title of *God's Voice in the Stars*. There are other books—also on Amazon on the topic, but I want to mention Dr. Chuck Missler who referenced these works and this topic in his study, *Signs in the Heavens* in 1994.

This study all began from the Bible verse Luke 1:67–70. This is the father of John the Baptist:

"And his father Zacharias was filled with the Holy Spirit, and prophesied, saying,

"Blessed be the Lord God of Israel; for He has visited and redeemed His people,

"And has raised up a horn of salvation for us in the house of His servant David;

"As He spoke by the mouth of His holy prophets, *which have been since the world began:*" [Emphasis added]

Zacharias was speaking prophetically by the power of the Holy Spirit. In other words, God was speaking through him. The last part of his prophecy is what caught the eyes of these three early researchers. They asked, "How can you have a prophet before the world existed?" Before the world existed, all you had were the heavens. What was in the heavens? It was the stars. That began this research. It is based upon that statement, and it is based upon the fact that God declared that the sun, moon and stars were to be for signs and seasons. Genesis 1:14:

"And God said, 'Let there be lights in the firmament of the heaven to divide the day from the night; and let them be for signs, and for seasons, and for days, and years:'"

How can the lights in the heavens be for signs? What are they a sign of? And the last part of this presentation, in order for this to make sense, God—not man—named the stars. The names of the stars that we have in the ancient star charts are the names given to them by God. All of this brings us to Genesis 15:5:

"And [God] brought [Abram] forth abroad, and said, 'Look now toward heaven, and tell the stars [list them in order by name], if you be able to number them:' and [God] said unto [Abram], 'So shall your seed be.'"

Paul makes a very important observation concerning this verse in Galatians 3:16:

"Now to Abraham and his seed were the promises made. He said not, 'And to seeds,' as of many; but as of one, 'And to your seed,' which is Christ."

The reference to "*seed*" in Genesis 15:5 is singular. God was speaking of a single seed coming from Abraham. Paul tells us that God was specifically speaking of Jesus. This forces us to go back and look at God's instructions to Abram, especially in light of Genesis 5:16:

"And [Abram] believed in the Lord; and [God] counted it to [Abram] for righteousness."

When Abram went outside and listed the stars by name, there was information there. In the Hebrew, God told Abram to list the stars of the Zodiac in order, by name. Chuck Missler points out that this listing by name also referred to listing each star in each constellation by its brightness. You list the name of the brightest star in that constellation. Then you list the second brightest star in the constellation. Then the third brightest star and so forth.

We are listing these names of stars by constellation, and then by brightness to put them in the correct order. We begin with the constellation of Virgo the Virgin. We add in the minor constellation in that major constellation. You then follow the Mazzaroth—the Hebrew name for the Zodiac—and you go from constellation, star names and minor constellations. You keep doing this until you come the Leo the Lion.

There was a code set forth in ancient Egypt as to where to start this reading of the constellations. That code was the Sphinx. This is a statue of a lion, but it has the face of a woman. You start with the woman—Virgo—and read through to the end of the lion—Leo.

According to these experts and researchers, listing the names and meanings of these stars in this order, you will have the message of Jesus who will be the "*seed*" of the woman born to a virgin. He will have this conflict with the forces of evil. He will be wounded. He will fulfill prophecy, and He will return to earth as the Lion of the Tribe of Judah.

What God instructed Abraham to do was to go outside and read the Gospel of Jesus, which God had displayed in the heavens for signs. They were His prophets set in the heavens to speak God's message before earth was even created. When Abraham read this message, he believed what God told him in the names of the stars. It was not that Abram believed God, it was that Abram believed *in the Lord*. There is a difference here. Pay attention to the actual words God used in writing His Bible.

This belief resulted in Abram's salvation or being declared righteous before God. It was not that Abram believed he was going to have a lot of children. He did that in Genesis 13:16. He believed God was going to give him a lot of children back in Genesis Thirteen, but that belief did not translate into God declaring Abram to be righteous. What is the difference?

The difference between Chapter Thirteen and Chapter Fifteen is that in Chapter Thirteen, Abraham was just looking at stars. He was counting them if it were possible. In Chapter Fifteen, he was paying attention to their names. He was listing them in order. He was reading information God encoded in the constellations.

Here is just a quick sample: you begin with the constellation of Virgo, the Virgin. The brightest star is a star in one of her hands. This star in the ancient star charts means, *The Seed*. [Again, the "*seed*" of the woman.] There is a star in her other hand that means *The Branch*. Both of these are names assigned by God to the Messiah. There is still another star whose name means, *The Gloriously Beautiful*. Then there is a fourth star whose name means *Shall Come Down*. As part of the constellation of Virgo, there are smaller constellations. One of these is Coma. The picture created by Coma is the Virgin with her child on her lap. We are starting with God fulfilling His contract by sending the Messiah who will be the male born of the Seed of the Woman. He will enter our world and become human. He will be related to us by birth. The Gloriously Beautiful shall come down into our world.

If you follow the constellations, and pay attention to their names and what they mean in the older star charts you have the telling of Jesus being born of a virgin and dying for our sins. He then returns to judge the earth.

A lesser-known constellation in Hebrew is called Ophiuchus. This depicts a powerful man stepping on a scorpion and contending with [wrestling with] a serpent to keep it from stealing the crown. In this constellation, there are stars whose names mean: *The Head of Him Who Holds*, *Treading Underfoot*, *The Wounding* and *Contending*. The Scorpion is wounding the heel of this man and he is stepping on its head—or near its head depending on the illustrator. This constellation depicts the seed of Satan bruising the heel of the Seed of the Woman while the Seed of the Woman bruises the head of the serpent. It is a picture of the prophecy found in Genesis 3:15.

Libra the Scales, which represents judgment, has two stars in its constellation. One means *The Price is Insufficient*. The other has a star that means *The Price Has Been Covered*.

This happens over and over again, in constellation after constellation. It is too consistent and too numerous for someone to be making this up. It shows an intelligent design in how these stars were arranged, and how they were named.

God wrote His Plan for this man born of a virgin in the stars of the sky. Abram read this message and believed what he saw. He believed in the Lord. I believe the verse is worded this way because Abram read about the Lord [Jesus] in the stars and believed this person born of a virgin would come and die for his sins. I also believe that Abram believed that God would be this man born of a virgin and would be the sacrifice for sin. God would then return to rule the earth and defeat evil. That is what Abram read. That is what Abram believed. That is why God saved Abram and declared him to be righteous.

This explains how Abram [now Abraham] was able to speak prophetically to his son, Isaac. God had instructed Abraham to take Isaac to Mount Moriah, and offer him there as a sacrifice. As Abraham and Isaac were climbing to the top of the mountain, Isaac asked, "Here are the wood and the fire. Where is the lamb?" Genesis 22:8:

"And Abraham said, 'My son, God will provide Himself [as] a lamb for a burnt offering:' so they went both of them together."

Abraham now knew that God was going to become the sacrifice for sin. Abraham knew this because God revealed it to him as he read the story of this man born of a virgin in the night skies.

***

Notice that the promise that God would bless the entire earth through Abraham was given by direct revelation. God told this to Abram directly.

This same promise is given directly to Isaac by God, and then again directly to Jacob. The information about this man to be born of a virgin was also revealed to Abraham by God.

***

This is a point that we need to stress. There are two forms of *religion* in the world. I am using the term very loosely at this point to include Christianity and Judaism. The first kind of religion is intuitive. Those who belong to these intuitive religions, such as Buddhism or Hinduism, look at the clues in the world around them, and use intellect [intuition] to figure out who God is and what God is doing. The other form of religion is revelation—God reveals who He is and what He is doing.

The intuitive religion can never be sure if they have figured it out correctly. Their faith and teachings will always be nothing more than a guess. God is not speaking to them. God is not revealing Himself to them. They have to figure God out. They might be good at this. They might even be close. But it will always be nothing more than a guess.

With regards to those religions based upon revelation, the question is always: "Who is doing the revealing?" and "Are they revealing the truth?" When you are dealing with a religion based upon revelations from a supernatural source, you must always "*test the spirits*." I John 4:1:

"Beloved, believe not every spirit, but [test] the spirits whether they are of God: because many false prophets are gone out into the world."

John even gives us a test that we can use to see if a revelation is from God or of Satan. I John 4:2–3:

"[This is how you can know] the Spirit of God: Every spirit that confesses that Jesus Christ is come in the flesh is of God:

And every spirit that confesses not that Jesus Christ is come in the flesh is not of God: and this is that spirit of antichrist, whereof you have heard that it should come; and even now already is it in the world."

This phrase "*come in the flesh*" is referring to the Incarnation. God was born into the human race and God became one of us by birth—the virgin birth. Jesus existed as God prior to His birth in Bethlehem. He was still God when He was human and lived among us. He is still both human and God when He returned to Heaven. He will be God-made-human throughout all eternity.

Jesus is God. God is Jesus. Now God is a Trinity [Three]. God the Father is a spirit and is still a spirit. God the Holy Spirit is a spirit and is still a spirit. God the Son was a spirit, but became flesh and dwelt among us. John 1:14:

"And the Word was made flesh, and dwelt among us, (and we beheld His glory, the glory as of the only begotten of the Father,) full of grace and truth."

This is why John began his Gospel with this declaration John 1:1:

"In the beginning was the Word, and the Word was with God, and the Word was God."

The contract requires that this man born of a virgin who will be the offering for sin must be God. I will discuss this in more detail in later chapters.

***

As I was working on my research into the Bible as a legally binding contract, I came to the realization that the Old Testament serves as the terms of the contract. In a contract, Party One who wrote and makes the contract and offers it to Party Two outlines what Party One will do. Therefore, throughout the entire Old Testament God is revealing directly, through prophets and through something called similitudes [this is similar to that] all the requirements of this male born of a virgin will be and do.

This is a very exhaustive and lengthy list. Because it is part of what Party One of the contract is offering, then Party One must fulfill each of these terms to meet Party One's obligations under the contract. If Party One fails to meet a single term of the contract, the contract becomes null and void.

This is an important part of contract law. Both parties must come before the court "*with clean hands.*" That is the actual legal term. This means you cannot go before the civil court and sue the other party to a contract if you have not met all of your obligations first. Party One must meet all of its obligations listed in the contract before it can cry "*foul*" on the other parties. Party

Two [and other parties] must then fulfill their obligations under the contract before they can cry *"foul."*

If the parties take a contract to civil court and ask the court to enforce the contract, both parties or the party filing the suit must have met and fulfilled all of the terms they agreed to.

There are over 300 prophecies that God revealed concerning Jesus relating to His Virgin Birth, Crucifixion and Resurrection. If God did not [or Jesus did not] meet and fulfill each of these prophecies, the contract is not fulfilled, and it cannot be enforced. This means that the contract becomes null and void. It will be as if the contract never existed.

The New Testament is the documentation that God has fulfilled each of the terms of the contract. Now in terms of an insurance policy, this means that God has written an insurance policy for the human race. He promised to do specific things throughout the Old Testament. God fulfilled His legal obligations under the terms of the contract and these are documented in the New Testament.

As a claim adjuster, it would be my job to pull the policy and see what was offered, what promises were made, and the terms of the contract. Then I would need to conduct an investigation into the events surrounding the claim made against the policy. Did Party Two do everything they were required to do? Did Party One fulfill all the terms of the contract on its part. If both parties have fulfilled the terms of the contract and met all the obligations under the contract, then the claim is covered and whatever was promised is released to the parties.

Now in this case, God has established jurisdiction over the human race. He is the Creator. He has authority to do whatever He chooses to do with His Creation. God created the contract with the human race based upon a violation of the restrictions God placed upon the human race: do not eat the forbidden fruit. They ate the forbidden fruit. The penalty for eating the forbidden fruit is death.

There was now a need to avoid the penalty—a way to avoid the spiritual death and the physical death. God created this contract wherein He would become part of the human race. He would die in the place of the human race. Through this contract any member of the human race could avoid the consequences of sin—which would be death.

Jesus outlined the requirement on the part of Party Two to obtain this coverage under the contract. Normally this would be payment of a premium. You pay so much money each month or year, and you have this coverage. As God does not need money, the terms of the contract is a little different. John 3:16:

"For God so loved the world that He gave His Only Begotten Son; that whosoever believes in Him should not perish but have everlasting life."

This contractual obligation was first introduced at the time of Abram through the Book of Job. Job 33:27–30:

"[God] looks upon men, and if any say, 'I have sinned, and perverted that which was right, and it [did not profit me];

"[God] will deliver his soul from going into the pit, and his life shall see the light.

"Lo, all these things works God oftentimes with man,

To bring back his soul from the pit, to be enlightened with the light of the living."

How is God going to accomplish this? That answer is also from the Book of Job. Job 33:22–24:

"Yea, his soul draws near unto the grave, and his life to the destroyers.

"If there be a messenger with him, an interpreter, one among a thousand, to show unto man [God's] uprightness:

"Then [God] is gracious unto him, and says, 'Deliver him from going down to the pit: I have found a ransom.'"

Now when man approaches the grave his flesh is old and dying. He is facing death. Job 33:21:

"His flesh is consumed away, that it cannot be seen; and his bones that were not seen stick out."

Through this contract, death and old age will be reversed. Job 33:25:

"His flesh shall be fresher than a child's: he shall return to the days of his youth:"

Both sin and death are undone through this contract.

This contract is activated by two actions on the part of a member of the human race. First the person must confess his/her sins. "I have sinned." Sin is defined in this contract as, "I have perverted that which was right." [A contract will define the terms of the contract in the contract.]

The second action must be repentance; turning away from the sin: "And it did not profit me."

So confession of sin and repentance of sin activates this contract with God. On God's part He is going to provide someone to appear with this person when this person stands before God at death. This person is an interpreter. This is not someone who interprets languages, but it is someone who interprets the law. This would be an attorney. God will provide a public defender to represent us when we come near the grave and stand before Him. This public defender is guaranteed to win. The soul of the person coming before God who has confessed their sins and repented of their sins will be spared from the pit [death and the grave] and they will see the light. Their bodies will be restored [at the Resurrection].

Paul puts it this way in Ephesians 2:8–9:

"For by grace are you saved through faith; and that not of yourselves: it is the gift of God:

Not of works, lest any man should boast."

This is something that God gives you free of charge. Go back to Romans 6:23 and see the entire verse:

"For the wages of sin is death; but the gift of God is eternal life through Jesus Christ our Lord."

God adds another part to the contract. He notes that once this gift is given, there is no clause in the contract to take back that gift. Once given, it cannot be lost. Consider this like a clause in an insurance policy which forbids the insurance company from ever cancelling your policy. Romans 11:29:

"For the gifts and calling of God are without repentance."

Another way of wording this promise is: "For the gifts [salvation] and callings of God are [irrevocable]." They can never be invalidated or taken back. The policy can never be cancelled.

Now this is the contract God has written and offered to the human race. In order to avoid the consequences of sin, which will be death—both physical and spiritual; God is going to become a male born of a virgin and will pay for our sins. If anyone confesses their sins to God and repents of those sins, God will provide a defender when we stand before Him who will represent us and win the case. As a result, there will come that time when our flesh shall be made new, we will avoid the pit, we shall see the light and we will live forever.

God will perform all the work in obtaining salvation. God will perform all the work in maintaining salavation. God will provide all the costs in fulfilling this contract. The legal obligation on our part is to believe that God will do this, and to trust Him to save us.

***

Now one last point about contract law. Most contracts have a clause that states how the contract can be changed. It normally involves a change to the contract in writing and endorsed [signed] by all the parties. Without this written addendum, changes to the contract are not valid and will not be honored.

God makes it clear that He does not allow any change to His contract.

God first placed a restriction on making any changes to the contract. This was listed in the last of the five Books of Law. Moses was giving a farewell address, and as part of that farewell address he made it very clear that there could not be any changes to the Law given by God. Deuteronomy 4:2:

"You shall not add unto the word which I command you, neither shall you diminish ought from it, that you may keep the commandments of the Lord your God which I command you."

As I teach on the Bible as being a legally-binding contract between God and man, I need to stress the actual contract is the Law. This would be the Torah, the Pentateuch, the first five books of the Bible: Genesis, Exodus, Leviticus, Numbers and Deuteronomy. But a contract does have what is called *addendums*. These are documents that are added to the original contract to clarify any points of the contract that might need clarifying. In the case of the Bible, the other books of the Old Testament can be seen as addendums. Some parts of the New Testament can be seen as an addendum.

An addendum is an added document. It is written by the party writing the contract and the parties have agreed upon the addition. The addendum must be endorsed by the party that wrote the contract. It is requested by the party signing it. In my manuscript, *Contract Written in Blood*, I note that the blood that Jesus shed is how the contract was written, and the Resurrection of Jesus from the grave is how God endorsed the agreement.

So the party here in Deuteronomy Chapter Four that is adding to the agreement is God. His addendum do not change the contract, but it does give more information to help a claims adjuster like me make a correct decision as to when something is covered or not by the policy.

Now let me shift over to the New Testament and discuss another restriction God placed on His contract. This is found in Revelation 22:18–19:

"For I testify unto every man that hears the words of the prophecy of this book, If any man shall add unto these things, God shall add unto him the plagues that are written in this book:

"And if any man shall take away from the words of the book of this prophecy, God shall take away his part out of the book of life, and out of the holy city, and from the things which are written in this book."

Some suggest that this warning only applies to the Book of Revelation. But each contract must contain a clear warning regarding changes or failure to comply with the contract. Such changes or failures will render the contract null and void. That is exactly what these two verses are doing. You change the contract at your own risk. If you change the contract, God has no legal obligation to honor the changes that you have made.

This is why it is so important to look at the teachings of various religions in light of contract law. This is not a collection of beliefs. It does matter what you believe. If what you believe is incorrect, then God's contract does not apply.

Christianity is a legal system. There were promises made by God. These promises involve specific physical events taking place in our world. There was the Virgin Birth. There was the Crucifixion, and there was the Resurrection. If these promises were not fulfilled as described by the contract, then God failed to fulfill His part of the contract. The contract becomes null and void.

Have you noticed that most Cults attack these three events directly or indirectly. They challenge the Virgin Birth. They deny that Jesus is now God among us [the result of the Virgin Birth]. They challenge the Crucifixion. They deny or challenge the Resurrection of Jesus. The physical evidence in our world of what God is doing is challenged, denied and altered. They try to hide what God has promised and what God has done.

The contract requires action—not just beliefs—on the part of those entering into this contract. There is the confession of sins. There is the repentance of sins. There is the need to accept Jesus as our defender [Savior] when we stand before God.

How we do this is outlined in the contract. Our obligations are outlined under the contract. It is a very one-sided contract. We endorse the contract—accept it; and God does everything else. But it is a contract. We do not have the legal authority to alter it or replace it. To do so will result in the contract becoming null and void.

***

In the light of this, let us go forward and examine those belief systems that claim they are Christian and covered by this contract but they are not. They are deceptions. They are deceptions by the enemy—Satan. They are deceptions that if we fall for them will result in our damnation before God. This is why I entitled this book, *Damned Deceptions*. These are deceptions that will result in your being damned before God.

I know that this is harsh. We do not like to speak of this. But as I noted before, the person writing the contract has the obligation to make the contract as clear as possible. This means we have to address the unpleasant and unpopular topics. Therefore I want to make this legal analysis and its consequences as clear as possible.

There is another difference between Christianity and other faiths. It is also a difference that makes Christianity a legal contractual system. It provides guarantees. This is the entire basis for contract law. One or more parties guarantees or promises to do something for other parties. The guarantees are written down and all the parties agree to these promises in writing and sign the agreement. If one or more of the parties fails to do what they have promised to do, the contract has been broken, and there is a court of law the parties can appeal to in order to force the violating party to do what he/she promised to do.

In this case, I am talking about salvation. This is the theme of the entire Bible. We need to be saved. God wants to save us. God has provided a way to save us. And here is where Christianity is different from all other faith systems: it guarantees salvation. I John 5:13:

"These things have I written unto you who believe on the name of the Son of God; *that you may know* that you have eternal life, and that you may believe on the name of the Son of God." [Emphasis added]

Consider these other verses:

Romans 10:9: "That if you shall confess with your mouth the Lord Jesus, and shall believe in your heart that God has raised Him from the dead, you shall be saved."

Notice that little word of "shall." That is what we call in the legal field, a "*legal imperative*." When you see this word in a law, compliance is mandatory. When you see it in the negative [shall not], then the action is forbidden. If there are no exceptions listed; then there are no exceptions.

Romans 10:13: "For whosoever shall call upon the name of the Lord shall be saved."

There it is again. "*Shall*"—it is mandatory that you will be saved. There are no exceptions listed here. There are also places where the "*shall*" is implied by the logic and internal composition of a verse. Consider John 3:16: "For God so loved the world that He gave His only begotten Son, that whosoever believers on Him shall not perish but have eternal life."

Now it does not say, "shall have eternal life;" but it is implied because of the way this verse is constructed. This verse links the "shall not perish" with the "have eternal life." By linking these phrases, they must be the same thing—the same promise. Since the "shall not perish" is mandatory; then the "have eternal life" also becomes mandatory and could be translated "shall have eternal life."

Let me add in something else I shall keep coming back to throughout this legal argument. This salvation is not something you work for. It is not something you earn. It is not something you are worthy of. All the other faith systems in the world suggest that somehow we have to earn salvation. We have to be worthy of it. But not Christianity. It makes it very clear that salvation is a gift given by God. Ephesians 2:8–9:

"For by grace are you saved through faith; and that not of yourselves: it is the gift of God:

Not of works, lest any man should boast."

Also Romans 6:23:

"For the wages of sin is death; but the gift of God is eternal life through Jesus Christ our Lord."

The Bible is God's contract. God wrote the contract, and He is offering it to us. I mentioned earlier that there is an important rule in contract law: the person writing the contract has the obligation to make the contract as clear as possible. Any ambiguity in the contract will be judged in favor of the party accepting the contract, not the party writing the contract. The person writing the contract has the ability to clear up any questions or ambiguities in the contract. Failure to do so goes against the one writing the contract.

This contract deals with salvation. God is offering salvation; and this is how we can obtain salvation. In these two verses, salvation is identified as a gift that God gives. It is ours for the asking. Now if a contract has conflicting statements, the courts will identify the statement that is in the best interests of the party accepting the contract, and those statements will be used to override any conflicting statements.

Here God offers salvation as a free gift. It is ours for the asking. Any other requirement mentioned in the Bible—if it contradicts these statements will be deemed null and void, and this requirement for free salvation will prevail. Now other passages do not contradict these two statements if you do proper research into what they are saying in the original language; and so salvation is a gift offered by God. It is free for the asking.

Now because God prepared the Bible as a contract, this requires that the other party must accept the offer and enter into the contract. People can have great contracts and offer great things, but they are not automatically ours. Because they are part of the contract, you must enter into the contract. Therefore, if someone does not enter into the contract and accept the terms of the contract, the free gift of salvation does not become theirs. No one can force you into a contract, nor can anyone enter into a contract on your behalf. It is something you must do personally. And you must do it of your own free will.

So unlike other faith systems, God's Bible makes promises. God guarantees these promises. He ensures that if we enter into His contract we will have salvation, and we will be saved. This guarantee is missing from all other faith system.

If we enter into this contract He has offered, and all parties abide by the terms of the contract [i. e. we ask God to save us]; then these guarantees are ours. As Romans 8:1 points out that once we enter into this contract, it is in force immediately:

"There is therefore *now* no condemnation…" [Emphasis added]

The promises will be fulfilled. The guarantees will come true, and God will never withdraw from this contract. Romans 11:29:

"For the gifts and the callings of God are without repentance."

CHAPTER TWO

THE KINSMAN REDEEMER

As we are dealing with the concept of the Bible being a legally-binding contract between God and man, we need to take a few moments to examine and understand the terms of the contract and the laws that are controlling it. The Laws in this case are the Laws God gave to Moses.

Keep in mind that the basis for a contract is that one party is offering something to one or more other parties. The contract specifies what is being offered and how the other parties can obtain it. In our case, the contract is offering salvation, and the contract [the Bible] outlines how God is going to provide this for us, and how we can obtain it. This is an important concept because no one can enter into a contract on your behalf. No one can force you into a contract. If either of these happens, the court will declare the contract null and void.

This is why God has to define how we obtain salvation. Salvation cannot be automatic because it is provided through a contract. To make salvation automatic for everyone would mean that God has removed free will, and God has entered into the contract on our behalf without our knowledge or permission. The courts would not allow that.

So God is establishing the contract. He has identified His legal authority to set standards for us, and His jurisdiction to judge us for violation of these standards. God has also made the contract so simple and so desirable that it is hard to conceive of anyone not wanting to enter into this contract; but people will choose to reject it. When that happens, we are dealing with very unusual people, or people who have been deceived, and do not know what they are doing. However, the Law still requires that if you want the benefits this contract is offering, we must choose to enter the contract, and this choice must be of our own free will.

Now God is choosing to not pass down the legal sentence of physical and spiritual death. To do this, He must work within the legal system and prove His legal right to suspend or transfer the sentence. Once He has established this; then He will have the legal authority to withhold judgment upon us.

We have already seen how the verbal contract was created in the Garden of Eden. God will send a male through a virgin birth. This male will confront sin and death, and break the power of sin and death. God then gave Adam and Eve a visual example of how this would happen by killing an innocent animal to cover the results of their sin [nakedness].

This initial example played out from the time of Adam down to Noah. He offered sacrifices when he and his family came out of the ark. It continued from Noah to Job and Abraham. They continued the practice of offering innocent animals on the altar to cover their sins. There is no discussion concerning formal and specific sacrifices until God brings Moses to Mount Sinai, and gives Moses both a verbal account of His Law and then has Moses create a written account of God's Law. The written account of God's Law expanded into five books: Genesis, Exodus, Leviticus, Numbers and Deuteronomy.

Now God had selected the Children of Israel to be His Chosen People. There is an initial promise by God to the Children of Israel. In Exodus 15:26 God makes His initial offer:

"And said, 'If you will diligently hearken to the voice of the Lord your God, and will do that which is right in His sight, and will give ear to His commandments, and keep all His statutes, I will put none of these diseases upon you, which I have brought upon the Egyptians: for I am the Lord who heals you.'"

When the Children of Israel came to Mount Sinai, God clarified His offer to the Children of Israel. Exodus 19:5–6:

""'Now therefore, if you will obey my voice indeed, and keep my covenant, then you shall be a peculiar treasure unto me above all people: for all the earth is mine:

""""And you shall be unto me a kingdom of priests, and a holy nation." These are the words which you shall speak unto the Children of Israel.'"

You will notice that there are actions required by the Children of Israel to enter into this contract. There are works involved in this contract. They must hear, obey, do and perform. This is because this is a contract of service. It is not a contract for salvation. They will serve God and be used of God. This offer is finalized and sealed with blood in Exodus Chapter Twenty-Four. Exodus 24:3:

"And Moses came and told the people all the words of the Lord, and all the judgments: and all the people answered with one voice, and said, 'All the words which the Lord has said will we do.'"

In response to this verbal agreement to the terms of this contract, Moses sets up an altar and twelve pillars—one for each tribe. Moses performed sacrifices before the Children of Israel. Then we find in Exodus 24:6–8:

"And Moses took half of the blood, and put it in basins; and half of the blood he sprinkled on the altar.

"And he took the book of the covenant, and read in the audience of the people: and they said, 'All that the Lord has said will we do, and be obedient.'

"And Moses took the blood, and sprinkled it on the people, and said, 'Behold the blood of the covenant, which the Lord has made with you concerning all these words.'"

We then see God coming down, and verbally giving His Ten Commandments to the Children of Israel. They freak out, and ask Moses to be the one to listen to God and tell them what God has said. So throughout Exodus, Leviticus, Numbers and Deuteronomy, Moses documents all that God is saying to the Children of Israel.

In an over-simplified summary, the Law of Moses deals with the concept of salvation. It identifies God's Law and defines in detail what sin is. It identifies the need for a Redeemer. It promises that God will send a Redeemer. The Law then teaches/preaches who and what this Redeemer will be, and what this Redeemer will do.

This message for the world will be presented in three forms. The first form will be a visual aid. Through sacrifices, the Children of Israel will repeat over and over again the message of God: "An innocent must die in the place of the guilty." Through seven Feasts, God will set timetables, create more visual aids, and ensure witnesses will be present to see God do what He has promised to do; i.e. provide a Redeemer. This way, the Children of Israel will become witnesses that God has fulfilled the contract and done as He has promised.

Finally, through another visual aid, God has created pictures [similitudes (this is similar to that)] through the Tabernacle, its structure, furnishings and the garments of the High Priest. Each part of the Tabernacle can be used to teach people more about the Redeemer.

Everything about the Law of Moses and the religion of Israel is designed to prepare the world for the coming of the Messiah [Redeemer], and to identify Him when He arrives.

The Law of Moses set forth various pictures, procedures and similitudes relating to the contract God was providing. The Feasts of Israel were pictures of this coming male born of a virgin. The various sacrifices were also pictures of this coming virgin-born man. Even the Tabernacle, its furniture and priestly garments, were all pictures of this coming virgin-born male, and what He would do as His part of the contract.

However, with the declaration that an animal used in the sacrifices had to be without spot or blemish, the Law of Moses made it impossible for any normal male to fulfill the legal requirement.

A "*spot*" refers to something that the animals have inherited. This would be any defect passed down through genetics—a birth defect. The "*blemish*" refers to an acquired defect, something that happened either at birth or after birth. Because sin is an inherited defect, any normal human could never meet the legal requirement for this virgin-born male to serve as the sacrifice for sin.

This means that this coming male, born of a virgin, must actually be from outside the human race and not inherit the sin nature the human race has been tainted with. But if this male is from outside the human race, it creates a serious legal issue about His authority to redeem us.

God made it clear that this virgin-born male would be God—the Son of God—through prophets and other revelations. A Psalmist during the Babylonia Captivity makes it clear that it is God who will be this Redeemer. Psalm 49:15:

"But God will redeem my soul from the power of the grave, for He shall receive me. Selah."

The reason why it has to be God is because no one in the entire human race can qualify. Psalm 49:7:

"None of them can by any means redeem his brother, nor give to God a ransom for him."

Isaiah gave more details about this virgin-born male. Isaiah 7:14:

"Therefore the Lord Himself shall give you a sign; Behold, a virgin shall conceive, and bear a son, and shall call His name *Immanuel*."

Matthew tells us what "*Immanuel*" means. It means that *God is with us*—physically present among us. So through the virgin-birth of this man, God will come to live among us. Isaiah also noted in Isaiah 9:6:

"For unto us a child is born, unto us a son is given: and the government shall be upon His shoulders: and His name shall be called Wonderful Counselor, The Mighty God, The Everlasting Father, The Prince of Peace."

Here the names of this child Isaiah is speaking of are names that apply only to God. "*The Mighty God*" and "*The Everlasting Father*" are titles that belong to God the Father. This child shall be the same as God the Father. He shall be equal to God the Father.

Finally, the prophet Micah adds to this description. Micah 5:2:

"But you, Bethlehem Ephratah, though you are little among the thousands of Judah, yet out of you shall He come forth unto me who is to be ruler in Israel; whose goings forth have been from of old, from everlasting."

This ruler who is born in Bethlehem will have existed before His own birth. In fact, the way this verse is worded tells us that this ruler has always existed. It also notes that this ruler will exist forever. He will have no beginning or end. If we cross-reference this prophecy with how the Psalmist describes God in Psalm 93:2 we will see the same description is used:

"Your throne is established of old, You *are from everlasting.*" [Emphasis added]

This will exclude every human since we have a beginning. It will also exclude every angelic being as each of them was created and, therefore, had a beginning. The only person who meets this description is God. This is another way of telling us that God will be this Redeemer.

***

To better understand God's Plan, we need to look at the Law of Moses. The Law of Moses is the template for how God will save the world from sin. There is a law that does allow for redemption. It is called The Kinsman Redeemer, and it is found in Leviticus 25:25:

"If your brother has become poor, and has sold away some of his possession, and if any of his kin come to redeem it, then shall he redeem that which his brother sold."

Now this law relating to redemption always allows for the person in debt to redeem himself. If the person in debt cannot redeem himself, he is required to sell his possessions to pay the debt. If that is not enough; then he must become the slave of the one he owes the debt to. He will be a slave for seven years.

This is our legal problem: when we sin, we create a debt. That debt is to sin. Romans 6:23 tells us that "the wages of sin is death." The price of sin is death. Now if this were speaking of just a physical death, then when we die physically, our debt would be paid. But it also includes spiritual death. When we die physically, we continue to die spiritually forever.

The Bible also adds to the problem. Romans 3:23 tells us that "all have sinned." Each person in the human race has

41

sinned; therefore, none of us can redeem ourselves. We all lack the price to redeem ourselves, and so we do not have the price to redeem someone else. If there is any hope for redeeming mankind, it must come from outside of the human race.

But it is not that easy. This Law requires that if someone wants to redeem a person who has fallen into debt there are three legal requirements. First of all, they must be related to the one who is in debt by birth. Second, the person must have the funds or resources to pay for the debt. Finally, the person redeeming the one in debt must be willing to redeem the man in debt. All three requirements must be present.

God wanted to redeem us, but this law created some problems. First of all, God was not related to us by birth. God was our Creator. He was not our brother. Therefore, God lacked the legal status to redeem us. No matter how much God qualified under the third requirement—in other words, no matter how much God wanted to redeem us, He lacked the other two legal requirements.

The Law of Moses also laid down the legal requirements to remove sin. Leviticus 17:11:

"For the life of the flesh is in the blood: and I have given it to you upon the altar to make an atonement for your souls: for it is the blood that makes an atonement for the soul."

The author of the Book of Hebrews puts it this way. Hebrews 9:22:

"And almost all things are by the law purged with blood; and without shedding of blood is no remission."

This poses a serious problem for God. The price to redeem from sin is shedding your blood until you die. God the Father is a spirit. Prior to the Virgin Birth, God the Son [Jesus] was also a spirit. God the Holy Spirit is a spirit. As a spirit, the Trinity has no blood of its own to shed. The Trinity, as a spirit, cannot die. Therefore, the Trinity is not only not legally entitled to redeem, God lacks the payment to redeem us [blood and death].

Now the first term of this contract focuses on the "*Seed of the Woman*" [Genesis 3:15]. God has established His jurisdiction. He has established His legal right to impose restrictions and to punish violations. He has established that death is the result of sin. He has imposed a suspended sentence through the use of an innocent dying in the place of the guilty. So the first vital clause in this contract with humanity is providing this virgin-born male. This is one of the promises God makes through this contract.

As we noted earlier, this male must be without inherited sin. This disqualifies any son of Adam as the sin nature is passed down from father to child. But God has also blocked the use of any other being from stepping in and becoming this virgin-born male. The contract notes that this person must have existed forever—must be without a beginning or an end. All of the angelic and heavenly hosts have a beginning. They were created beings. Even if God created a special male to be born of this virgin, that person could never qualify under the contract. That person would have a beginning. The only person who could qualify is God. God literally wrote Himself into a corner through the prophecies. The virgin-born male must be God, and only God. No one else will qualify.

This is an important legal point to make here. The person who becomes the virgin-born male must be God. If this virgin-born male is anything less than God; then this virgin-born male does not fulfill the terms of the contract. The contract becomes null and void. It cannot be enforced.

This is why John noted in John 1:1:

"In the beginning was the Word, and the Word was with God, and the Word was God."

Paul described Jesus in this way. Philippians 2:6–8:

"Who, being in the form of God, thought it not robbery to be equal with God:

But made Himself of no reputation, and took upon Him the form of a servant, and was made in the likeness of men

And being found in fashion as a man, He humbled Himself, and became obedient unto death, even the death of the cross."

Jesus is God. Jesus is equal to God. The only reason Jesus became obedient to God was by His own choice. He chose to obey God the Father. He did not have to obey God the Father.

Now Jesus could have assumed a human form. There are accounts of Him doing so throughout the Old Testament. The Angel of the Lord, in most cases, was Jesus appearing in either a human or angelic form to men. Now as such, Jesus had part of the payment to redeem. He had blood. But He could not die, and He was not related to the human race through birth. So God had to take the DNA material of a woman, and place Himself into that DNA.

Now if this had been a human sperm joined with a human egg, then a new soul would have been created. We become living souls at the moment our parents' sperm and egg join in the womb. This was not to be a new soul. This was to be an old soul, an eternal soul that had no beginning or end. Therefore, the male DNA could not be involved. This is why it had to be a virgin birth. God took the female DNA and caused her body to create a sperm. This provided the male chromosome so that the virgin-born child would be male.

Now because this sperm and egg were of the woman, it created a unique form of life. The embryo created a body, but it did not generate a new soul connected to it. It was soulless. Jesus joined Himself to the embryo. It would grow into a normal body, but Jesus would be the soul for this human body. This way sin could not be passed down from parents to child.

This resolves all the legal problems. God, as Jesus born into the human race, is now related to us by birth. Jesus now has His own blood that can be shed. Jesus can now die. He is legally qualified to redeem us. He is related to us by birth. He has the price for the redemption in that He has His own blood that can be shed; and He can die. This will fulfill the contractual requirements.

If we remove the Virgin Birth, this male would not fulfill the contract. If this male born of a virgin is anyone other than God, it invalidates the contract. If this male born of a virgin had a new soul or the birth process created a new soul in the embryo, it would have inherited sin and disqualified the virgin-born male from being the sin offering. He would not be innocent. He could not die in our place. If this male born of a virgin does not fulfill each and every one of the prophecies relating to His First Coming to earth, the contract becomes null and void.

If the contract becomes null and void, then Jesus cannot save us. He cannot remove sin and death from our lives. If Jesus is not everything the contract requires, then there is no other virgin-born male who can meet the legal requirements of the contract. In other words, we are all going to Hell, and there is nothing to stop us or save us. Even God cannot forgive our sins and spare us, because that was not a clause in the contract.

Everything must follow the contract. All parties must fulfill their obligations under the contract or the contract cannot save us. As we look at the two main Cults, which serve as templates for most Cults, we will see that if what they profess is true; then there is no salvation, and we are all still lost in our sins. It is not that they can create an alternate Plan of Salvation that will work for them. God is only offering one contract so that means that there is only one Plan of Salvation. If you reject the contract or try to alter the contract, you run the risk of invalidating the contract. If the contract becomes invalid, there is no other contract available to us.

CHAPTER THREE

IS GOD A JUST GOD?

I am going to spend a little bit of time looking at God and what God has revealed about Himself. This information is important, as Cults will make statements concerning God that contradict what God is saying about Himself. In order to understand the actions of God, we need to understand the nature and character of God. So I want to ask, "What does God say about Himself?"

I mentioned earlier that all religions fall into two categories. There is the intuitive category and there is the revelation category. The intuitive category relies on intuition, observation, logic and analysis of clues to determine who and what God is, and what God requires of us. Unfortunately, there is no way to know if you got it right until that moment that you stand before God. And if you got it wrong, there is no way that you can change things at that point. Intuitive religion does not know. Intuitive religion cannot know. At best, it is guessing. But, to be honest, it is seeking. This applies to most of the eastern religions.

They have founders and teachers that were presenting their ideas of how the universe worked, and what God required of us, and where we would spend eternity. None of these founders knew for sure. All of these founders were characterized as being seekers. They were all seeking the truth. Unfortunately, they would never know for sure if they had guessed the truth correctly until it was too late.

For lack of a better description, these religions are building their own God(s). They are picking up this trait and this action. They are building a jigsaw puzzle from all the pieces lying around them and trying to make them fit into who God is. C. S. Lewis, in his book, *The Problem of Pain*, made the observation that if man were going to build his own God to explain the way life is; then why would anyone present Him as kind and loving?

The world is not kind. The world is not loving. There is a lot of pain and misery. In a story featuring Robert E. Howard's fictional fantasy character, Conan the Barbarian, the central character describes his god, Crom. Conan came from the icy wastelands of Cimmeria, which would be present-day Germany. "Crom sits up on his icy mountain. If Crom notices you, he will torment you and test you." For this reason, you spend your entire life trying to make sure that Crom does not notice you.

To be honest, if I were going to build my own god; I would model him after Crom. That would explain the pain and suffering in the world. It would explain the wars, torture, cruelty and disease. Yes, having a god like Crom would explain a lot. So C. S. Lewis asked a very reasonable question: "If the Christian made God up; then why would you make Him loving and kind? The world does not support such a picture of God."

If you follow the logic, then no one in their right mind would describe the god of this world as loving and kind. But that is the problem. The god of this world is not God the Creator. The god of this world is Satan the Usurper. He tried to usurp the throne of God and lost. He was cast out. And he uses the power that he has to try to destroy what God the Creator loves.

Why do we claim that God is loving and kind if we have made God for our own benefit? The answer is simple. We did not create God. We are not going on intuition. We are not looking at the clues and guessing what God is like. The revelation religions claim that God has revealed who His is, what He is doing; and what He expects of us.

C. S. Lewis had an interesting argument that he used during his days of being an atheist. He would argue that it was impossible for us to meet our Creator just as it was impossible for Hamlet to meet his creator: Shakespeare. This is because they existed in two different planes of existence. Shakespeare existed in the three-dimensional real world. Hamlet existed on a printed page of a play. Hamlet could not leave the book. He could not rise from the printed page. He could not enter our world. He could never meet Shakespeare. His logic was good, and C. S. Lewis presented the problem correctly. From our point of view, it is impossible for us to ever meet our Creator. This is why the intuitive religions were our best bet. We would look at clues around us and deduce from them what we could about God. We would then try to guess what God was like, and what God expected of us.

It is interesting that almost all of these intuitive religions suggested that there would be a judgment at the end of our lives. They all portrayed God as some sort of judge. The concept of good and evil was important to them. They all wanted to avoid punishment.

However, when C. S. Lewis accepted Jesus as his Savior, he came up with a solution to his Shakespeare/Hamlet Dilemma. He had only looked at it from the point of view of Hamlet. It was impossible for Hamlet to meet Shakespeare. It is also impossible for us to leave our plane of existence and enter Heaven to meet God.

"But," suggested C. S. Lewis, "is the same true for God?" He came to realize that there was a way for Shakespeare to meet Hamlet, but only if Shakespeare took the initiative. What if Shakespeare wrote a new play? And in this play, Shakespeare created a character that represented him. And in this new play, Shakespeare wrote a scene in which the character of Shakespeare met the character of Hamlet. Shakespeare could write dialogue for the Shakespeare character, and reveal things about Shakespeare to Hamlet without having to have Hamlet leave the printed page.

It is possible for us to meet our Creator if our Creator takes the initiative. If our Creator speaks to us, then we can hear Him. If our Creator is born into our world and becomes one of us; then we can meet Him and learn from Him. This is the basis of Christianity. Judaism and Islam do not have God coming into our world as part of Creation and interacting with us. The Jews are expecting this; but it has not happened yet in their understanding. Islam does not have God becoming one of us and meeting us in this life.

They both accept revelations and God speaking to us through prophets and other means; but God becoming one of us and entering our world to reveal Himself is not part of their religion—at least not yet. The Jews believe a Messiah is coming, and that Messiah will be God coming among them; but they reject this claim concerning Jesus, and they are still waiting for their Messiah to appear even though the appointed time per their prophets has passed.

The Incarnation of Jesus into the world is God's solution to the Shakespeare/Hamlet Dilemma. God becomes part of His Creation in order to reveal Himself to us directly. Jesus was not a man God used to speak to us. Jesus was God as man coming among us to reveal Himself in person.

Now, as I mentioned earlier, this poses a serious problem. How do we know that it is God who is speaking to us? The entire basis for the *Church of Jesus Christ of Latter-Day Saints* is based upon what they claim to be revelations from God to them through prophets, angels and ancient books. These revelations contradict traditional revelations. How do we know which revelation is of God, especially when the revelations contradict?

I John 1:4 instructs us to test the spirits when information is given to us from a supernatural source:

"Beloved, believe not every spirit, but [test] the spirits whether they are of God: because many false prophets are gone out into the world."

John even gave us the way to test the spirits. We test the spirits by what they teach, not by how they look, or what they do. I John 4:2–3:

"[This is how you can know] the Spirit of God: Every spirit that confesses that Jesus Christ is come in the flesh is of God:

And every spirit that confesses not that Jesus Christ is come in the flesh is not of God: and this is that spirit of antichrist, whereof you have heard that it should come; and even now already is it in the world."

The "*Jesus is come in the flesh*" refers to the Incarnation. Is Jesus Christ God, who was born into the human race and is now human—now one of us? There are three core events that are required by the contract offered by God. These core events are actual physical events that took place in our world that we can research and investigate as proof of the contract, and that God is fulfilling the contract He has offered us. Because of these three physical, historical core events, Christianity is not a faith-based religion. It is a fact-based legal system offered by God to each one of us.

The first historical core event is the Incarnation. Was Jesus born into the human race via a virgin birth? Is Jesus God? Is God now human; and is He now related to us by birth?

The second historical core event is the Crucifixion. Did Jesus die upon a cross? Did He die at the time and in the manner predicted by God through the Old Testament prophets?

The third historical core event is the Resurrection. Did Jesus rise from the grave in the manner and at the time the prophets predicted?

There were over three hundred prophecies given in the Old Testament relating to these three historical core events. Part of these prophecies also mentions other actions Jesus would perform with regards to healing and teaching. These are historical events that took place in our world, so it should be possible to investigate them, and examine the evidence for ourselves.

We should find it an important point that Cults attack these three core events. They change how Jesus entered our world, or who He was when He entered our world. They change how He died, or why He died. They change the Resurrection into something else. By attacking these three core events, they seek to remove the physical proof offered by God and the Bible. They attack the salvation God offers through His Bible. They even attack the Bible.

The message of the Bible, the proof of the Bible, and the gift of salvation is what humanity wants and needs. It is a Win-Win Situation for God and mankind. So why are the Cults seeking to destroy it? There is no sense to these efforts until you recognize the force behind these Cults and behind these efforts: Satan. He wants to see everything that God does and loves destroyed. This is the only way these efforts make any sense.

***

But what I wanted to do for this chapter was to examine what we do know about God as a result of revelation and how we can test revelations concerning God.

As I noted concerning the Intuitive Religions, they all teach that there will be a time when we are judged by God. The four Revelation Religions all have a similar point in common. They teach that there will be a judgment at some point in the future. There will be an accounting for our actions and inactions.

They also teach that God is a just judge, so let me start with this point. As none of the main Revelation Religions contradict this statement, we can assume that it is true. If God has revealed Himself to Judaism, Christianity, Islam and Mormonism as being a just God, then we can safely begin with this information concerning God, and use logic and common sense to build on this foundation.

Now let me begin this discussion of God being a just God by the logic and meaning of such a statement. The concept of being a just God means that God is fair. In order for God to be fair, then He must deal with and treat the first man and woman [Adam and Eve] the same way He will deal with and treat the last man and woman—and every man and woman (or child) in between. That is the working definition of being just and fair.

This requires announcing how things work. God announced to Adam and Eve that they had only one restriction: "*Do not eat the fruit of the Tree of Knowledge.*" God announced the punishment for violating this restriction: "*You shall surely die.*" This was fair. God told them the restriction. God revealed the result of violating that restriction. God is a just God.

Now they violated that restriction, and they were placed under a sentence of death. There was immediate spiritual death in that they were now separated from God by their sin. There was eventual physical death as they began to die, and death would eventually claim them when their souls separated from their bodies. God offered a suspended sentence regarding the spiritual death. They were considered dead spiritually, but the sentence would be suspended if they believed that God would eventually send a man born of a virgin to break the power of sin and death. As a physical way of demonstrating this belief, they would offer an innocent animal to die in their place.

Notice what I have done. I have gone all the way back to the first revelation of God dealing with the first man and woman. This is how God first revealed how He dealt with the first man and the first woman. Now for God to be just, He must deal with each and every man and woman the same way until He deals with the last man and woman. I can say this with confidence because that is the definition of a just God.

Each and every person is facing both spiritual and physical death because of sin. That is the status of every living person in the world: past, present and future. God has suspended that sentence of spiritual death in order to give each and every person time to consider if they will accept the offer of this man who is to be born of a virgin. By doing this, God is being fair. God is being just.

This practice continued prior to the Jewish faith. No other plan was offered. Even when the Book of Job—possibly the oldest book ever written—presented the concept that confession of sin and repentance of sin would result in our avoiding being sent into the pit [Hell]; it was still based upon the belief that God would provide someone to come and stand before Him with us, and that this person was a male who would serve as a public defender. He would become our "*ransom*."

Even when we see God calling the Children of Israel to be His Chosen People, there was not a change in the Plan of Salvation. Many people get this wrong. They look at the Law of Moses, and they begin to believe that keeping the Law would result in salvation. If anyone could keep the Law of Moses in all points, they would not be in danger of going into the pit.

This is because it would also mean that they had never sinned, and so there was no sin in their life. But that is NOT a Plan of Salvation. If there is no sin; then salvation is not required. There is nothing to save us from.

So even though there will be those who claim that by keeping the Law of Moses—or the Ten Commandments—they are saved, they are not saved. The truth is more correctly stated that they are *not condemned*. Not being condemned is not the same thing as being saved. Being saved suggests that there is a danger, and somehow we have been spared from that danger. If you keep the Law of Moses, there is no danger for you. You are not subject to being judged by God. How can God judge you, if you have done nothing wrong? If there are no charges filed against you, then you will never go to court and you will never stand before the Judge. But James noted in James 2:10:

"For whosoever shall keep the whole law, and yet offend in one point, he is guilty of all."

Think of the Law of Moses as a chain hanging over the pit of Hell. The chain is securely fasted to the edge of the cliff, and you are securely fastened to the other end. Now you can imagine ten links of chain as in the Ten Commandments, or you can imagine 613 links of chain as the Jews believe that there are 613 basic parts of the Law. It really does not matter. If you are hanging over the pit of Hell by this length of chain, and just one link breaks, it really does not matter which link breaks. The end result is that you are going to fall into the pit.

So, yes, if you can keep each and every Law that God handed down through Moses, and not violated a single point of that law or the spirit of that Law; then there is no sin in your life. If there is no sin in your life, then death has no power over you. It is a basic premise of law that if you do not break the law; then the law has no power over you. It cannot do anything to you. But this level of compliance is physically impossible. We have all sinned. We have all earned death. We are all going to Hell because of that single sin.

If we go back and look at the covenant God made with the Children of Israel, there is no promise of salvation in that covenant. Take a look for yourself. Exodus 15:26 this was the initial verbal agreement:

"And said, 'If you will diligently hearken to the voice of the Lord your God, and will do that which is right in His sight, and will give ear to His commandments, and keep all His statutes, I will put none of these diseases upon you, which I have brought upon the Egyptians: for I am the Lord who heals you.'"

This was a covenant of protection. There was no offer of salvation in this agreement. When the Children of Israel came to the base of Mount Sinai, God had Moses perform a more permanent contract. Moses set up pillars—one for each tribe. He set up an altar. He offered sacrifices upon the altar and caught the blood in a basin. He repeated the formal agreement God was offering to them. When they gave verbal assent, Moses sprinkled the blood from the basin over all the people using a branch of hyssop. Exodus 19:5–8:

"'Now therefore, if you will obey my voice indeed, and keep my covenant, then you shall be a peculiar treasure unto me above all people: for all the earth is mine:

"And you shall be unto me a kingdom of priests, and a holy nation.' These are the words which you shalt speak unto the Children of Israel.

"And Moses came and called for the elders of the people, and laid before their faces all these words which the Lord commanded him.

"And all the people answered together, and said, 'All that the Lord has spoken we will do. And Moses returned the words of the people unto the Lord."

This is a contract of service, not salvation. Obviously, if you can keep every part of the Law of Moses, then there is no sin in your life, and you do not need the contract of salvation. But no one, other than Jesus, has ever been able to keep the entire Law.

Some will challenge my position here, and suggest that Jesus taught that keeping the Law was the Plan of Salvation. It was not. He did not. And a closer examination of this event will reveal the truth of what Jesus was doing.

There was a rich young ruler who came to Jesus, and asked Jesus what he must do to have eternal life. Matthew 19:16–22:

"And, behold, one came and said unto Him, 'Good Master, what good thing shall I do, that I may have eternal life?'

And He said unto him, 'Why [do you call] me good? There is none good but one, that is, God. But if you will enter into life, keep the commandments.'

He said unto Him, 'Which?' Jesus said, 'You shall do no murder, You shall not commit adultery, You shall not steal, You shall not bear false witness,

Honor your father and your mother: and, you shall love your neighbor as yourself.'

The young man said unto Him, 'All these things have I kept from my youth up: what [am I still lacking]?'

Jesus said unto him, 'If you will be perfect, go and sell what you have, and give to the poor, and you shall have treasure in Heaven: and come and follow me.'

But when the young man heard that saying, he went away sorrowful: for he had great possessions."

Let me walk you through this one step at a time because the opening comments are very important and key to why Jesus said the things that He said. The rich young ruler came to Jesus and called Him, "Good Master." Notice the response of Jesus. He is leading the rich young ruler to a very important conclusion. "Why are you calling me good? No one is good except for God."

Notice that Jesus did not deny that He was good. And in doing so, He was suggesting that He was God. He was testing how the rich young ruler came to Jesus in the first place. Did God the Father send him to Jesus? If God the Father sent people to Jesus, it was because God had revealed to them that Jesus was the Christ, and that being the Christ, Jesus was God among us. Jesus is asking if this rich young ruler had realized that Jesus was God. If so, His response would have been different. The rich young ruler would have identified Jesus as God's solution to sin. Jesus would have been the solution to his problem. All he would need is faith in Jesus.

But the rich young ruler missed the point entirely. He did not even begin to believe that Jesus was God. In fact, he did not even answer the question. He was not coming to Jesus to be saved. Therefore, God did not send the rich young ruler. He was not going to be one who believed that Jesus was the Messiah. Since he was not trusting in the Messiah to save him, then he fell under the Law of Moses. Remember if you can keep the entire Law and all the points of the Law, then there is no sin in your life and you do not need the contract—you do not need a Messiah to die for your sins. This is what the rich young ruler was claiming. So Jesus put him to the test.

Now notice that it is Jesus who is listing the commandments. Notice also that there are some commandments missing. I do not believe Jesus intended for this to be a complete list. When Jesus was asked to identify the greatest commandment [Matthew 22:36–40] Jesus listed Deuteronomy 6:5 ["You shall love the Lord with all your heart, soul and mind/might."] Then Jesus offered His opinion regarding the second greatest commandment. For this, He cited Leviticus 19:18 ["Love your neighbor as yourself"]. Then Jesus declared that if you could keep these two commandments, you would fulfill all the requirements under both the Law of Moses and the prophets.

Jesus left off the Law regarding coveting. Jesus did not mention keeping the Sabbath. Jesus did not mention the Law about having no other god before God, or not taking God's name in vain. When the rich young ruler declared that he was sin free—"All these I have kept since my youth"—Jesus put the Law into practice. If you claim to keep the entire Law; then by the Law you shall be judged. Jesus judged the rich young ruler by the Law, and the rich young ruler was found guilty.

I, personally, believe that Jesus was applying the Law of having no other god before God. He told the rich young ruler to give away all his wealth and follow Him. The rich young ruler put his wealth above Jesus. He put his wealth above God. He loved his wealth, and his wealth had become his god. He failed the test. He was not sinless. He needed a Messiah to save him.

So God never offered the Jews one way of salvation and a different way of salvation to the Gentiles. He offered the Jews a contract of service. If they did everything God told them to do and obeyed His voice, God would make them a nation of priests. He would use them to teach the world of the coming Messiah. All the sacrifices, feasts, garments, furnishings and other requirements of the Law were pictures of the coming Messiah—who and what He would be, and what He would do to fulfill God's contract.

***

Now God's earliest revelation concerning the Plan of Salvation was in Job Chapter Thirty-Three. This was the confession of sin and the repentance of sin. This was God providing someone to stand with us and defend us when we came before Him. This person who would stand with us was identified by God in verse 33:24 as being the "ransom."

Job is believed to have lived at the time of Abraham, and this puts him 400 years before Moses and the Law of Moses. The Law of Moses does not alter the Plan of Salvation.

Now Moses wrote all of this down as God instructed him to. There was a written account of the events and the information. There were around three million people who were present and heard God directly, and who saw the miracles Moses performed. They saw the Cloud by day and the Pillar of Fire by night. They ate the manna. They saw the fire come down and consume the sacrifices. They saw the glory of God fill the Tabernacle. All of this documents what the first five books of the Bible claimed.

No one who was present challenged this account. They challenged God's choice of leaders; but no one challenged the Red Sea account. No one challenged the manna to feed them. No one challenged God speaking to them. No one challenged that God gave Moses the Five Books of Law. That means that we have somewhere around three million eyewitnesses to these events. Three million witnesses would be more than enough to convince any court that these events did happen, and that they happened exactly as recorded.

Now God gives additional information through His prophets. In Isaiah, God declares one of the proofs that He is God and that He does exist. Isaiah 46:9–10:

"'Remember the former things of old: for I am God, and there is no one else; I am God, and there is none like me,

"Declaring the end from the beginning, and from ancient times the things that are not yet done, saying, "My counsel shall stand, and I will do all my pleasure:"'"

God gives us proof that He exists. He is outside of our time/space continuum and He knows the future. The reason He knows the future is that He is causing it to happen. To prove that He does exist, and that He is God, He cites prophecy as the proof. A prophet of God is correct 100% of the time.

Then God gives additional information through his prophet Malachi. Malachi 3:6:

"For I am the Lord, *I change not*; therefore you sons of Jacob are not consumed." [Emphasis added]

God does not change. We learn in the Book of Hebrews that it is impossible for God to lie. Hebrews 6:17–18:

"Wherein God, willing more abundantly to show unto the heirs of promise the immutability of His counsel, confirmed it by an oath:

"That by two immutable things, in which *it was impossible for God to lie*, we might have a strong consolation, who have fled for refuge to lay hold upon the hope set before us:" [Emphasis added]

The two immutable things referred to things that cannot be changed. That is what *"immutable"* means. The first is that God made an oath. The second is that God cannot lie. So if God declared it and sealed it with an oath, we can trust what He said/ did completely.

So with these two additional revelations by God about Himself, He locked everything into place. All that has come before Malachi is set and cannot change because God does not change. He does not lie. Notice that this declaration took place before Christianity, Islam or Mormonism. The God of the Old Testament, as God has revealed Himself, is who God is and how He works. Any revelation that comes after Malachi and claims to be a new revelation is to be questioned and tested. If it contradicts what God has already said about Himself and how He works; then it is to be rejected. This would even apply to Christianity as it came after God's revealing of Himself. If Christianity contradicts what God has already revealed about Himself; then we must reject it, and cannot trust it because God does not change; and God does not lie. This is another harsh reality of contract law. It's not what we want. It's what the contract says.

It is possible to take information concerning God prior to Malachi—or even after Malachi—and for God to give more information to understand the earlier revelations. That is allowed because they are still the earlier revelations. As long as it does not contradict what God has already revealed about Himself, it should be considered. The minute it contradicts the earlier revelations, it must be rejected.

In contract law there is the contract. This is what the person writing the contract promises to do. These are the terms of the contract, and how you enter into the contract. But there is also a concept in contract law called *addendums*. This literally means "*add ons*." These add ons cannot change the original contract. That is still in place. These add ons give additional information to clarify points of the original contract. God's contract or promise of salvation is found in Job, Genesis, Exodus, Leviticus, Numbers and Deuteronomy. But the rest of the Bible becomes addendums. They clarify what God has promised. They prove that God has kept His promise, and done what He promised to do. These addendums give more information and a better understanding about the contract and how it works. But they do not change the contract.

For example: Psalm Twenty-Two becomes an addendum. It quotes the words the Messiah will say as He is dying: "My God, my God why have you forsaken me?" It reveals that the Messiah will have His hands and feet pierced. It reveals that the Messiah will have His bones pulled out of their sockets. It tells us He will be thirsty as He is dying. It tells us people will mock Him as He dies. It tells us that people will gamble for His garments.

This does not change the original requirement in the contract that an innocent shall die for a guilty. But it does give us additional information about *how* the innocent will die for the guilty.

Now God, being a just God, will deal with Adam and Eve the same way He deals with the last man and woman, and everyone in between. He will not change. He will not lie. This means that any new revelation about God must line up perfectly with what God has already revealed about Himself. It can expand and clarify what has already been revealed; but it cannot change it.

We always test new revelations relating to God and what He is doing, and compare it to the first revelations concerning God and His actions. If it is not supported by the earlier revelations, it must be rejected. Those religions that test the old revelations by the new ones have the legal process backwards. That is not how the legal system works. There is the original contract. Everything must comply with the original contract.

***

Another point I need to make... Christianity fulfilled the prophecies given by God up to and including Malachi. It expands on what God has revealed about Himself and what He is planning on doing. There is no conflict between Judaism and Christianity except for the identity of the Messiah, and the Old Testament explains why that is so. God has placed a spiritual blindness upon the nation of Israel as to the identity of the Messiah. This is found in Psalm 69:23:

"Let their eyes be darkened, that they see not; and make their loins continually to shake."

Why is David asking God to do this? He explains in Psalm 69:26:

"For they persecute Him whom You have [beaten]; and they talk to the grief of those whom You have wounded."

The Jews' own spiritual documents disqualify them and their testimony concerning the identity of the Messiah. Where the Jews question and reject Jesus as the Messiah, their testimony is lacking in credibility because their actions have resulted in their being spiritually blind to the Messiah's identity.

Many people will suggest, "Well, if anyone should know who the Messiah will be, it should be the Jews. After all, it is the Jews' Messiah."

That legal argument and reasoning is flawed because it does not take into account God's decision to make the nation of Israel blind as to the identity of the Messiah. David asked God to make the Jews blind to the identity of the Messiah because of how they treated Him. Jesus approved the curse and activated the blindness when the priests rejected Him as the Messiah at the Triumphant Entry. Jesus goes off and weeps over the city because of this rejection. He gives the prophecy of the destruction of the city because of their rejection, and He makes this statement. Luke 19:42:

"Saying, 'If you had known, even you, at least in *this your day*, the things which belong unto your peace! but *now they are hid from your eyes.*" [Emphasis added]

With that statement, the spiritual blindness requested by David in Psalm 69:23 was activated. From that point forward, the Jews, as a nation will be blind as to the identity of their Messiah. This blindness will continue until God removes the Church and Zechariah 12:10 takes place:

"And I will pour upon the house of David, and upon the inhabitants of Jerusalem, the spirit of grace and of supplications: and *they shall look upon Me whom they have pierced*, and *they shall mourn for Him*, as one mourns for his only son, and shall be in bitterness for Him, as one that is in bitterness for his firstborn." [Emphasis added]

The day is coming when God will pour out His spirit upon Jerusalem. The result of this anointing will be that their eyes will be opened. They will look upon God, and they will recognize that Jesus was God among them. They will realize that they have pierced God. They will have missed their Messiah, and they will mourn for all those lost years.

***

There is still one more comment I need to make about God's nature. The Cults suggest that God allowed His Church, Bible, and message to be corrupted. They claim that they have the true Gospel, and that all others are wrong. Jesus has declared that this is impossible. Jesus made this declaration in the New Testament, and it is important when dealing with Cults and deception. Matthew 16:18:

"And I say also unto you, 'That you are Peter, and upon this rock I will build my church; and *the gates of hell shall not prevail against it.*'" [Emphasis added]

There is an entire discussion about what Jesus was talking about concerning the rock and His plans for Peter, but the key point of this verse for our purposes is that Jesus declared that the Gates of Hell could never prevail against His Church. So when we deal with someone claiming that the enemy or Satan was able to overcome the Church or suppress the truth of the Church or take over the Church; their claims fly right into the face of this declaration. We then have to ask, "Who are you going to believe: Jesus or someone teaching something different than the contract?"

I am not ignoring the corruption regarding the organization of the Church. Where there is power, corrupt people will always seek to attain it—whether in politics, business or religion. But the message was preserved. The Bible was preserved. It is the same message and Bible today as it was when God presented it. That is the difference.

Because God is a just God, and God does not change, nor does God lie; we can take what God has laid down in the Old Testament as an accurate revelation of who He is and what He is going to do. As a just God, God will not allow His message to be altered or lost. God must preserve the offer He made to Adam and Eve so that every person in ever generation can hear it. That is what "*and everyone in between*" means. If God does not do that; then God is not a just God. God would not be a fair God.

As we study the New Testament and compare what it teaches about God and what God is going to do, we see that the New Testament is not in conflict with God's original revelation. The New Testament compliments the Old Testament. The New Testament explains passages of the Old Testament that did not make sense. The New Testament can also be considered a further and expanded revelation of God and His plan for the human race.

Unfortunately, we cannot say the same regarding the religion of Islam or Mormonism. Other religions that claim revelation from God to support their beliefs and which contradict the Bible must also be called into question. According to John, these were the deceptions presented by antichrist that were sent to deceive us, and which we should watch out for and not believe.

CHAPTER FOUR

CAN WE TRUST THE BIBLICAL DOCUMENTS?

I have spent three chapters talking about the Bible being a legally-binding contract between God and mankind. I have quoted numerous passages from the Bible. However, the world has attacked the Bible on so many levels that we must stop for a moment and ask if the Bible we have today is reliable, and is there evidence to support that the Bible is truly inspired by God, or has it already been altered to satisfy political motives?

Let me just point out Genesis 3:15 to set the stage for this discussion:

"And I will put enmity between you and the woman, and between your seed and her seed; it shall bruise your head, and you shall bruise His heel."

God declared war on Satan all the way back in the Garden of Eden. "*Enmity*" is another word for "*hostility*." The relationship between Satan and the human race has always been a hostile relationship. Have you ever wondered why so much has happened to the Children of Israel? They were made slaves in Egypt for four hundred years. They were sent into Captivity into Babylon for seventy years. They were invaded by Rome and their Temple and capital city were destroyed. The Jews were scattered throughout the entire world. They were persecuted, and in World War II, Hitler sought to wipe them out through the concentration camps.

From the day they were given back their homeland, the surrounding countries have attacked them, hated them and vowed to destroy them. Has any race ever dealt with this level of hostility? And America is pulled into this hostility because it supports Israel. This is the enmity God spoke of all the way back in the Garden of Eden.

Even now, we are seeing the rise of an anti-Semitic attitude not just in Europe and throughout the world; but it is growing even here in America, and in our political system in Washington D.C.

Satan is at war with this promise God made in the Garden. He has sought to destroy the line that would produce this virgin-born male. The Children of Israel went into Egypt as welcomed guests under Joseph, and were then enslaved. When Pharaoh feared their growing population, he ordered all male babies born to the Children of Israel thrown into the Nile River. New excavations in Egypt show an increase in infant mortality in the city of Avaris, where the Jews were believed to have lived.

When Mary gave birth to Jesus, Herod sent in troops to wipe out every male Jewish baby age three years old and under in Bethlehem. If Joseph had not heeded the warning of God's angel, Jesus would have been killed when He was young.

In Revelation Chapter Twelve, John describes the conflict between the dragon [Satan] and a woman about to give birth. The symbols surrounding the woman suggest that this is Israel. The dragon is Satan. The child she is about to give birth to is Jesus.

There is a war between Satan and God. That war is centered on the Children of Israel, Israel and Jesus. And the first casualty in any war is truth. So it is no wonder that the Bible is attacked over and over again. It is not surprising that the Bible is called into question to the level that it is.

***

When you go to trial, there are two basic strategies. The first is to discredit the evidence that goes against you. If the evidence the other side is preparing to submit to the court to prove that they are right and you are wrong can be called into question and found to be unreliable; then the judge will not consider it when making the final decision. If you cannot discredit the evidence, then you seek to block it and make it inadmissible.

I have been in enough legal arenas to know that the truth is not always presented. I taught those taking cases to trial in the Workers' Compensation system that all issues [points of disagreement between the parties] fell into two categories when preparing to take the case to trial. The first category is issues of credibility. Can you believe what the evidence is saying? The second category is issues of admissibility. When I was acting as an expert witness regarding workers' compensation, the other side tried to bar me from testifying in several cases. Even though I had twenty years of personal experience relating to Workers' Compensation and had taught various topics for several years, they refused to accept that I was an expert. They knew I was an expert, but they knew they could not discredit me or my testimony. They came up with crazy arguments before the court and tried to block me over and over.

This is how the legal war is waged. You build up your evidence while tearing down or blocking the opposition's evidence. So it is no wonder that Satan seeks to tear down, discredit or even block the Bible as evidence.

However, these tactics will only work in this world to confuse and deceive us. These arguments will not work when we stand before God in Heaven. God knows the Bible is true. He wrote it. If Satan were to try to challenge the Bible before God, God will shoot down any argument by noting that He wrote the Bible—end of discussion. He knows what it is. He knows what is says. He knows what it means.

So Satan can only work his deception in this world. And as part of his hostility toward God, the Jews and Jesus, he is trying to discredit the Bible. There are different resources on the internet and books and DVDs that deal with many of the deceptions Satan has submitted.

One of the first arguments Satan raised is that there was no evidence of the Jews being in Egypt. There was no evidence of the Plagues. There was no evidence to support the Exodus. Fortunately, a filmmaker put together a DVD entitled *Evidence of Proof, the Exodus*. It is available on Amazon if you wish to view it.

This filmmaker asked the hard questions and expressed the point very clearly. If the Exodus did not take place, then Judaism and Christianity are built on a lie. When he questioned those who held that there was no archeological evidence to support the account of the Exodus, they had no problem with keeping the Passover, even though—in their opinion—it never took place. They could not see the conflict there.

To make the discussion short, if you place the Exodus in the Later Kingdom Period of Egypt, then there is no evidence. However, if the Exodus took place in the Middle Kingdom Period of Egypt, everything is there. The evidence supports the events and there is proof available. He did a brief discussion raising issue with how the events were dated in Egypt's time line and there is evidence that the time line may need to be adjusted. What was so ironic is that he spoke to several experts and museum curators who oversaw the documents and the evidence. However, they kept insisting that even though the facts lined up perfectly, it could not be the Exodus because the evidence came before the dates they had set for the Exodus.

The next issue was that Moses could not have written the first five books of the Bible because writing did not exist that far back. The same filmmaker produced another DVD entitled *The Moses Controversy*—also on Amazon. He used his same methods of tracking down evidence outside of the Bible that there was a written language. It was present in Egypt at the time of the Exodus, and it was a written language that could be available and known to the Children of Israel. It seems that before the Babylonia Captivity, the Jews used a different alphabet rather than the one we see used today. In this alphabet, the symbols are not only letters, but represent pictures and concepts/themes. These letters were pictographs.

As the filmmaker was conducting his research, a guide took him to a cave in the desert area where the Children of Israel had been, and showed him images cut into the cave wall. It surprised me because as soon as they showed the images, I recognized them as Paleo-Hebrew letters from my own study on Bible Codes. He also found these Paleo-Hebrew letters on pillars in Egypt from the time of the Exodus.

When you are in a court of law, you will make a statement and the opposition will challenge you. They will not let the statement or information be placed into evidence. You then have to show that the information is credible—you can believe it. You have to show how you got the evidence, and that you followed proper procedure in obtaining it. If you did not follow regulations and laws in obtaining the information and evidence, it can be blocked no matter how true it is, or how important it is to your case.

What we have seen with this filmmaker is his willingness to listen to the objections Satan makes and then lay the foundation to prove the statement and evidence is true. The truth is that Satan misrepresents our information to the point of making it questionable. What is even more surprising is that God knew Satan would do this and prepared a defense before we even knew we would need a defense.

Dan Brown, in his novel/film *The DaVinci Code,* made several allegations that the Bible could not be trusted. It is the old argument that those putting together the Bible only allowed documents in that supported their power base. Other documents were intentionally suppressed. Some are alleged to have been altered. We can see documents were suppressed and rejected; but the motives behind these decisions are completely different from those presented by Dan Brown.

In my previous chapter, I spoke about the test for various revelations from supernatural and other sources. Those putting the Bible together went back to the earliest revelation of God and tested each new revelation by the old. Those new revelations that contradicted the earlier revelations were rejected based upon the declaration of God that He does not change.

Back in my college days, when I was first saved, and had read through the Bible for the first time, I wanted more information about God. I came across a collection entitled, *The Lost Books of the Bible and The Forgotten Books of Eden.* There were a lot of older manuscripts that never made it into the Bible. However, they are still available if you want to track them down and read them. I did.

Even at that young age, and with my limited education and experience, it was obvious that these works contradicted the Bible. They were also historically inaccurate. And in some cases, the writings contradicted each other. Given the above method for testing revelations from God, all of them were rejected and should be rejected. Just as a quick example: *The Gospel of Pilate* gave three versions of how Pilate died. According to history, he retired from public office and died of old age.

But God had something else in mind for His defense. Two hundred years before Jesus was born, God arranged to have hundreds of scrolls hidden away in clay jars in a settlement called Qumran. This was located near the Dead Sea. These scrolls remained undisturbed until the 1940's when a young shepherd accidentally found the clay jars in a cave. These are the Dead Sea Scrolls, and contain every book of the Old Testament except for Esther.

When Dan Brown made the statement that the Church had altered the early Bible to make it say what they wanted it to say, he ignored the Dead Sea Scrolls and the evidence they provided. The Dead Sea Scrolls are the earliest copies we have of the Old Testament. They were from two hundred years before Jesus was born. They were a thousand years before the Church fell into corruption. A comparison of the Dead Sea Scrolls versions of the Old Testament and modern translations show a less than a three percent variation. And the parts that are different do not change any doctrine or teaching. They are grammatical differences and other minor variations.

We also have the Jews translating their Old Testament into Greek. It is called the Septuagint [LXX] because it was the result of the work of seventy scholars. This was done in 250 B.C.

Another point I need to make is that the Jews and the Christians had a very hostile relationship throughout the Dark

Ages and during the time Dan Brown claims the Church altered the Bible to say what they wanted it to say. But God placed the Old Testament documents into the care and protection of the Jews during this time. They would not allow any changes to their Holy Scriptures—especially changes designed to favor the Christian faith.

Finally, Dan Brown made the mistake of thinking that the Catholic Church was the only Church at that time. He ignored other groups such as the Anabaptists and others who refused to join the Catholic Church over doctrinal issues. They were remnants preserved by God during the dark times. They, too, had their copies of Scriptures and they protected and preserved these copies as well.

Take early copies of Homer or of Caesar's writings and compare them to the Bible. You find that Homer's Iliad was written about 800 B.C. The earliest copies we have of the *Iliad* come from 400 B.C. This means that there is a four hundred year gap between the writing and the earliest copy of the text. For Caesar's *Gallic Wars* it was written about 100 B.C. But the earliest copies of this manuscript date back to 900 A.D. This creates a 1,000-year gap between the writing and the earliest copy. If you compare changes from one copy to the next of either of these manuscripts, there are numerous changes.

However, the care given to making copies of the Torah [Genesis, Exodus, Leviticus, Numbers and Deuteronomy] and other books from the Old Testament is greater than secular manuscripts. There are some sects of Jews who believe not only were the first five books of the Bible inspired by God, these sects believe God dictated these books to Moses, and he wrote them down exactly as God gave it to him on Mount Sinai. Some sects even believe that not only did God dictate the words to Moses; God dictated the words letter-by-letter. [More on this in a moment.]

When a copy of the Torah is made, each page has to be an exact copy of the original. There must be the same lines of words on the copy as was on the original. The letter in the top right-hand corner must be the same letter on the top right-hand corner of the original. The same is true with the letter in the top left, bottom right and bottom left. The letter in the center of the page must be the same letter in the center of the page on the original. In addition, to the copy having to have the same number of lines, each line must have the same number of letters as on the original.

As a final test, each Hebrew letter has a numerical value [they use letters not numbers to record numbers]. The priests add up the numerical values of the original page, and add up the numerical values of the copy. It the numbers are not exact, the copy is destroyed. The Jews have tried as hard as they can to become human Xerox machines and make their copies as precise and exact as possible.

There have been sects of Jews and Jewish Rabbis throughout the ages who believed God placed codes into the Torah and other books of the Old Testament. There was various information they found hidden away in the texts, but the most amazing came to light in the 1980's with the creation of personal computers.

Ancient Rabbis would create a ten-by-ten grid, and write out passages from the Torah letter-by-letter. They felt that this was the best way to discovery messages encoded in the original text by Equidistance Letter Sequencing [ELS]. To put this simply, they believed that if you took every third letter, or fourth letter or fifth letter, it would spell out other words with information hidden in the passage.

In the 1980's a Jewish cryptographer who had cracked codes in World War II used a personal computer to run a program to search for codes using Equidistance Letter Sequencing. He took the book of Genesis, and removed all the punctuation and spacing between letters so it was a long stream of letters. He had even removed all the vowels [a, e, i, o and u] from the words, as the Torah prior to the Babylonian Captivity did not use vowels. He then had the computer run a search for words hidden in Equidistance Letter Sequences. His test proved successful, and he ran various tests on his theory.

There is an excellent work on this subject written by Jews and entitled, *Cracking the Bible Codes*. They were very careful to avoid the marketing hype and sensationalism others added to their books. It is a careful, scholarly study of the phenomena. It is available on Amazon. This code only happens with the Old Testament. It does not work with the New Testament. Rabbis and scholars have been researching and studying this phenomenon for years. They have found names, dates and information encoded in equidistance letter sequences throughout the Torah and other books. The most interesting find for them was in the account of Judah and Tamar from Genesis Thirty-Eight. Encoded in this passage was the event of Chanukah. The name of the Maccabees who led the rebellion is encoded there. Other words and names relating to the rebellion are encoded there. And even the date of the rebellion is encoded there.

I can recommend this book and other studies to help you investigate this phenomenon. The team took other lengthy literary works and removed the spacing and punctuation [such as War and Peace] but they could not find codes there. Apparently, it does not happen by accident.

They took the Samaritan Torah. This is a copy of the Torah preserved by the Samaritans who were left behind in the Babylonia Captivity. It says the same things and teaches the same things as the Jewish Torah, but the same care was not taken in copying from the original. Those small changes were enough to erase the Bible Code from that version.

As some of these passages, such as the Judah and Tamar passage give information concerning the future, this code could not have been created and inserted by humans. It had to be added by someone who knew the future and had access to these names, details and dates.

Now that we have established that the Old Testament has not been altered, but has been carefully preserved to be as close to the original as possible, keep in mind that the doctrines of the New Testament are based upon the teachings and prophecies of the Old Testament.

Let me spend just a few moments discussing God's proof that He exists and that He is in charge: prophecy. I mentioned Isaiah 46:10 earlier and that God would tell us the end from the beginning. I could spend time on the prophecies relating to Jesus, but as I am trying to establish the divine origin of the Old Testament—since it is the source by which all other revelations are tested—let me share a couple of examples from the book, *Science Speaks* by Peter Stoner. [This book is out of print, but you might find a copy at ABE Books.com.]

He discusses God's prophecy regarding the city of Tyre, which was made in 590 BC by the prophet Ezekiel. Ezekiel 26:3 - 5:

"Therefore thus says the Lord God; 'Behold, I am against you, O Tyre, and will cause many nations to come up against you, as the sea causes his waves to come up.

And they shall destroy the walls of Tyre, and break down her towers: I will also scrape her dust from her, and make her like the top of a rock.'"

We also see this from Ezekiel 26:7:

"For thus says the Lord God; 'Behold, I will bring upon Tyre Nebuchadnezzar, king of Babylon, a king of kings, from the north, with horses, and with chariots, and with horsemen, and companies, and much people.'"

Ezekiel again adds to this prophecy one more time in Ezekiel 26:12:

"And they shall make a spoil of your riches, and make a prey of your merchandise: and they shall break down your walls, and destroy your pleasant houses: and they shall lay your stones and your timber and your dust in the midst of the water."

Ezekiel continues to add to the prophecy in Ezekiel 26:14:

"And I will make you like the top of a rock: you shall be a place to spread nets upon; you shall be built no more: for I the Lord have spoken it,' says the Lord God."

Finally, Ezekiel adds this information concerning the city of Tyre in Ezekiel 26:16:

"Then all the princes of the sea shall come down from their thrones, and lay away their robes, and put off their broidered garments: they shall clothe themselves with trembling; they shall sit upon the ground, and shall tremble at every moment, and be astonished at you."

Now this is not some vague prophecy that Tyre is going to fall. God gave Ezekiel some very specific details concerning the city of Tyre. Let's list the various things that God declared through Ezekiel that He was going to do to Tyre:

1. Nebuchadnezzar would take the city.
2. Other nations would take the city.
3. Princes of the sea will come from their thrones, lay aside their robe and be frightened because of Tyre
4. The walls and houses would be broken down.
5. The dirt would be scraped off.
6. The walls, timber and dirt would be cast into the sea.
7. The place would become like a rock used for spreading out nets.
8. The city would never be built again.

These are eight predictions concerning the city of Tyre. Let's take them one-by-one and consider the odds. Now when calculating odds, it is a simple process. Consider this example: Suppose that one man in every ten is bald. We will call this factor [A]. Suppose that every man in 100 has lost a finger. We will call this factor [B]. So we ask the question: "What are the odds of one man being bald and losing a finger?" We would multiply the factors together. In this case, we would multiply [A] by [B]. [One man in ten is bald times one man in 100 has lost a finger.] The formula would be like this $[10 \times 100 = 1,000]$. This means that the odds of a man being both bald and losing a finger are one in a thousand. Note: the more accurate your factors, the more accurate your calculation will be.

Now let's do a very conservative estimate. Nebuchadnezzar was in the process of conquering the entire world. So the odds of Nebuchadnezzar conquering Tyre would be pretty good. Let's set it as a one-in-three chance. It would all depend on which direction Nebuchadnezzar sent his army. There are four directions [north, south, east and west] and three of those directions lead away from Tyre. One leads toward it.

When did this happen? According to history, Nebuchadnezzar came against Tyre in 586 BC. That is four years after Ezekiel gave his prediction [590 BC]. Well, that's not too impressive. We could do that good just looking at the newspaper today. But keep in mind that this is only one of multiple parts to this prophecy.

Nebuchadnezzar laid siege to the city in 586 BC. But the siege lasted for thirteen years. It seems that Tyre was a pretty strong city, and could hold its own. At the end of this thirteen-year siege Nebuchadnezzar finally took the city in 573 BC only to discover that Tyre had relocated its city and everything of value to an island one-half mile off shore. Nebuchadnezzar fulfilled the first part of the prophecy, but he did not gain anything for all his efforts. The city of Tyre continued as Nebuchadnezzar left it for 241 years. So what happened 241 years later?

In 322 BC, we have Alexander the Great making his effort to conquer the world. He came to Tyre [the one on the island], but he was unable to take the city. What did Alexander do? He raided the surrounding cities, captured them and seized their fleets. This fulfilled the prophecy about the princes of the sea coming off their thrones and laying aside their robes and being terrified. They all surrendered to Alexander because they were terrified of him.

Even with the ships from these costal cities, Alexander could not take Tyre, so what did he do? He took the walls, timbers and houses of the original city and cast them into the sea. He scraped off the dirt down to bare rock, and used the dirt and rubble to build a causeway from the shore out to the island. This is how he took Tyre. He took the city in seven months, and completely destroyed the city.

With all the ruins of the city gone and the dirt scraped away, it is now a place for the fishermen to spread their nets to dry. Oh, and by the way, the city still has yet to be rebuilt. Let's try to calculate the odds of this happening on it own by accident.

We already consider the odds of Tyre being attacked by Nebuchadnezzar were pretty good: a one in three chance. The fact that other nations would end up attacking Tyre would depend on if the city had anything of value or if Nebuchadnezzar is the one to destroy it. These odds are going to have a lot of variables and be pretty high. I am going to leave these odds out of my calculation just so you can see what we can calculate accurately.

The fact that the city would be completely destroyed...let's be conservative and given how barbaric kings were back then the fact that Tyre would be completely destroyed would be a one in five chance.

I'll be honest and the idea of scraping everything off and casting it into the sea contains a lot of variables. Peter Stoner suggested we just accept the prophecy that Tyre would become like a rock His calculation was pretty conservative. He set it at one in five hundred.

Now this is a fishing area so there will be many fishermen and lots of fish. If they need to spread their nets and Tyre is now like a rock, he calculated the odds of Tyre becoming a place to spread nets at one in ten.

The facts that other nations would be terrified by what happens to Tyre are pretty good. Stoner put this at a one in five chance.

Tyre was in a good location. It had a good fishing industry. There is the chance that others might come and rebuild the area and take advantage of the location. So stoner puts the odds of Tyre NOT being built again at one in twenty.

Now let's use his calculations and determine the odds of all of these things coming true by accident on their own. Remember we are taking the odds of each factor and multiplying them out: [3 X 5 X 500 X 10 X 5 X 20 = one chance in 7,500,000. That is just an example of a single prophecy and I left out the details of things being tossed into the sea.

Peter Stoner calculated the odds for four other prophecies concerning cities and countries. He reviewed the prophecy concerning Samaria found in Micah 1:6:

"Therefore I will make Samaria as a heap of the field, and as plantings of a vineyard: and I will pour down the stones thereof into the valley, and I will discover the foundations thereof."

During the reign of Ahab, there were two sieges against Samaria. Both proved unsuccessful, but both involved great slaughters. During the reign of Jehoram, the city was once more under siege and nearly defeated. Finally, in 723 BC it was taken by Sargon who removed many of the inhabitants into captivity. Although the city is still inhabited, the ruins of the ancient city are still scattered across the landscape.

Stoner calculated the odds of this prophecy coming true at one in 40,000. He then calculated the odds relating to the prophecy regarding Gaza and Ashkelon found in Zephaniah 2:4 and 6 and Jeremiah 47:5 of coming true by accident on their own:

"For Gaza shall be forsaken, and Ashkelon a desolation: they shall drive out Ashdod at the noon day, and Ekron shall be rooted up."

"And the sea coast shall be dwellings and cottages for shepherds, and folds for flocks."

"Baldness is come upon Gaza; Ashkelon is cut off with the remnant of their valley: how long will you cut yourself?"

Gaza fell to Alexander the Great who killed everyone who survived the siege of the city. Ashkelon was the site of many bloody battles between the Saracens and the Crusaders. However, the cities did continue after their destruction.

Adding these factors relating to Gaza and Ashkelon into the calculation the odds of these events happening on their own by accident would be one in twelve thousand five hundred.

Stoner then brought in the prophecy Joshua made concerning Jericho found in Joshua 6:26. This prophecy was very precise and detailed:

"And Joshua adjured them at that time, saying, 'Cursed be the man before the Lord, who rises up and builds this city Jericho: he shall lay the foundation thereof in his firstborn, and in his youngest son shall he set up the gates of it."

What does this mean in common English? It means that if someone tries to rebuild the city, his firstborn son shall die when he lays the foundation. He will then lose his youngest son on the same day that he hangs the gates of the city.

We see in I Kings 16:34 where Hiel the Bethelite did rebuild the city and his firstborn son died when he laid the foundation for the city; and his youngest son died when he hung the gates.

This is very precise and very specific. It predicts not only two deaths, but also when those deaths would occur and which one would be the one to die. Stoner puts the odds of this happening by accident on their own as one in two hundred thousand.

Now this is the point that I need to make here. If you do not understand mathematics and how to calculate the odds of something happening, it is a progressive process. Each time you add another factor; you need to multiply your previous odds by the new factor. So where we had one in seven million five hundred thousand for Tyre as a stand-alone prophecy, we would then take that number and multiply it by the factor for Samaria [one in 40,000]. We would take that number and multiply it by the odds of Gaza and Ashkelon [one in 12,500]. Then you would multiply that by the odds of Jericho [one in 200,000]. I will be honest; my calculator does not have that many zeroes available.

Stoner tried to create a visual picture for these kinds of odds. He noted that about a million earths would fit inside our sun. Unfortunately, our sun is not big enough for this visual aid. You would need ten suns the same size as our sun. You would fill all ten suns with silver dollars [hopefully they would not melt.] Then you would paint just one silver dollar red and push all ten suns together and mix the silver dollars thoroughly. Take a blind person, or a person wearing a blindfold, and send him in. He has one selection and only one selection.

The odds of him selecting the silver dollar painted red the first time is the same odds as just these four prophecies coming true on their own by accident. When the odds of something happening by accident reach this level, they become nonsensical. No intelligent person would accept that this could have happened on its own by accident.

Theses are just four prophecies. The Old Testament is filled with these kinds of prophecies. Add in the hundreds of prophecies concerning Jesus, and there is no way all of these prophecies could have happened as predicted in the Old Testament. They could not have happened on their own by accident. But this is what God is telling us. Prophecy is proof that God does exist. Prophecy is proof that God is in charge.

When you add in the factors that God does exist, and God is controlling everything, and God will cause these things to happen; then these astronomical, nonsensical odds drop to a chance of one in one every time.

The evidence tells us that the only way this could happen is if this were written by God and God told these writers what He was going to do. This proves that God does exist, and that God did make it happen on purpose. It could not have happened on its own by accident.

This gives us a very credible proof concerning the reliability of the Old Testament documents. All the arguments about altering documents or "cherry-picking" only those documents you want to accept fail to convince when faced with this kind of evidence. Those still challenging the credibility and reliability of the Old Testament documents would have to overcome this body of evidence.

Now Satan will also try to discredit the documents of the New Testament by claiming that these documents are not actual accounts but were written by others using the Disciples' names. Satan claims they were written hundred of years later.

However, there is an important event in history. This event is so important that it would have been mentioned in any document written after it. This was the destruction of Jerusalem and the Temple in 70 AD. This was forty years after the death and resurrection of Jesus. Jesus predicted that this would happen, and so anyone writing about His prediction after it happened would have mentioned that He was correct and the prophecy came true exactly as He said. None of the accounts do that, and this suggests that they were written before the Temple was destroyed—before 70 AD.

We have eleven men who chose torture and/or death over altering their account of the events in the life of Jesus. They died to prove their accounts were true. This kind of evidence would carry great weight in a court of law.

Just as a quick discussion of a couple of the documents we have relating to the New Testament. One of these documents is a fragment of the Gospel of John. It is part of a collection of thousands of papyrus fragments and documents discovered in Africa and Greece. These documents are a collection housed at the John Rylands University Library in Manchester in the United Kingdom.

In the Rylands Collection, there is a portion of the Gospel of John. It is identified in the collection as P52. It was written around 80–100 AD. The Rylands fragment is dated at 125 AD. This puts this copy within 25 to 45 years of the original writing. It was found in Egypt in 1920, so we need to add in how long it would take for this manuscript to be copied by hand and passed from believer to believer until it came to Egypt. Given the culture and technology of that day, it would not be unreasonable to suggest twenty or thirty years for copies to be made and spread into Egypt.

Another portion of the Gospel of John is the Bodmer papyrus. This is a collection of twenty-two papyri discovered in 1952. The collection is named after Martin Bodmer who purchased them. These are housed in Cologny, just outside of Geneva Switzerland. This collection contains fragments of the Old and New Testaments as well as early Christian Literature, Homer and Meander. The collection was found in Egypt, assembled in Cairo. From there they were smuggled into Switzerland where they were purchased by Bodmer.

One of the documents is referred to as P66. Its preservation surprised those who discovered the document. Its first twenty-six leaves were intact and even had its original stitching. This part of the collection contains John 1:1–6:11, 6:35b–14:26, 29–30; 15:2–26; 16:2–4, 6–7; 16:10–20:20, 22–23; 20:25–21:9, 12, 17. It is one of the oldest well-preserved New Testament manuscripts known to exist. The original document is believed to have been written in 70 AD. The Bodmer papyrus is dated to 200 AD. This puts it within 130 years of the original writing. One scholar is suggesting an even early date for the papyri, and suggests the early to middle part of the Second Century [100 AD]. We are not talking about manuscripts written five or six hundreds of years after-the-fact here as critics of the Bible like to suggest.

There is another phenomenon these Bible critics do not like to consider, but let me introduce it into evidenced here. Believers liked to quote the Bible. They would quote portions of the Bible in letters to each other. They would quote portions of the Bible in their diaries. There is an entire body of non-Biblical sources that document much of the Bible within the first couple of hundred years after the death and resurrection of Jesus.

As a final piece of evidence, I would like to introduce the number of documents available for study and research. If you only had the two parchments mentioned above, then you would have nothing to compare them to. But if you had three or four more documents, and they agreed with these two documents; then that would strengthen their authenticity.

So, as my final legal argument on this topic, let me just note that there are 5,838 total Greek Manuscripts available. There are 18,524 early New Testament manuscripts. There are 42,000 copies of Old Testament manuscripts. This gives us 66,362 manuscripts to use to compare and test against our current Bible. [Consider that there are only 251 copies of *The Gallic Wars* and 1,757 copies of *The Iliad*.]

The Bible is one of the most carefully documented, tested and preserved documents in the world. The Old Testament documents are believed to be 97% accurate renditions of the original texts, and New Testament copies are found to be 99.5% accurate despite their many years of hand copying. Again, these differences do not affect the doctrine or teaching of the documents.

So when Dan Brown and others claim documents were suppressed or altered from the original, there is no credible evidence to support such a claim. If this claim was presented in a court of law to attack the credibility of the Bible, it would not hold up and it would not be allowed. It is speculation and conjecture, which is contradicted by the evidence.

CHAPTER FIVE

THE MATHEMATICS OF THE CULTS

I do apologize for spending so much time dealing with the Bible and God's Plan of Salvation before getting to the topic of the Cults, but if this were to be a legal argument we could submit to a court of law, then we must lay the foundation for each of our claims and statements before they would be allowed by the court. As the issues we are dealing with concern our souls and their eternal destiny, I want to make sure that these legal arguments are as solid and admissible as possible.

It is a sad reality of our court system that if the opposition can suppress and block important evidence, then the court will have no choice but to render an incorrect verdict. I do not want anyone coming to an incorrect verdict based upon a technicality. Fortunately, when we stand before God the truth will win out.

So my next point is to define what a Cult is. There are many differences of opinions, and doctrines change from one denomination or Church to the next. Some denominations focus on one part of the Bible. Others use non-Biblical sources in order to support what they believe. So at what point does a difference of opinion shift over into deception and into being a Cult?

As I mentioned before, this discussion on Cults was passed on to me by my daughter, Shalom Knotts, and was a presentation she heard in Chapel at college by The Watchman Fellowship, Inc. out of Arlington Texas. There is also a website for Brent Cunningham presenting the same material so I will give credit where I can.

I found this description of the Cults so simple and so to-the-point that I share this whenever discussing Cults. Math has four actions: Addition, Subtraction, Multiplication and Division. The Cults have four actions as well.

1. They **Add** to the Bible. In other words, they replace the Bible with their own versions or additional literature.
2. They **Subtract** from Jesus. They take away from Jesus. They will have many theories about who Jesus is, but they have removed His Godhood from Him in the process. They allow Him to be anything but God.
3. They **Multiply** the ways of salvation. The Bible makes the Plan of Salvation very clear and notes that there is only one way that we are saved. The Cults will create multiple ways of getting saved apart from what the Bible teaches. None of their plans of salvation can save us.
4. They **Divide** the Body of Christ [the Church]. They create division whenever they come into a True Church.

Let's look at each of these teachings in light of the Bible. We will then come back and consider what the Cults are telling us about each topic.

ADDING TO THE BIBLE:

I believe that the Bible is exactly what God intended it to be. I believe this because I see the Bible as God's contract with His Creation. I did my own research on the Gnostic Gospels and other books that were considered and then cast aside and not allowed to be part of the Bible. Dan Brown in his fictional work, *The DaVinci Code* suggests that these decisions were politically-motivated decisions, and those works which did not support the Church were set aside. I have had people make these claims to me, so let me take a moment to discuss these other books.

When I was first saved, I found myself hungry for the Bible and what it had to say. I, therefore, made it a part of my meals. I would read the Bible whenever I sat down to eat. When I finished going through the Bible, I wanted to learn more about Jesus. I came across a collection of books entitled *The Lost*

Books of the Bible and The Forgotten Books of Eden. I knew nothing about these works or why they were forgotten or lost, but I began to read them whenever I sat down to eat.

To my surprise, these books did not speak to me. They did not fill the need in my life the way the Bible did. I pushed on to get through them because they claimed to be written by those who were mentioned in the Bible. However, I began to see that they contradicted each other. They had historical facts wrong. I finally came to the conclusion that these were all fictional works that someone wrote because they did not like how the world actually worked or what history actually said. In short, I could not trust these works to give me any real, credible information about God, Jesus or the work of the Holy Spirit.

What I did not know at the time is that several of the books were call the Gnostic Gospels. The Gnostics were one of the very first Cults. They were there at the time of the Apostle John, and he wrote many of his lessons to deal with their false teachings.

There are two passages of Scripture I want to discuss in this section. The first is Revelation 22:18–19:

"For I testify unto every man that hears the words of the prophecy of this book, If any man shall add unto these things, God shall add unto him the plagues that are written in this book:

"And if any man shall take away from the words of the book of this prophecy, God shall take away his part out of the book of life, and out of the holy city, and from the things which are written in this book."

Every contract—especially an insurance policy—will contain a clause that identifies how any part of the contract or policy can be changed. Basically, the clause notes that the policy cannot be changed. The exception is only if all parties agree with the change, and then only if the change is made in writing and endorsed [signed] by all the parties. Any changes to a contract/policy after they are endorsed [signed] are invalid and a court will not recognize it unless it follows the instructions set down in the contract.

Here, John, speaking of the Book of Revelation, makes it clear that there are no changes allowed to the Book of

Revelation—period! There is no clause giving anyone the authority or procedure to change the book. Nothing can be added to it. Nothing can be removed from it.

Now I grew up on the King James Bible version. Fortunately, I am an English major and after classes on Shakespeare, I know what the words mean. For many years, when I would quote a Bible verse I would use the King James Version and copy it exactly—even the "*thees*," "*thous*," and the "*yea verilies*." It was because of this warning at the end of Revelation. I did not want to be adding to the verse or taking away from the verse. I imagine those who were called upon to translate the Bible into English from Greek, Hebrew, Aramaic and Latin had the same concerns.

Over the years, God has shown me that I can replace the "*thees*" with "*you*" and up-grade all the other King James expressions that might confuse others, so long as I keep the translation as accurate at possible. The rule is that I cannot change the meaning of the verse. It must mean the same thing as it did in the King James Version.

Now each of the Gnostic Gospels and all these other works were adding to the Bible. I believe that even though John meant the statement to apply only to the Book of Revelation, I believe that God had it placed as the last book in the Bible and intended it to refer to the Bible as a whole. [Take that belief for what it's worth.]

Now the other passage I want to bring up comes from II Timothy 3:16–17:

"All scripture is given by inspiration of God, and is profitable for doctrine, for reproof, for correction, for instruction in righteousness:

That the man of God may be perfect, thoroughly furnished unto all good works."

I believe that the Bible is God's complete contract. Within the Bible, we have everything we need to guide us and to make an informed decision concerning God's offer of salvation— that is what the contract is promising. So I do not believe that anything else will ever be added to the Bible. It is complete.

But do not misunderstand this statement. This does not mean that God does not speak to us today, or that He has not spoken to believers throughout the centuries. In the legal system of contract law, you have the actual laws. These were created by the legal authorities and processed to become laws that govern contracts. From time to time, there are lawsuits filed in Civil Court to seek understanding or enforcement of a contract. Each time a judge hears a case and renders a legal opinion regarding the contract; this opinion becomes part of another body of legal authority called: *case laws*.

The case laws do not have the authority to change or repeal a law. Case laws only have the authority to clarify the laws, the contract or the application.

God continues to speak to His followers. God continues to reveal things about Himself and about His Plan for the world.

Now Cults will try to convince you to accept their new revelation without following proper legal procedure. You cannot do that. The law is the law. The contract still prevails. And according to II Timothy 3:16–17, God has placed everything we need to test any new revelation to ensure that it is from God. We always test new revelations by using the original revelation as the basis. If the new revelation does not line up with the original revelation, then it must be rejected.

This is exactly what early Church fathers did when it came to the Gnostic Gospels.

ALL SCRIPTURE—and this would include the Old Testament, as it was the only Scripture Paul had access to as he was writing his letters. There were no Gospels. There were no New Testament copies to tap into. People seem to forget this when they talk about the New Testament. God will continue to inspire people to write. I believe that much of the poems and Bible studies I have written were inspired by God. Should they be considered the same as the Bible? Of course not! That contract is now complete.

The Old Testament—as we shall learn later in this book; is the original contract. It is the terms of the contract. It outlines what God is going to do for His Creation. He is going to send a Messiah to save us. It outlines how we become a party to this contract. We confess our sins and repent of them to become a party to God's contract. The contract gives us test after test so that we will know who the Messiah is when He comes. That is the Old Testament.

***

If I were to compare the New Testament to contract law, it would be the same as a claim made against the contract [an insurance policy]. Again, my expertise is workers' compensation insurance. When a person files a claim for benefits, I must examine their claim and compare it to the insurance policy. Are they covered? If they were covered, I would then compare it to the Labor Code to see what benefits they are entitled to. What benefits should be provided? And for how long should benefits be provided?

Jesus made the claim to be the Messiah. He claims that He is the fulfillment of God's promises made in the Old Testament. He has called forth witnesses. There are two Disciples who wrote Gospels outlining what He taught and what He did. They give careful details relating to the Crucifixion and the Resurrection. I would contact these witnesses in my investigation and get all the information I can from them to see if this Jesus meets the legal requirement to be the Messiah.

There were two second-hand statements. Normally a second-hand statement would not be allowed into evidence in a court of law. However, these two second-hand statements are actually investigations conducted at the time Jesus made His claim to be the Messiah. Mark wrote what he heard from Peter, so this is his deposition of Peter's statement. Luke went to many eyewitnesses and collected their statements for his investigation. Investigations are allowed as evidence in a court of law. Depositions are allowed in a court of law. Therefore, all four Gospels would be admissible if this needed to go to court.

We then have letters from those who knew Jesus. There is Peter. There is John. There is James. There is Jude. James and Jude are half-brothers to Jesus.

Then there is another witness who was not an eyewitness, but he claims to be an eyewitness. There is a statement this witness makes which we must consider. In I Corinthians 15:5–8 Paul is listing the various people who physically saw Jesus after His Resurrection:

"And that He was seen of Cephas, then of the twelve:

After that, He was seen of above five hundred brethren at once; of whom the greater part remain unto this present, but some are fallen asleep [have died].

After that, He was seen of James; then of all the apostles.

And last of all He was seen of me also, as of one born out of due time."

Paul never refers to himself as a Disciple, but he does claim the title of Apostle in each of his letters. He speaks of various revelations and visions given to him in preparation for his ministry. Some will point to his encounter on the road to Damascus as a fulfilling of Christ appearing to Paul, but Paul is not speaking of visions of Jesus here. He is speaking of actual physical appearances. And he includes himself into this list. It appears that Paul is claiming that he may have had various physical appearances of Jesus coming and teaching him as a way of preparing him for the ministry he was called to. He did spend several years in the desert after his conversion. I would make that argument to have Paul included as witnesses I would need to investigate to make a final decision on this claim of Jesus to be the Messiah. I might even list Paul as an expert witness since he spent so much time studying the Old Testament Scriptures and making legal arguments [like mine here] in his letters. The other side might challenge and disqualify him as an eyewitness; but the courts would have to allow his writings in as an expert witness. The Church accepted his teachings, arguments and statement and authorized him to establish Churches throughout the known world at that time. The Church listened to and considered Paul an expert on the Scriptures and Jesus Christ's ministry; the court would have to listen to what he had to say.

This would bring the New Testament under the umbrella of contract law. It is the evidence and investigations to support

Jesus' claim to be the Messiah. If He is the one God sent to be the Messiah; then God has fulfilled what He promised to do in the Old Testament. This means that all 300+ prophecies concerning the Messiah would have been fulfilled by Jesus in order for the contract to be fulfilled and valid in a court of law.

**

There is another concept of law. It is called *prima facie evidence*. *Prima facie evidence* is the prime evidence—it is the evidence by which all other evidence is tested. *Prima facie evidence* is accepted by the court without having to prove that it is credible. An example of this might be a law that controls contract law. For workers' compensation, it was any Labor Code or Regulation created by the state. In this case, the *prima facie evidence* would be the Bible.

I state that the Bible would be *prima facie evidence* because the Bible is the contract God is offering mankind. In any civil court dispute over the interpretation and application of a contract, the contract is accepted into evidence. It is proof of what the Party #1 has offered.

You will notice that I have been slipping in various Bible verses to support the comments I have been making. I am using *prima facie evidence* to prove that what I am saying about the Bible is true. In other words, you can believe what I am saying. These statements have credibility and could be submitted to a court of law. Of course, the statements I am making are not evidence until the court accepts them. I have to prove that what I am saying is true. In a court of law, I would cite a legal authority or *prima facie evidence* when I make a statement to document that my statement is supported by the evidence. This is what we do in a court of law.

This is why I am citing Bible verses as proof that what I am saying is true. I don't have to prove the Bible to the court. It carries the *prima facie evidence* status. It is automatically accepted. I have shown how the Old Testament is 97% exact to what was first written in the Old Testament, and 99.5% accurate in documenting what the New Testament originally said. We have provided ample evidence that the current documents of the Bible are the most accurate copies of the contract that we can produce. My statements, however, do have to be proven.

If this were a lawsuit involving a contract, it would be completely acceptable to bring a copy—or even the original copy—of the contract into court. "This is what the contract says," I would say. And then I would be allowed to read that portion of the contract into evidence. This is what I am doing here. In this case, the Bible is the contract, so I can read portions of this contract into evidence as proof that this is what the contract actually says. The courts would allow this.

Using the Bible as my legal authority for my statements and conclusion is how it is done in a court of law.

Now, if God were to provide a new revelation, II Timothy 3:16–17 requires us to take this new revelation and compare it to the original revelation from God—the Old Testament. This is what the writers of the New Testament Documents did. The teachings that make up the final version of the New Testament comply with each of the teachings of the Old Testament. The dispute between the Jews and the New Testament centers on the identity of the Messiah. The Christians cite the Old Testament to prove that Jesus has met the legal requirements and has fulfilled the terms of the contract.

The Jews reject the claim of Jesus. They insist the Messiah is still coming. However, if you look at Daniel 9:25, there was a very specific timeframe in which the Messiah would reveal Himself. For this reason, no new or recently revealed Messiah would qualify:

"Know therefore and understand, that from the going forth of the commandment to restore and to build Jerusalem unto the Messiah the Prince shall be seven weeks, and threescore and two weeks: the street shall be built again, and the wall, even in troublous times."

Threescore and two weeks plus seven weeks equals sixty-nine weeks. A week in this prophecy is a period of seven years [this is documented in Revelation]. A prophetic year is 360 days long, not 365 days long. So we are looking at [69 X 7 X 360 = 173,880] days from the signing of the decree to return to Jerusalem from Babylon and rebuilt the walls of the city. This historical event took place only once and is documented in the Book of Nehemiah. One hundred seventy-three thousand, eight hundred and eighty days have passed. Jesus rode into Jerusalem on the 173,880[th] day after the signing of decree. He fulfilled the prophecy. But rather than accept Jesus as the Messiah, the Rabbis claim that they did something wrong and it made God change His mind.

Again, someone claimed a revelation from God, but did not check it with the contract. Malachi 3:6:

"For I am the Lord, I change not; therefore you sons of Jacob are not consumed."

God does not change. He does not change His mind. If God did change His mind, the Children of Israel would have been wiped out completely. So whoever claimed that God changed His mind and did not send the Messiah as promised and when promised is wrong. It contradicts what the Bible declares. It contradicts the *prima facie evidence* and so his statement would not be allowed in a court of law.

Also, as I mentioned before, the *prima facie evidence* [Psalm Sixty-Nine] notes that God is going to intentionally make the Jews blind as to who the Messiah will be, and so any statement by them would lack credibility and not be admissible in a court of law.

The appearance of Jesus and the timing of His declaration to be the Messiah comply with the timeframe set by the Old Testament documents. If the Jews are going to challenge His claim to be the Messiah; then the Jews will have to present someone else who made that claim at that time. If Jesus is not the Messiah, and there is no other Messiah who made that claim on that date; then there is no Messiah. He will not be coming at a later date. The terms of the contract were broken, and the contract is now null and void.

So when each of these Cult claims to have a new revelation from God, we are required to test the new revelation—not the old. If the new revelation does not comply with the terms of the contract, these revelations are not from God. Therefore, they cannot be accepted. They must be rejected.

SUBTRACTING FROM JESUS:

The Bible outlines very carefully who the Messiah will be. It outlines very carefully what the Messiah must do to fulfill the terms of the contract. It also makes it very clear what the Messiah must be in order to legally qualify as the Messiah to fulfill the terms of the contract. Let me be brief here. When God led me to conduct my own investigation into the nature and legal requirements of the Messiah, I ended up with a 700+ page manuscript. But as part of my investigation then, I used something called *similitudes*. Hosea 12:10:

"I have also spoken by the prophets, and I have multiplied visions, and used similitudes, by the ministry of the prophets."

What is a similitude? A similitude is showing how something is similar to something else. This is an imperfect picture of that—they are similar. The Tabernacle is a wealth of similitudes. For example: Gold is a metal that represents God. Acacia wood is a wood that is resistant to corruption. As a similitude, acacia wood would represent a sinless man. Gold would represent God. The Ark of the Covenant is a box made of acacia wood [the sinless man]. It is covered within and without by gold [God]. This is a picture of the Incarnation—God becomes man.

This box contains three items: the Tablets of Stone, the Jar of Manna and the Rod of Aaron. The tablets represent the rejection of God's standard for living. The jar represents the rejection of God's provision. The rod represents the rejection of God's authority over us. This is a three-fold rejection of God. It is a perfect picture of sin. Jesus took the sin of the world into Himself when He was on the cross. How could He do this without becoming sinful and being disqualified as the sin offering?

It is possible because the Ark is under the Mercy Seat. The Mercy Seat is pure gold, and so it represents God the Father.

The Mercy Seat is where you come when you are guilty and seek mercy before the sentence is handed down.

Jesus was under the authority of God the Father. He was submissive to God the Father in all things—including taking the sin of the world within Himself. He was doing what God wanted Him to do. God was doing this to Him and He was submitting. This is how He avoided becoming sinful when He was filled with sin. This is how He continued to remain qualified for the sin offering. He submitted to God and allowed God the Father to do this to Him.

That is just one quick example. If I tried to deal with all the similitudes [that I have found] concerning Jesus, this book would cover multiple volumes. So I will keep it brief and pull out those things that are key to this topic. Who is Jesus?

First of all, Jesus must be God. If He is not God, He is not the Messiah described in the terms of the contract. If Jesus is not the Messiah spoken of in prophecies; then He cannot save us, and His death was nothing more than a tragedy and the miscarriage of justice for an individual.

I have been discussing the concept of the Kinsman Redeemer found in Leviticus 25:25. Jesus—as the Messiah—will be the Kinsman Redeemer. But Psalm 49:15 makes it very clear that God will be the one to redeem our souls:

"But *God will redeem my soul* from the power of the grave; for He shall receive me. Selah." [Emphasis added]

To fulfill this part of the prophecy, Jesus—as Redeemer—must be God. If He is not God; then this prophecy is not fulfilled.

***

Now I want to take a moment and revisit an argument proposed by C. S. Lewis. It has come to be called the *Liar, Lunatic or Lord Position*. It boils down to the belief that if Jesus claimed to be God, then there are only three possible views that we can consider of Jesus. If Jesus claimed to be God, and He knew He was not God; then He is a liar. If He is a liar, we cannot trust anything that He said or taught, and everything He said and taught must be rejected. All of His statements would be barred in a court of law because He had perjured Himself and lied.

If Jesus claimed to be God, and He did not have enough grasp of reality to realize that He was not God; then He was a lunatic and had lost touch with reality. Again, everything He said or taught must be rejected as the babblings of a lunatic. Before a person would be allowed to testify in a court of law, he must prove that he is competent to testify. Not knowing what was real and not real would disqualify him as a witness.

But if Jesus claimed to be God, and He was God; then He is our Lord, and we must obey Him and do what He says. There are no other options.

Those who claim that Jesus was a good man, but not God; are not following the logic of their statement. Those who claim that He was good man, a moral man, or a great teacher; and deny that Jesus is God, are making statements that are contradictory of the logic surrounding Jesus. Any assessment of Jesus that claims that He is not God; can only logically result in Jesus being a liar or being a lunatic. You cannot ignore the logic of C. S. Lewis' statement.

As we shall see in later chapters, Jesus did make claims to be God. He made direct claims and said He was God, or that He was equal to God. He made indirect claims to being God, and accepted titles and worship reserved only for God. So we are limited to only these three options when we consider who and what Jesus was.

When I took classes from the late Dr. Walter Martin, he focused on defining terms. Whenever someone would tell him that they believed in Jesus, his response was to ask, "Which Jesus?" Paul made this observation in II Corinthians 11:4:

"But I fear, lest by any means, as the serpent beguiled Eve through his subtlety, so your minds should be corrupted from the simplicity that is in Christ.

"For if he who comes preaches *another Jesus*, whom we have not preached, or if you receive *another spirit*, which you have not received, or *another gospel*, which you have not accepted, you might well [believe] him." [Emphasis added]

Paul knew that there were others who would come after him. His fear was that his spiritual children would be deceived and that they would accept another Jesus, or that they might believe in a different spirit or even another gospel. We will discuss the other Gospel in just a moment in our overview of the ways of salvation. But the Cults are good at confusing believers by using the same terminology and names; but they have given them different definitions.

The Mormons downgrade Jesus to a spirit brother. They identify him as Lucifer's spirit brother and make Jesus one of many spirit sons of God. The Jehovah's Witnesses downgrade Jesus to the Archangel Michael—a created being. God used Michael rather than the only begotten Son of God. God did not beget Michael. He created him. That is an important difference.

We will discuss terminology in more detail later in the book. But if Jesus is anything less than what He claims to be and what the Bible teaches Him to be, you have just fallen for the Cult practice of subtracting from Jesus.

MULTIPLYING THE WAYS OF SALVATION:

Jesus made it very clear when He spoke to His Disciples the night before He was crucified. John 14:6:

"Jesus said unto him, 'I am the way, the truth, and the life: *no man comes unto the Father, but by me.*'" [Emphasis added]

With this statement, Jesus transformed Christianity into an exclusive system. Paul made it clear in I Timothy 2:5:

"For there is one God, and *one mediator between God and men*, the man Christ Jesus;" [Emphasis added]

All other faith systems will fail to get you to God. All roads do not lead to God. Jesus—and only Jesus—knows how to get to God, and we must follow what Jesus said and taught in order to come before God.

I know this offends people. People get angry when they hear that Jesus is the only way of salvation. But let me point out two things. The first is that Jesus is the one who made this claim. He is the one who made Christianity exclusive. Second, it is not my place to make you comfortable about this. When I served as an expert witness for the court, it was not my role to say what people wanted to hear. It was my role to testify as to the truth whether it benefited one side in the argument or not. As an expert witness, I am called upon to present the facts, the evidence and the information as accurately as possible. It is up to the judge and/or the jury to accept my testimony or not.

Jesus established only one way to be saved—come before God. Any other faith system that teaches or suggests other saviors, or other ways of being saved are false and they will fail to help you reach your goal. Paul made this observation in Galatians Chapter One:

"I marvel that you are so soon removed from Him who called you into the grace of Christ unto *another gospel*:

"Which is not another; but there be some who trouble you, and would pervert the gospel of Christ.

"But though we, or *an angel from Heaven*, preach *any other gospel* unto you [other] than that which we have preached unto you, let him be accursed.

"As we said before, so say I now again, 'If any man preach *any other gospel* unto you than that [which] you have received, let him be accursed.'" [Emphasis added]

We will discover in later chapters that there is a Cult that prides itself on being based upon another Gospel, which they claim, was presented by an angel from Heaven. It will surprise you how carefully God wrote the Bible to address the false teachings that would come centuries later. This is just one example.

THEY DIVIDE THE BODY OF CHRIST:

Whenever these Cults come into a Church [body of Christ], they create division. They cause people to be deceived and led away. They cause conflict and challenge the teachings of the Bible. They will declare that they have a new revelation. They know something no one else knows. They have a better doctrine. They have a better way to be saved. The reason they cause division is because of the first three positions: they add to the Bible, they subtract from Jesus and they multiply the ways of salvation.

I had a discussion the other day with a friend, and it became obvious that if we wanted to do a discussion on Cults, there were so many points on which we disagreed; we could have hundreds of points of disagreement. My focus in this work is to keep things simple and to keep things focused, and so I will be looking at just some basic doctrines. It dawned upon me the old question: "*How many times does a person have to tell a lie before they become a liar?*" The answer is "*just one.*" Once a single lie has been spoken, the person speaking becomes a liar and everything that person says must be tested to see if it is a lie or not. This is why I use as many Bible verses as I can. I might slip up. I might state something that is not true, but I thought it was true. I might be misinformed. It is not what I say; it is what the Bible says that matters.

So I will look at the Creation because it establishes God's legal jurisdiction over us. I will look at the Virgin Birth as it established Jesus legal claim to redeem us. I will look at the Crucifixion as this is how Jesus paid for our sin. I will look at the Resurrection as this is the proof that the sacrifice of Jesus was successful in removing sin. Finally, I will look at the Plan of Salvation as this is the contract God is offering the human race.

There are many other points where we may disagree. There are many points in which Christians disagree with each other; but it does not establish them as a Cult. I want to narrow the focus and show the important lies so that the reader can make a decision for himself/herself.

CHAPTER SIX

"WOLVES IN SHEEP'S CLOTHING"

I am not comfortable using the kind of word that I used in the title of this book. I do not like the word "*damned.*" I do not like it because I know exactly what I mean when I use it. I do not want anyone to be damned and spend eternity in Hell. However, with this book there is no better description of the kind of deceptions we are dealing with. The Cults are Satan's counterfeit for God's Church. They are not just stealing your life savings. They are stealing away your eternity. Not that you can lose your salvation once God has given it; but they make you believe that you are saved when you are not, and so you reject God's offer of true salvation because you do not believe you need it. They are deceiving people right into Hell, and these people have no idea that they are going there.

As I noted previously, the person writing the contract has the greater obligation to make the contract as clear as possible. The person writing the contract has the obligation to remove any ambiguity. This is what I am trying to do in this book: make things clear, and remove ambiguity. Therefore, the title of this book makes it as clear as I can. If you allow yourself to be deceived; then you run the risk of being damned to Hell.

There is one of the problems when dealing with deception. People who are deceived do not know that they are deceived. If they knew they are deceived, then it is not deception. But how do you know if you are being deceived?

Paul gave advice to believers to come back to the Scriptures occasionally and test what they believed against what the Scriptures say. He was fully aware that deception can slip in and we will not recognize it. The Scriptures are the test. Truth will line up with the Scriptures. If it does not line up with Scriptures; then it is not truth and should not be believed. II Corinthians 13:5:

"Examine yourselves, whether you are [still] in the faith; prove your own selves. Know you not your own selves, how that Jesus Christ is in you, except you are reprobates?"

Even if you are attending what appears to be a Bible-believing Church, take the time to test your beliefs against Scripture. Now if you find that you are believing something that is false, change your beliefs; don't change the Scriptures to say what you want. That is the error of the Jehovah's Witnesses. They could not prove their doctrines using the Bible, so they altered the Bible to support what they taught.

The title of this chapter is "Wolves in Sheep's Clothing." This is a term that Jesus used when He spoke of false prophets, false Christs and false teachings. Matthew 7:15:

"Beware of false prophets, which come to you in sheep's clothing, but inwardly they are ravening wolves."

These counterfeits of Satan are described by Jesus as ravening wolves. A ravening wolf does not slip into the flock just to hang out with the sheep because it likes the grass in the field they are feeding on. They are there to kill the sheep. They are there to do damage and harm.

This is why I believe that we are not just dealing with deceptions. We are dealing with damned deceptions—deceptions designed to lure you into a system that cannot and will not save you; so that you will end up in Hell for all eternity.

Jesus knew the danger. We warned us of the dangers. Matthew 24:4–5:

"And Jesus answered and said unto them, 'Take heed that no man deceive you.

"For many shall come in my name saying, "I am Christ" and shall deceive many.'"

Back in the 1960's and 1970's we saw several Cults where the founders of those Cults claimed to be Jesus. One leader claimed that Jesus died before He was supposed to die, and so God had come to this Cult leader and made him the new Christ.

Others just elevated themselves a little bit higher and higher until they were trusted and worshiped as if they were God.

These kinds of Cults are easier to identify, but Jesus was speaking of wolves in sheep's clothing. These are wolves who look like a sheep and pretend to be sheep. There are Cults where the members honestly think that they are sheep. They believe that they are saved. The founder of the Cult dressed them up like sheep so that they would believe that they were sheep. Even they do not know that they are not sheep. They act like sheep and come together once a week to worship and fellowship. They use the same words that we use. They go out like sheep and try to teach others to be like them. These are the kinds of Cults that are difficult to identify and harder to reach because they are convinced that they are sheep—that they are Christians.

The people are deceived. They are not the wolves per se. They are those whom the wolves have taken control of. In fact, in these kinds of Cults, you can go further and further toward the top of the organization and each will honestly believe that they are sheep. In these organizations, Satan is the wolf. He is using those who are sincere, but deceived, to lure as many people as possible into his trap.

I really want to make it clear that those who have been deceived into thinking that they are sheep are not the wolves. They honestly are deceived and honestly believe that they are sheep. The enemy, in these cases, are those who know they are deceiving others and continue to do so.

So I want to make it clear that this book is designed to help each person—sheep and non-sheep—to examine the truth and come to make the correct decision as to whether they are sheep or not. I do not want you attacking people on your doorstep. I do not suggest screaming and getting into their faces. Those who think that they are sheep and are not, are the victims here. Those who created this deception are the wolves. They are the true enemies. Unfortunately, those who created this deception and turned it loose on the world have passed away. They wound this wolf up, and it continues to grow on its own.

Jesus warned us in Matthew 24:11:

"And many false prophets shall come and deceive many."

How crazy is all of this going to get? Jesus taught that as we get closer to the End Times these deceptions would become more prevalent. Matthew 24:23–27:

"Then if any man shall say unto you, 'Lo, here is Christ,' or 'there;' believe it not.

"For there shall arise false Christs, and false prophets, and shall show great signs and wonders; insomuch that, if it were possible, they shall deceive the very elect.

"Behold, I have told you [this] before [it happens].

"Wherefore if they shall say unto you, 'Behold, he is in the desert;' go not forth: 'Behold, he is in the secret chambers;' believe it not.

"For as the lightning comes out of the east, and shines even unto the west; so shall also the coming of the Son of man be."

Let me go through this warning line by line and pull out the information we need to know. There are going to be those who will claim that Jesus has come back. There is one Cult whose leader purchased a very nice, expensive mansion for the Second Coming. The Cult set dates when Jesus would return and bring Abraham, Moses and David with Him. This leader had the Cult buy this mansion. He would live in it until they arrived. [The Cult leader has passed and the mansion has been sold since then.]

This same Cult kept setting dates and nothing happened. They finally claimed that Jesus did return, but He was invisible. Now you see where the advice of Jesus is so valuable. Don't listen to these lies.

Next, do not pay attention to what they are doing. Pay attention to what they are saying and teaching. Jesus gave us this warning that these false prophets and false Christs will be able to perform wonders and miracles. They will do this to draw people in and to convince them that they are Christ or that they are of God.

Paul gave this warning in II Corinthians 11:14:

"And no marvel; for Satan himself is transformed *into an angel of light*." [Emphasis added]

If the devil can change his appearance and make himself appear to be a messenger from God, imagine what his followers can do with his help. Paul warned in II Thessalonians 2:8–9:

"And then shall that Wicked [One] be revealed, whom the Lord shall consume with the spirit of His mouth, and shall destroy with the brightness of His coming:

Even him, whose coming is after the working of Satan *with all power and signs and lying wonders*," [Emphasis added]

Satan and his servants have the ability to appear as something different from what they are. They have the ability to perform miracles, signs and wonders. These are all for the purpose of drawing people in and deceiving them

Jesus noted that these false Christs and false prophets would show "*great signs and wonders*." They will be very good. They will be hard to detect. He warned that if it were possible, they could deceive true Christian believers. Fortunately, by the way Jesus words this warning it suggests that "*the elect*" will not be taken in, but will see these deceivers for what they are. Keep in mind that Jesus describes them as wolves in sheep's clothing. Everyone looking at them will see sheep. They will look like sheep, and act like sheep; because they have been deceived into thinking that they are sheep.

Jesus tells us that when He returns, it will be obvious. In this case, He is speaking of His Second Coming. There is the Rapture where Jesus comes FOR His Church. He does not touch down. He does not announce Himself to the world. He comes in the air and we all rise to meet Him. But when He comes WITH His Church, then everyone will see Him. He used the example of a flash of lightning. It starts in one part of the sky. Everyone sees it. It continues to spread across the sky until everyone has seen it. That is how it is going to be when Jesus returns WITH His Church to reclaim the earth and set up His Kingdom out of Jerusalem.

Jesus told us this was going to happen. He told us the kinds of things they will say and do in order to deceive us. He gave us this warning ahead of time so when it does start to happen, we will remember and say, "Wait a minute! Jesus warned us about this. Don't fall for it."

Again, don't pay attention to how they look or to what they do. Follow John's example in I John 4:1 -3:

"Beloved, believe not every spirit, but [test] the spirits whether they are of God: because many false prophets [have] gone out into the world.

[This is how you can know] the Spirit of God: Every spirit that confesses that Jesus Christ is come in the flesh is of God:

And every spirit that confesses not that Jesus Christ is come in the flesh is not of God: and this is that spirit of antichrist, whereof you have heard that it should come; and even now already it is in the world."

As we confront the deception, it is not what they do. It is what they say. And John warns us that those who are of God will confess that Jesus is God who was born into the human race— that He came among us "*in the flesh*." All those who challenge that teaching and make Jesus into anything or anyone other than God born into the human race are the deceivers. Do not trust them. Do not accept them. Do not follow them.

CHAPTER SEVEN

"WHICH JESUS?"
PART ONE

I mentioned in a prior chapter that the late Dr. Walter Martin was one of the experts on the Cults. In his classes, he noted that whenever anyone tells him that they believed in Jesus, he would ask them, "Which one?" or "Which Jesus?"

Paul expressed his concern that after he had taught the members in various Churches and he moved on that someone would come in and teach a different Jesus, or a different Spirit, or a different Gospel. His concern is that his converts might believe these false teachers.

Whenever we teach on the Cults, we normally have to spend an entire class discussing terminology. When someone tells you that they believe in Jesus does not mean that they believe the same things that you believe. Satan loves to offer counterfeits. I believe it was C. S. Lewis who made the observation that Satan does not create anything. Satan will take what God has created and twist it to a different meaning or purpose.

One of the problems we encounter when dealing with those trapped in the Cults is that we can generate a great deal of heat; but that does not produce any light. There are so many topics that we can disagree on, and we can debate and argue these for hours on end. They can inflame the emotions; but if it does not produce light so that the other party can see the truth and come out of the darkness; then all you are doing is fighting for fighting's sake. We do not want to do this. You should not be doing this. The minute you are in a discussion and you feel you must win—especially at any cost—then you are no longer letting the Holy Spirit guide you. This is not competition. This is not winning. We win when those who have been deceived come out of their deception and accept Jesus as their Savior. Scoring points, shutting them down, and beating them into submission will not win them to Christ. Every encounter should be about them, and not you or your ego. This can be very hard.

What Dr. Walter Martin would tell us in our classes is to focus on what is important. There are certain topics that we cannot be wrong about. It does not matter what day of the week you attend Church. It does not matter if you eat meat or not. It does not matter if you wear a suit and tie to Church or not. Those issues do not affect where you will spend eternity. When it comes to the issue of salvation and where you will spend eternity; these are the issues that we cannot make a mistake with.

We've identified the method of salvation. God outlines His Plan of Salvation in His Bible. The Bible is God's contract and it contains the promises God has made in writing to us. Three events are predicted in the Old Testament, and these three events are the physical proof that God has kept His promise. The first is the Incarnation. God the Son separated from the Trinity and entered the human race through the process of a virgin birth. He is born without sin. He lives without sin. He is legally qualified to be a sin offering for the entire human race.

The next event is the death of Jesus. The death of Jesus is carefully controlled. There can be no deviation from the legal requirements. If the sin offering is not exactly according to procedure and prophecy, then the sin offering will not be accepted by God. So we must make sure that the Crucifixion we are talking about meets all the legal and prophetic requirements laid down in the Old Testament.

The last historical event is the Resurrection. The Resurrection is the proof that God has accepted Jesus' sin offering. The Resurrection must be according to prophecy and if not; then it can be called into question. Without the Resurrection, there is no proof that the sacrifice of Jesus worked. At best, we can "*hope*" that it worked; but we can never "*know*."

***

I want to take a moment and focus on prophecy. I want to stress prophecy because prophecy is the proof that God offers. He offers it to prove that He does exist. He offers it to prove that He is in charge. Isaiah 46:9 - 11:

"Remember the former things of old: for I am God, and there is no one else; I am God, and there is no one like me,

"Declaring the end from the beginning, and from ancient times the things that are not yet done, saying, 'My counsel shall stand, and I will do all my pleasure:

"... I have spoken it, I will also bring it to pass; I have purposed it, I will also do it.'"

If I were to write you a letter, and in this letter, I made a prediction, this would be like prophecy. In this letter, I would tell you that on December 27th three years from now, a man will walk through the front door at a very specific address. He will walk from inside the house to outside the house. He will be wearing blue pants. He will be wearing a white long-sleeved shirt with the sleeves rolled up. He will be wearing boots. He will pass through this door at 2:00 in the afternoon. He will use his right hand to open the door. In his left hand, he will be holding a book. That book will be a collection of poems by Robert Frost. The man will not be wearing glasses. He will be clean-shaven. He will be balding.

There are many factors here. We would start to calculate those factors. I want to keep this conservative and so some factors I will just leave out. The odds of male versus female, and how many addresses are there to choose from, and how many kinds of shoes the person has; are intentionally left out by me. I want to keep this example simple. You can add them in if you want to. However, even when I leave these factors out, the odds of my being correct still rise dramatically. Again, we take each factor and multiply it with the next. We take that result and multiply it by the next factor until we have combined all the factors.

There are three ways to enter or exit that house. Therefore, our first factor is one in three. There are two directions you can go when passing through the door. So the next factor is one in two. Let's suggest that the man owns three colors of pants: black, blue and brown. Therefore, this is one in three. The man owns seven different colors of shirts. This factor would be one in seven. Of these seven shirts, four are long-sleeved. Long-sleeved shirts can be worn with sleeves down or rolled up—a one in two chance. There are twenty-four hours in the day so our next factor is one in twenty-four. The man has two hands so this would mean a one in two chance of getting the correct hand. He owns three thousand books—the man loves to read. This brings those odds to one in three thousand. He has three thousand books to choose from. Glasses or not is a one in two chance. Clean-shaven or not is a one in two chance. Balding or not is also a one in two probability.

Now getting all of these predictions correct would be the chance of one in 1,548,288,000 [if my calculator is correct]. If I can make that prediction, and it happens just like I predicted; then I must be pretty good. The odds are too great of it happening on its own by accident.

However, when you come to that address three years later and see me walking out of the house wearing blue pants and a white shirt at two o'clock in the afternoon carrying a collected works of Robert Frost, you're going to scream "*Foul!*" I did not *predict* the event. I *caused* the event. I do not disagree. But that is exactly how God is able to predict the future with such great detail. He planned it. He controlled it. He caused it. This moves the odds from being as high as they are down to the odds of one out of one. It happens the way He said every time.

Many years ago there was a television game show called *To Tell The Truth*. The show opened with three people all introducing themselves as the same person. Only one person was that person. The other two were lying. The panel had to ask questions to figure out who was telling the truth.

Back in my college days, there was a Christian comedy team that traveled from Church to Church doing skits as their ministry. They produced some record albums, which I have in my collection. The name of the group was *Isaac Airfreight*, and they did one skit called *The Saving Game*. In their skit, a person gets to interview three contestants [similar to *the Dating Game*] and pick their Savior.

If it were not so serious this can be a pretty funny skit. But it illustrates how Satan will slip in several versions of Jesus and try to deceive you into selecting the wrong one. If you pick the wrong one, you are not saved. Your eternity depends on making the right choice.

So let's blend *To Tell The Truth* and *The Saving Game* for a moment. Multiple people stand up and tell you, "*I am Jesus Christ*." They all claim to be Jesus Christ. So like *To Tell The Truth*, we will ask questions to figure out which one is actually Jesus Christ. But like *The Saving Game*, when the round is over, we must choose one of them to be our Savior. If we choose a counterfeit, that person cannot save you. You loose. You go to Hell for all eternity. That is exactly what is taking place in our lives when we are dealing with Cults.

Since the decision is that serious, we really need to do some research before making the decision. We do conduct research so that we can know which questions to ask in order to get the answers that will give us the information we need in order to pick the correct Savior. I suggest that we use the Bible to conduct our research. As mentioned before, the Bible is our *prima facie evidence*. It is the evidence by which all other evidence is tested.

John begins his description of the Messiah by going back before the birth of the Messiah, and even before the Creation of the heavens and the earth. John 1:1–3:

"In the beginning was the Word, and the Word was with God, and *the Word was God.*

"The same *was in the beginning with God.*

"*All things were made by Him*, and without Him was not anything made that was made." [Emphasis added]

John uses the title "*The Word*" to refer to the Messiah. Keep in mind, the Messiah did not have a name until the Messiah was born of the virgin. John moves the Messiah prior to His birth to the same status as God. He moves the Messiah all the way back to the beginning of all things. John moves the Messiah above all created beings and elevates the Messiah to the level of Creator. Nothing was made unless the Messiah made it. He then brings the Messiah from being God prior to the Messiah's physical birth, and moves the Messiah into the human race. John 1:14:

"And *the Word was made [into] flesh* and lived among us, (and we beheld His glory, the glory of the *only begotten* of the Father) *full of grace and truth*." [Emphasis added]

John identifies himself at this point as being an eyewitness to the identity of the Messiah. In John 1:17 John connects Jesus with the reference to "*grace and truth*." In doing so, John equates Jesus with the Word:

"For the law was given by Moses, but *grace and truth came by Jesus Christ*." [Emphasis added]

Remember, in verse fourteen John described the Word as being full of grace and truth when the Word became flesh. Here Jesus brings grace and truth. Therefore, Jesus is the Word. Jesus is the Messiah.

John's description of Jesus lines up perfectly with the prophecy of Micah 5:2:

"But you, Bethlehem Ephratah, though you are little among the thousands of Judah, yet out of you shall he come forth unto me who is to be ruler in Israel; whose goings forth *have been from old, from everlasting*." [Emphasis added]

This Messiah described by Micah is not a created being. The Messiah has always existed. He has no beginning and He has no end. He is eternal. This is just one reason why we believe that the Messiah—this person born of a virgin—must be God. He must have existed before He was born. He must have been born into the human race via a virgin birth. This person born of the virgin bears the titles of God, has no beginning, and has no end. He has always existed. He will exist forever. Prior to His being born into the human race, He was God. He was involved in the creation of the heavens, the earth and mankind. By being born into the human race, God is now human and related to us by birth.

Now according to prophecies, there are some additional requirements. This Messiah must be of the line of Abraham. He must be of the Tribe of Judah. He must be of the line of David, but not of the line of Solomon. He had to be born of a virgin, and that birth had to take place in Bethlehem.

One of the arguments by non-believers as they look at the life of Jesus, and how He fulfills prophecies, is that in several scenarios it is clear that Jesus is doing something specifically in order to fulfill a prophecy. Take for example John 19:28:

"After this, Jesus, knowing that all things were accomplished, that the Scriptures might be fulfilled said, 'I thirst.'"

Psalm 69:21 describes the Messiah as drinking vinegar as part of the prophecy. By announcing to the guards around the cross that He was thirsty, Jesus caused the guards to give Him vinegar to drink. He caused that part of the prophecy to happen. If He had kept quiet, they would not have given Him vinegar to drink. Right after drinking the vinegar He dies. So the only reason He asked for something to drink was to ensure that this prophecy was fulfilled.

Non-believers will look at this passage, point to it and say, "See! He was deliberately doing something because it was in the prophecy." And to this, I will respond, "Of course!"

People will get into an argument over those portions of prophecy that Jesus fulfilled which He had no control over, such as being born in Bethlehem, or being of the line of David. But let me refer back to the discussion of my prophecy of someone walking through a specific door. My prophecy was correct and happened exactly as I described it because I caused it to happen. If we look at Jesus as limited to just the events of His life, we will point to various events and say, "He controlled this." or "He did not control this one." But that is not true.

Because Jesus is God and existed before His birth, He was able to control each and every event of the prophecy to ensure that each and every event was exactly as God had described it. Asking for something to drink while He was on the cross was controlling events to ensure everything happened the way it was predicted. God said that He would declare it, and that *He would cause it to happen* [Isaiah 46:11]. There is no deception here. God is not trying to trick anyone. God disclosed His secret of how He could make prophecy after prophecy, and each one would come true exactly as He described it. He declares the prophecy. And then He causes the prophecy to happen exactly as He described it.

There were events before Jesus was born, but as God, Jesus had control over those events and ensured that they happened exactly as God said they would. When God needed to get Mary down to Bethlehem in time for the birth of Jesus, He caused a Roman Emperor to order a census, and as part of that census, everyone had to return to their hometown. This forced Joseph to transport Mary in her condition all the way down to Bethlehem. Yes, God controlled the events; but there was no deception in doing so. The test is not that things will happen this way. The test is: *"Can God make these things happen this way?"* Don't misunderstand the test.

There were events in Jesus' life where He had control over events, and He did things to ensure they happened exactly as God described them. Jesus chose to go to Jerusalem for Passover on the same Passover that would correspond with Daniel 9:25's prophecy. He was an active participant in going to the Passover in Jerusalem exactly when all of these events would take place. Being an active participant does not invalidate God's prophecy—especially if you are God.

If God is God, and God is in control; then God had the power to prevent Jesus from going to Jerusalem if He was not the Messiah. God has the power to make events happen, and to keep events from happening. Both are proof of God's control over events, and proof of God's power.

Let me comment on a prophecy concerning the Eastern Gate in Jerusalem. This was the gate Jesus rode the donkey through on Palm Sunday—the 173,880th day from the decree to rebuild the walls of Jerusalem. Ezekiel 44:1–2:

"Then He brought me back the way of the gate of the outward sanctuary which looks toward the east; and it was shut.

"Then said the Lord unto me; 'This gate shall be shut, it shall not be opened, and no man shall enter in by it; because the Lord, the God of Israel, has entered in by it, therefore it shall be shut."

If you go to Jerusalem and stand in the Garden of Gethsemane on the Mount of Olives, you get a good view of this Eastern Gate. It is just across the street. It is sealed. It was bricked up. No one can pass through it. Various people have tried to open the gate and pass through it, but God has kept it sealed. As one point, the King of Jordan sought to blow open the gate and pass through, but a war broke out in his country before he could complete his task. God can both cause events to happen, and God can block events from happening. If Jesus were causing prophecies to be fulfilled to prove He was the Messiah, and He was not—God could have stopped each event Jesus caused to happen. God declares it, and God causes it to happen.

The fact that Jesus was able to cause these events to happen was further proof that He is God.

There were events after Jesus' death where He was no longer in His body. God controlled the events after Jesus' death to ensure that it happened exactly as God described them. God the Father controlled events so that the legs of Jesus were not broken. God controlled events to ensure that the blood of Jesus would be poured out at the foot of the cross. God the Father controlled events to ensure Jesus' body would be placed in a rich man's grave. God the Father controlled events so that the Roman government would seal the tomb and place guards around it to ensure no one could have access to the body of Jesus until it was time for Him to resurrect.

God said He was going to do these things. God did these things. There is no foul in this process because God is doing this to prove that He does exist and that He does control all things. He is proving to us that when He says something is going to happen, then it will happen the way He said it would because He is the one who is making it happen.

When we discussed prophecies and we were calculating the odds of just a single event happening the way God said it would; there was no danger of it not happening. There was no possibility of it happening some other way. God removed all possibilities except for His scenario because He is that powerful and controlled the events that meticulously to ensure it would happen the way that He said it would.

Prophecy, when it comes to God, is not a guess. It is not a chance. It is nothing more than a declaration. "I said it would happen this way. It will happen this way. I will leave nothing to chance. I will remove chance, odds, and probabilities from the equation because I will make it happen. I will control the events so that they do happen the way I said they would."

So from a human point of view, these other requirements of the prophecy appear to be things that the Messiah has no control over. But that is an illusion. We need to look at these events from God's point of view. If Jesus is God, and He existed in Heaven before He was born; then God does have control over these things and God can and did make them happen. God is sharing His knowledge of what He is going to do in the future; and so each and every detail is planned out and must line up perfectly.

***

I have touched on just one part of the Christian Jesus of the Bible. This is who He is. This is what He has done. Let's explore what the Jehovah's Witnesses say concerning Jesus? In Watchtower theology, Jesus is not God. In the *New World Translation of Scripture*, John 1:1 has been altered. Instead of reading: "In the beginning was the Word and the Word was with God and the Word was God," their translation reads, "In the beginning was the word and the word was with God and the word was a god." [Notice it is "god" with a small "g."]

If you press a representative of the Watchtower Society as to how many Gods there are, they will admit that there is only one God. They cannot explain how Jesus can be "*a god*" but not "*God*" if there is only one God. They will, however, have an explanation as to why they translated the verse the way they did—even if their translation become self-contradictory.

Let me take a moment to discuss a decision made by the Watchtower Society. When the Watchtower Society first began, they used the King James Bible. They liked the King James Bible because it used the name *Jehovah* for God in the Old Testament—but not in the New Testament. [The name "*Jehovah*" is very important to the Jehovah's Witness.]

When they came across a passage such as John 1:1, they would use creative interpretation to make the passage say what they needed it to say. In the above verse, the Jehovah's Witness will point out that there is no definitive article in front of the word "*God*." Without the definitive article [the] in front of "*God*" then it must be properly translated "*a god*." That would be correct if that were the only rule of grammar involved with this verse.

There is an entire study entitled "*exegesis*." I dealt with this in my Greek class in college. There are rules to guide you in extracting information from the passage to ensure you have properly and correctly translated that passage.

Unfortunately, for the Jehovah's Witnesses, there are other rules of grammar at play here. They ignore the use of the linking verb "*was*" by John—"the Word was God." When you use the linking verb of "was" or "is," the linking verb becomes a kind of grammatical *equals sign* [=]. The words being linked must be equal in all things. Since John used "*the Word*" and linked it to "*God*," then using proper grammar it should be translated "*The Word was The God*." You have to continue applying all rules of grammar until you get the most accurate translation. The Watchtower Society did not follow this rule. They stopped applying grammatical rules as soon as they got the translation that they wanted/needed.

This is the kind of creative manipulating of the King James Bible to make it say what they were teaching. In the 1950's the leaders of the Watchtower chose to address this problem. Rather than changing their beliefs to line up with what the King James Bible said, they created the *New World Translation of Scriptures* and altered the King James Bible to say what they needed it to say.

In creating this *New World Translation*, they did not go back to the Greek and Hebrew texts and translate them. When the

King James Bible was translated there were three councils, two groups of experts and constant review of the work to ensure it was saying what the original Hebrew and Greek manuscripts said as closely as possible. Rather than going back to the original manuscripts, they took the English version of the King James Bible and altered the wording to fit their teachings.

If you take a closer look, the New World Translation of Scriptures continues to be rewritten every so often as other passages come to light that cause problems for the Watchtower Society and their doctrines.

Let me put this back into a legal context. The Watchtower Society did not like the contract God wrote, and so they wrote their own version of the contract to say what they wanted it to say. They did not have the legal authority to do this. The *New World Translation of Scriptures* is not a valid contract. Anything it claims or promises will not be honored by God. Their contract is null and void. God did not write it. God will not honor it. Any Plan of Salvation it offers does not have the guarantee of God behind it.

***

When asked about who Jesus is, the Watchtower theology will teach that Jesus is actually the Archangel Michael. There is just one problem with this; Michael is a created being. Therefore, Michael did not always exist. He had a beginning. Michael as Jesus does not fulfill the prophecy in Micah 5:2:

"But you, Bethlehem Ephratah, though you are little among the thousands of Judah, yet out of you shall he come forth unto me who is to be ruler in Israel; *whose goings forth have been from old, from everlasting.*" [Emphasis added]

If Jesus is, in fact, Michael; then Jesus did not fulfill this prophecy. If Jesus did not fulfill this prophecy, then we have one of two choices. The first is that Micah is not a prophet of God since his prophecy did not come true. This puts all the teachings in Micah into question. Since it was made part of the Bible, this one false prophecy can actually call the entire Bible into question. If this prophecy is false; then those compiling the Bible made a mistake with Micah. If they made a mistake with Micah, how can we know if they made a mistake somewhere else? Maybe there was another book that should have been added. Maybe there are other books that should have been left out. Yes, it is that serious. You must follow the logic of the evidence.

Think of the Bible as a long line of dominos. Each domino is a prophecy God made. Each prophecy is proof that God exists. Each prophecy is proof that God is in charge. There is no greater force in all the universe that can alter, block or even delay a single prophecy of God. We tap the first domino, and it falls. As it falls, it must hit the next domino and knock it down. This process is repeated time and time again until all the dominos have fallen. In other words, each prophecy comes true exactly as God declared and at the time He determined. Each prophecy triggers the next prophecy until all the prophecies relating to this topic are complete. This is how we know it was God. This is how we know it is true.

Now into this long line of dominos, we have the domino of Micah 5:2—the prophecy of Jesus' birth in Bethlehem. When the domino before it falls, the Micah 5:2 domino does not. The prophecy did not come true as predicted. The process stops, and no further dominos fall. The line of prophecies cannot be completed. The line of prophecies was not from God. The existence of God can now be called into question. The proof He offered was invalid. The Supreme Authority of God must also called into question, as something was greater than God, and was able to stop God from fulfilling everything He promised. Again, it is that serious. We need to understand that just like a legal contract everything is connected. Everything is part of it. And any flaw in any part of the contract can invalidate the contract either in part or in the whole.

Our second option, if Jesus is Michael; then that Jesus cannot be the Messiah discussed in the prophecy. That Jesus does not fulfill the prophecy, and even though every other prophecy is fulfilled—including the death—it cannot qualify as a fulfillment of God's promises in the Bible. They all must come true or there is no salvation. We are all still going to Hell.

The only solution to these problems that maintains the Bible and God's contract with man would be that Jesus is not Michael, and that Jesus is, in fact, God who has no beginning and has no end. That is the only solution to the problem. Either the Jehovah's Witnesses are wrong, or Micah was wrong, or Jesus is not the Messiah. If the Jehovah's Witnesses are wrong, Jesus is God, He is the Messiah, and we are saved. If Micah is wrong, the entire Bible is called into question and we are not saved. If Jesus is Michel the angel, then Jesus is not the Messiah. His death cannot save us, and we are all lost and going to Hell.

If the Watchtower Society is correct, the end result of their position is a disaster for believers. If we take their argument and follow it to its logical conclusion—if Jesus is not the person in this prophecy; then He cannot be the Messiah. This means that His death was a tragic miscarriage of justice; but it cannot save us. In other words, we are all still doomed and destined for Hell. They have invalidated God's Plan of Salvation and God is not offering a different plan.

***

One of the points the Cults seem to miss every time, is that God set forth some very precise prophecies, events and timetables. To date, Jesus is the only person in all of history who has fulfilled all of these requirements. If you disqualify Jesus, God cannot just send someone else. God's timetable has already passed. If Jesus does not meet all the requirements, or if Jesus is not the Messiah; then there is no Plan B. God only has Plan A. God had such confidence that He could produce Plan A and everything would happen exactly as He described it, that He did not build in a safety net. He did not consider failure. He does not have a Plan B option. If Jesus is not the Messiah or if Jesus is disqualified from being the Messiah, then God's entire Plan of Salvation program fails. There is no new Messiah coming—He would not meet the requirements and time frames after-the-fact.

God does not lie and God does not change. Therefore, God has to get it right the first time; or there is no Plan of Salvation.

Consider that when you try to disqualify Jesus or create a new program.

***

The Watchtower Society theology teaches that Michael is the first created being, and so they conclude that this makes Michael the *firstborn son of God* in a figurative sense. With this statement, the Watchtower Society has "*introduced facts that are not in evidence.*" In other words, they are making a claim that there is no evidence to support. This would be a legal objection raised in court, and the statement would not be allowed into evidence for the court to consider unless they can prove their statement is true.

They would have to submit passages from the Bible that identifies Michael as the first created being. While it is true that Michael is a created being, and he was directly created by God, this would only make him *one* of the "*sons of God.*" It does not qualify him to be the *firstborn son of God.* Unfortunately, the Bible does not identify which angel was the first to be created.

Given the description and position of Lucifer as identified in Isaiah 14:12–17, and Ezekiel 28:13–17, someone could make a strong argument for Lucifer to be the first created being. His position was pretty exalted before his fall.

There are only two titles that Michael can claim according to Scripture. The first is that Michael is one of the "*sons of God.*" The second is that he is also an archangel. We can also prove that his assignments seem connected with the nation of Israel. But to extend that to declaring that Michael is the *firstborn son of God* intentionally leaves out information and it is designed to misrepresent the intent of Scripture. They are pulling titles and giving them new meanings in an attempt to support their doctrine.

Scripture makes a distinction between a "*son of God*" and the "*begotten son of God.*" Any creature that is a direct creation of God is called a "*son of God.*" We see "*sons of God*" used to refer to angels in Genesis 6:2. We see the angels referred to "*sons of God*" in Job 1:6. There is an entire category of created beings who bear this title because they were created directly by God. We even see this title applied to Adam in Luke 3:38 because Adam was created directly by God.

When John tells us that God will give us the power to "*become the sons of God*" in John 1:12, John is not suggesting that we will become angels. Hebrews makes it clear that we will be above the angels. John is referring to the spiritual part of us that will be directly created by God. We are all sons of Adam because of our physical state. But when God brings our spirit to life and we are born again, then our spirit self is a direct creation of God and qualifies as a son of God.

So when the Jehovah's Witnesses claim Michael is a "*son of God,*" they are correct; but Michael is a created son of God. The Messiah must be a "*begotten*" son of God. There is a difference. There are many sons of God; but there is only one Begotten Son of God—that is Jesus.

God fulfills His promises in a literal sense. His promises are literal, not figurative. The attempt by the Watchtower Society to take what is literal and make it figurative is dishonest in its interpretation and application of Scripture. Consider these Bible verses:

Psalm 2:7: "I will declare the decree: the Lord has said unto me, 'You are my Son; this day *have I begotten you.*'" [Emphasis added]

John 1:14: "And the Word was made flesh, and dwelt among us, (and we beheld His glory, the glory as of *the only begotten* of the Father,) full of grace and truth." [Emphasis added]

John 1:18: "No man has seen God at any time; the *only begotten Son*, which is in the bosom of the Father, He has declared Him." [Emphasis added]

John 3:16: "For God so loved the world, that He gave His *only begotten Son*, that whosoever believes in Him should not perish, but have everlasting life." [Emphasis added]

And finally…I John 4:9: "In this was manifested the love of God toward us, because that God sent His *only begotten Son* into the world, that we might live through Him." [Emphasis added]

Notice that in each of these verses, Jesus is described as the *"begotten"* Son of God, not the *"created"* son of God. There is a profound difference. When you *"beget,"* you beget something that is like you. Like produces like. Cats do not produce dogs. Dogs do not produce fish. If like begets like, and God begot Jesus; then God begat God, and Jesus is God.

When you *"create"* it is not of you, and it is less than you. Also note that God has begotten a Son, but there is only one Son that God has begotten. This is a single begetting of a Son. There is no way that Michael or any angelic being could qualify.

***

As noted above, Michael is not God; therefore, there are serious problems with Jesus—if He is the Archangel Michael—accepting worship that belongs to God, claiming titles that only God can claim, and in various direct and indirect ways making Himself equal to God.

The author of the Book of Hebrews will also be found to be incorrect. When speaking of Jesus, the author of the Book of Hebrews specifically elevated Jesus above all the angels and claims that God is the one who is doing the elevating. Hebrews 1:5–6:

"For unto which of the angels did God say at any time, 'You are my son, this day have I begotten you?' And again, 'I will be to him a father and he shall be to me a son?'

"And again, when He brings in the firstborn into the world, He said, 'And let all the angels of God worship him.'"

Also, the author of the Book of Hebrews quotes God in Psalm 45:6 when God refers to Jesus as being God:

"But unto the Son He says, 'Your throne, O God is forever and ever; a scepter of righteousness is the scepter of your kingdom.'"

Notice that the author of the Book of Hebrews is quoting from the Old Testament—the contract God wrote. These are terms and conditions set forth in the Old Testament and the author of the Book of Hebrews is citing them to support the teaching that Jesus is God. The author of the Book of Hebrews is quoting God as the One who is declaring Jesus to be God.

Either God is elevating Michael above all the other angels, and is equating Michael to being equal with Him; or God is speaking of someone else.

The Watchtower theology does not line up with the Bible, and so it must be questioned and rejected.

But what about the Jesus of the Church of Jesus Christ of Latter Day Saints [Mormons]? To be honest, it is a little more complicated than the problems with the Jehovah's Witnesses. To properly understand what the Mormons are teaching about their Jesus we must take a step back, even before the Creation of the world. We also discover different versions in the Mormon doctrines. When dealing with Mormon doctrine, there was one standard when the Latter Day Church began, and it has changed over the years. I am going to continue this chapter under the same title and devote that chapter to a discussion of the Jesus presented by the Latter Day Saints once I cover a few important issues.

CHAPTER EIGHT

SPIRITUAL AUTHORITY

I really wish I did not have to do this, but the more I worked on *Which Jesus Part Two* and dealt with the teaching of the *Church of Jesus Christ of the Latter Day Saints*, I realized that the first battle you may encounter with them will be over spiritual authority. There is a standard response by Mormon theologians when you quote a passage from the Bible—especially if it contradicts what the Latter Day Church teaches. *The Church of Jesus Christ of Latter Day Saints* will believe the Bible "*only in so far as it is correctly interpreted.*" I had mentioned in the discussion on the Mathematics of the Cults how the Cults ADD to the Bible.

The issue of what constitutes a correct interpretation, and who has the spiritual authority to interpret and apply Scripture, is a responsibility that the Mormon Church claims is their sole jurisdiction. They use their additional documents to correctly interpret Scripture.

The Church of Jesus Christ of Latter Day Saints refers to themselves as "*The Restored Church.*" Joseph Smith taught that with the death of the last Apostle—that would be John the Beloved—the Church lost its authority. He suggests that somehow the original message was lost. He taught that the original power and authority was lost, and so God chose him to restore what had been lost. This teaching completely ignores the concept of the Holy Spirit coming to live in each believer at the time of salvation, and leading and guiding each individual believer. For what Joseph Smith was teaching to have happened, the Holy Spirit would have had to have been removed from the earth. There is no proof of this; it is just his position.

According to the history of the Mormon Church, in 1820, Joseph Smith [at age 15] was deeply religious. He looked around him and saw corruption in all of the Churches. Joseph Smith struggled with the question of which Church should he join. This led to his first *"divine revelation."* According to the account in 1820, Joseph Smith came across the verse of James 1:15:

"If any of you lack wisdom, let him ask of God, who gives to all men liberally, and upbraids not; and it shall be given him."

Inspired by this verse, Joseph Smith went into the woods to pray. According to Joseph Smith's testimony, two men appeared to him as he prayed. In his own words, he received a vision:

"One of them spake unto me, calling me by name and said, pointing to the other *This Is My Beloved Son, Hear Him.*"

"I was answered that I must join none of them [the Churches] for they were all wrong; and the Personage who addressed me said that all their creeds were an abomination in his sight, that those professors were all corrupt, 'that they draw near me with this lips, that their hearts are far from me they teach for doctrines the commandments of men, having a form of godliness, but they deny the power thereof." [Joseph Smith, *History* 1:17 and 19]

If that comment sounds familiar, it should. It is what Jesus said of the Pharisees in Matthew 15:8–9. The verse was lifted out of the Bible—in other words, it was taken out of the context in which Jesus used it; and Joseph Smith claimed Jesus applied it to His own Church.

An observer will quickly notice how Joseph Smith speaks in King James English; and many of his comments are laced with references, expressions and passages from the King James Bible. When I discuss the background on the Book of Mormon I will also address an associate of Joseph Smith who was an excommunicated minister named Sidney Rigdon. This may have been the source for the many references and King James Bible terminology.

Joseph Smith taught that God and Jesus appeared to him in the woods and instructed him that all Churches were corrupt, and so he should not join any of them. Just to keep the record straight, there were two times when this vision was shared by Joseph Smith. It should be noted that in the 1832 version of this account, Joseph Smith only noted that Jesus had appeared unto him. God the Father was added to the account when Joseph Smith repeated the story in the 1838–1839 version six years later. Somehow, he had forgotten that God was there when he gave the first account of the vision. As an investigator, these kinds of details are important as they establish the credibility of a witness and that person's account of events.

According to Joseph Smith, three years later he went to bed on Sept. 21, 1823:

"I betook myself to prayer and supplication to Almighty God for forgiveness of all my sins and follies, and also for a manifestation to me so that I might know of my state standing before him for I had full confidence in obtaining a divine manifestation, as I previously had one." [Joseph Smith, *Pearl of Great Price* 1:29]

In response to this, the angel, Moroni, appeared to Joseph Smith and revealed to him a book made of plates of gold. These plates described the account of those who were the former inhabitants of America.

The angel also told him that the *"Fullness of the Gospel"* was contained in the book. The Savior had apparently delivered this Gospel directly to the inhabitants of America. [Joseph Smith, *History* 1:34 and 35]

The angel, Moroni, informed Joseph Smith that the *"Urim and Thummim"* were buried with the golden plates. The Urim and Thummim were *"two stones in silver bows"* and would allow him to translate the plates.

The angel, Moroni, appeared to Joseph Smith again—three times in the same night and once the next day. The angel, Moroni, appeared annually after that for the next four years. [Joseph Smith, *History* 1:29–42]

Although Moroni had *"presented"* the book to Joseph Smith, he was not permitted to retrieve the golden plates until given permission. He was not allowed to let anyone see the plates except for a chosen few or he would be destroyed. [Joseph Smith, *History* 1:29–42].

Joseph Smith had married Emma Hale in 1827. Nine months later, he was given permission to retrieve the golden plates. He was told to keep them safe until the angel "*should call for them.*" According to the Church, Joseph Smith translated the information on the plates, which had been written in "*Reformed Egyptian,*" into English. [*Book of Mormon* 9:32]

"…Thus the Book of Mormon was translated by the gift and power of God, and not by any power of man." [Dave Whitmer, *An Address to All Believers in Christ*, Concord, CA; Pacific Publishing Company, 1887, page 12]

[Please note that I will go into a discussion in more detail regarding the translation process and the various witnesses at a later section of the book. As I am approaching this book from a legal and investigation point of view, witnesses and their statements will be important. I want to focus on these at that time.]

According to Mormon Theology, in May of 1829, Oliver Cowdery and Joseph Smith went into the woods to pray about baptism for the remission of sins. While they were praying, John the Baptist appeared and conferred the Aaronic Priesthood upon them and gave them instructions about how to baptize each other. Later, Peter, James and John conferred the Melchizedek Priesthood upon them. [Joseph Smith, *History* 1:68–72]

The *One True Church* was founded on April 6, 1830 in Fayette, New York.

At the founding meeting, Joseph Smith received a revelation from God that he would be "a seer, a translator, a prophet and apostle." [*History of the Church of Jesus Christ Latter-Day Saints* (Salt Lake City, UT, Deseret 1978) pages 1:40–42].

Based upon the above, I want to take a few minutes to discuss spiritual authorities, the priesthood of a believer and the true nature and status of both the Aaronic Priesthood and the Levitical Priesthood. It is because the Latter Day Church claims to have both of these priesthoods that they will reject anyone else's application or interpretation of Scriptures. Therefore, unfortunately, we must address this issue before we can address any other issue or doctrine relating to the teachings of the Latter Day Church and the Bible.

As noted previously, the Bible is the *prima facie evidence* in this legal argument because it contains the actual contract God made with man. It is the ultimate ploy of attorneys to try to suppress evidence and not allow it to be submitted to the court. There was a vendor back when I fought liens before the WCAB that would cite the contracts it had with other vendors to support their positions, but would refuse to let the contract be reviewed by us or even to be submitted into evidence. They wanted to keep the terms of their contracts secret. By claiming that only they can properly interpret the Bible, the Latter Day Saints are using the same legal tactic. God is willing to be transparent—as transparent as possible—about what He is offering to the world. The Latter Day Saints try to hide it by saying that only they can read it and understand it. When they do interpret the Bible, they use Mormon doctrines to guide them rather than letting the Bible speak for itself.

The Mormon Church teaches that with the dying off of the original disciples in Israel, the Church lost both the revelation to guide it along with the authority to operate the Church. [*Church History in the Fullness of Time* page 4] For some reason, the Holy Spirit given to the Church to guide all believers was lost. Somehow, He stopped being available to non-Disciples—even if they believed and studied the Bible. How this happened is never adequately explained.

The teaching of the Mormon Church is that Jesus came to America when He left Israel after His Resurrection, and here He selected twelve more disciples. According to Mormon doctrine three of these disciples never died. [Book of Mormon 3 Nephi 28:7] This suggests that Jesus abandoned the believers in Israel after John the Beloved died off; and that Jesus chose instead to move His Church over to America. Again, the Bible is silent on this and no prophesy in the Bible suggests such a decision.

It is the position of the Latter Day Church that all other Churches have lost the ability to understand Scriptures, receive revelations from God or even operate the Church. It was the position of Joseph Smith that this is why God instructed him to not join any existing Church.

I will challenge this description of the modern Church and note initially that the kind of condition of the modern Church that Joseph Smith describes is impossible as it violates a promise made by Jesus Christ. First of all Jesus noted that the Gates of Hell cannot prevail against the Church [Matthew 16:18].

We also have the promises of Jesus in the Great Commission. Mathew 28: 20:

"Teaching them to observe all things whatsoever I have commanded you: and, lo, *I am with you always*, even unto the end of the world. Amen." [Emphasis added]

In order for the Church to lose its spiritual authority and power to the level Joseph Smith is suggesting, then Satan would have to prevail over the Church and Jesus would have to abandon the Church. While there was corruption through the Dark Ages, God always kept a remnant in place that protected the Bible, taught the Gospel and kept the Church going even when other denominations fell into corruption. God never left the world without a witness.

Just as an observation, it seems very unlikely that God would send Jesus into the world, put Jesus through so much pain and suffering to start the Church, and then allow the Church to be taken over and corrupted so that it was powerless within such a short period of time. If God had exerted that much effort to create the Church, He can also exert that much effort to preserve the Church—especially since the Holy Spirit was given to each believer. This was, after all, according to Jesus, the function of the Holy Spirit. The Latter Day Church, however, has a different view of the nature and function of the Holy Spirit.

In addition to the promise of Jesus that the Gates of Hell will never prevail over the Church, we also have a promise made by John the Apostle. John 1:12–13:

"But as many as received Him [Jesus], *to them He gave the power* to become the sons of God, even to those who believe on His name:

"Which were born, not of blood, nor of the will of the flesh, nor of the will of man, *but of God*." [Emphasis added]

In this verse, believers who have received Jesus as their Savior are given power and authority directly by God, not by the previous Apostles.

If there is any question as to what it means to receive Jesus, we could consider John 3:16:

"For God so loved the world that He gave His only Begotten Son, that *whosoever believes in Him* should not perish but have everlasting life." [Emphasis added]

The Latter Day Church has a very different concept of receiving Jesus, and how Jesus acts as their Savior. We will discuss this in more detail later on. However, the Mormon Plan of Salvation is not even close to the Bible's Plan of Salvation. Mormon theologians teach that their members must work for their salvation and earn it. They must prove that they are worthy to be saved. They do not trust in Jesus to save them. They trust in their own efforts. Therefore, they have not believed, nor have they received Jesus; and therefore, John 1:12–13 cannot apply to them. They cannot have this power mentioned by John.

Each Christian believer has spiritual authority and power because they have accepted Jesus as their Savior and not because they have the Aaronic or Melchizedek priesthood. Where Joseph Smith and the Latter Day Saints claim authority given to them by John the Baptist, Peter, James and John; we have power and authority given to us directly by God. God is greater than John the Baptist, Peter, James and John the Apostle. If there is any dispute, our power and authority outranks their power and authority.

However, I need to point out that there is no requirement in the New Testament for a believer to have either the Aaronic Priesthood or the Melchizedek priesthood, nor is it offered to any believer. In fact, just the opposite is demonstrated in the Scriptures. Matthew 27:50–51:

"Jesus, when He had cried again with a loud voice, yielded up the ghost.

And, behold, the veil of the temple was torn in two from the top to the bottom; and the earth did quake, and the rocks broke;"

The Veil is very important in this scenario. The Veil is what separated the Holy of Holies where God dwelt from the rest of the world. Only a priest could enter into the Holy of Holies. Only the High Priest could go behind the Veil and come into God's Presence. With the death of Jesus, the issue of sin was resolved forever; there was no need for the Veil. There was no longer any need for a priest here on earth. Therefore, God tore the Veil in two. He grabbed it at the top and tore it from top to bottom. There was no longer a need for a priest—any priest—to come on our behalf before God. Men and women could come before God directly. Hebrews 4:16:

"Let us therefore come boldly unto the throne of grace, that we may obtain mercy, and find grace to help in time of need."

The author of the Book of Hebrews makes it clear that believers can come before God on their own. There is no need for a priest to represent us when we come before God.

It is the Holy Spirit who comes to dwell inside each believer at the moment of salvation that becomes our link to Jesus and God in Heaven. He is the one who gives us the power and the authority to represent God to others just as the office of a priest used to do. All believers are given the title, role and authority as a priest of God. Revelation 1:6:

"And has made us kings and priests unto God and His Father; to Him be glory and dominion for ever and ever. Amen."

In this passage it is Jesus who has made us priests. It was not John the Baptist. It was not the Apostles. We are given our priesthood directly by Jesus. His authority is greater than the authority of John the Baptist or the Apostles. Therefore, our priesthood is greater.

We are also given the power to understand and interpret the Scriptures. I Corinthians 2:10:

"But God has revealed them unto us by His Spirit: for the Spirit searches all things, yea, the deep things of God.

"For what man knows the things of a man, save the spirit of man which is in him? even so the things of God knows no man, but the Spirit of God.

"Now we have received, not the spirit of the world, but the Spirit which is of God; that we might know the things that are freely given to us of God."

Now the Holy Spirit, according the Mormon Theology, is an impersonal force—like electricity. The Holy Spirit of the Latter Day Church is not God. It is not intelligent and does not have wisdom. The Holy Spirit of the Latter Day Church cannot do for them what the Holy Spirit of the Bible can do for believers. Our Holy Spirit is part of the Trinity. He is an actual person. He is God, so He knows the deep things of God and the mind of God. He is personal. He is our guide, and so He has wisdom and intelligence to lead us and to guide us.

This creates a serious problem for the Latter Day Saints. They reject the Spirit of God. Without the Spirit of God, it is impossible know the things of God. That is what this passage has just said. Without the Spirit of God, there is no one to reveal to them the things of God. This means that it is impossible for them to read the Bible and understand it. They claim that it is their priesthood that does this for them. That is why only they can interpret Scripture. However, as we shall see, their priesthoods are a deception. They do not have the Aaronic/Levitical Priesthood—and if they do, it is ineffective when dealing with the things of God. They cannot have the Melchezedek Priesthood, and we will explain why in a few moments.

***

So, what about the priesthoods that the Latter Day Church is claiming as their authority? The Bible has several things to say about both the Aaronic Priesthood and the Melchizedek Priesthood; and what the Bible says has a direct impact on any spiritual authority the Latter Day Church claims from these designations.

There is a difference between the Aaronic Priesthood and the Melchizedek Priesthood. It is a very important distinction. The author of the Book of Hebrews goes into a detailed discussion of both. The author of the Book of Hebrews notes that when God gave the Melchizedek Priesthood to the Messiah, He made an oath concerning this priesthood. Psalm 110:4:

"The Lord *has sworn*, and *will not repent*, 'You are *a priest forever* after the order of Melchizedek." [Emphasis added]

We have to ask why did God swear when He declared the Messiah to be a priest forever after the order of Melchizedek. Hebrews 6:18:

"That by two immutable things, in which *it was impossible for God to lie*, we might have a strong consolation, who have fled for refuge to lay hold upon the hope set before us:" [Emphasis added]

It is impossible for God to lie. If God makes an oath or if God swears; then God cannot change His mind. He cannot go back on what He has promised. What God said, He will do, and He will not change.

Now the Melchizedek priesthood was made with an oath. This means that the Melchizedek Priesthood can never change. If the Melchizedek Priesthood changes, then God has lied. God cannot lie. God made an oath, and He will not repent. He will not change His mind. He will never revoke the Melchizedek Priesthood from Jesus and give it to someone else [Psalm 110:4].

However, the Aaronic Priest was not given with an oath. Hebrews 7:21:

""(For those priests were made [priests] *without an oath*; but this [the Melchizedek was made] *with an oath* by He who said unto Him, 'The Lord swore and will not repent, "You are a priest forever after the order of Melchizedek:)"""" [Emphasis added]

The Levitical/Aaronic Priesthoods were created without an oath. This means that God can change His mind concerning the Aaronic Priesthood. God can set the Levitical/Aaronic Priesthood aside. And God did set the Levitical/Aaronic

Priesthood aside when there was no longer any reason for them to exist. It was a temporary system at best. It was only intended to be in place until the perfect sacrifice was offered. When the perfect sacrifice came, the imperfect priesthood that offered imperfect sacrifices was set aside. This is why the Veil in the Temple was torn in two.

The author of the Book of Hebrews makes it clear that the Levitical/Aaronic Priesthood was imperfect. It could not accomplish what needed to be done. Hebrews 10:1–4:

"For the law [being] a shadow of good things to come, and not the [actual] image of the things, can never with those sacrifices which they offered year by year continually make those [coming to offer the sacrifice] perfect.

"For then would they not have ceased to be offered? because that the worshippers once purged should have had no more conscience of sins.

"But in those sacrifices there is a remembrance again made of sins every year.

"For it is not possible that the blood of bulls and of goats should take away sins."

Let me put this is an easy to read discussion. The Law of Moses was a picture of what God intended to do. That picture was that an innocent would die in the place of the guilty. It was a picture of what God intended to do in Heaven. It was a picture, and not the real thing. Because it was only a picture it did not have the same power as the real deal. It was imperfect, and did not resolve the problem of sin on a permanent basis. People had to keep coming back each year and offer another sacrifice for their sins. If this system was the real deal and did what God was promising, then you would only have to make the sacrifice once, and there would not ever be a need to offer another sacrifice.

The reason this system was imperfect is because the priest was offering an imperfect sacrifice. The priest was offering the blood of animals. The sacrifice that God's system would offer would be the blood of the Messiah. Hebrews 10:10:

"By [this] we are sanctified through the offering of the body of Jesus Christ *once* for all." [Emphasis added]

Notice this last bit of information: *"once for all."* It only had to be offered one time, and that one offering would cover everyone. It would cover everyone throughout the entire world and throughout all of time. The offering of Jesus was perfect. He was the innocent that the picture was portraying. Because He was the fulfillment of the promise, the picture was no longer needed. There is no need to offer anything else. The sacrifice of Jesus resolved the issue of sin forever.

Now there is a legal problem with the offering of Jesus. It cannot qualify as a sacrifice offered by the Levitical/Aaronic Priesthood. Jesus was offering Himself upon the cross; and so He was both the priest offering the sacrifice, and He was the sacrifice being offered.

But Jesus was not of the Tribe of Levi. He was of the kingly Tribe of Judah. Therefore, it would be illegal for Jesus to offer a sacrifice to God through the Levitical/Aaronic Priesthood. Under the Law of Moses only a priest of the Tribe of Levi can offer a sacrifice to God. We see in II Chronicles 26:19 that King Uzziah sought to offer a sacrifice before God in the Temple. It was a bloodless sacrifice. He only wanted to burn incense to God; but he was the king, he was of the Tribe of Judah; and not a priest of the Tribe of Levi. The priests physically blocked him from entering the Temple:

"Then Uzziah was [angry], and had a censer in his hand to burn incense: and while he was [angry] with the priests, the leprosy even rose up in his forehead before the priests in the house of the Lord, from beside the incense altar."

God struck King Uzziah with leprosy, and he remained a leper for the rest of his life. A king cannot perform the functions of a priest. Someone of the Tribe of Judah can never perform the office of the Tribe of Levi.

But God had a solution. Jesus did not offer His sacrifice as a Levitical/Aaronic Priest. God used a completely different priesthood. God used the priesthood of Melchizedek. Psalm 110:4:

"The Lord has sworn, and will not repent, 'You are a priest forever after the order of Melchizedek.'"

This priesthood was given to Jesus by God. God swore an oath to make Jesus a priest after the order of Melchizedek. God will not change His mind about this. He shall not repent. He cannot repent. Jesus became a priest after the order of Melchizedek, and He will remain a priest after the order of Melchizedek forever.

The Levitical/Aaronic Priesthood was not qualified or authorized to perform the true sacrifice of the true innocent who came to die in the place of the guilty. The Melchezedek priesthood was created to offer this perfect sacrifice. The Levitical/Aaronic priesthoods were created to officiate over the picture—the temporary system—not the real thing.

***

So who was this Melchizedek? He was the King of Salem [Jerusalem]. *"Salem"* means peace [Shalom], and so he was the King of Peace. He was both a priest and a king. He was not under the Law of Moses because the Law of Moses would not be given to Moses for another four hundred years. Melchizedek was a king of the Most High God. He held two different offices. He came to meet Abraham when Abraham returned from freeing Lot who had been captured in a war.

According to Genesis 14:19, Melchizedek blessed Abraham. This is important. The author of Hebrews has this to say about the blessing. Hebrews 7:7:

"And without all contradiction the lesser is blessed of the better."

There is no dispute over this fact. It is accepted by all. The only way that Melchizedek could bless Abraham is if Melchizedek was greater than Abraham. This hierarchy is further demonstrated by the fact that Abraham paid tithes of the spoils to Melchizedek. Genesis 14:20:

"'And blessed be the most high God, who has delivered your enemies into your hand.' And he [Abraham] gave him [Melchizedek] tithes of all."

The author of the Book of Hebrews has something to say about this as well. Hebrews 7:9–10:

"And as I may so say, 'Levi also, who receives tithes, payed tithes in Abraham.'

"For he was yet in the loins of his father, when Melchizedek met him"

Let me break this part of the argument down for you. Abraham paid tithes to Melchizedek. In doing this, Abraham acknowledged that Melchizedek was greater than he was. Now Levi is of the line of Abraham. As a great grandson of Abraham, Levi is less than Abraham. That is how family hierarchies work. Abraham had Isaac. Isaac had Jacob. Jacob had Levi. Abraham, as the first in the line, is the greatest of all. He deserves the respect of all who come after him. Isaac is not greater than Abraham. He is less than Abraham because Abraham is his father. Isaac is required to honor the father and mother. Isaac is greater than Jacob. Jacob is less than Isaac because Isaac is his father. The Commandment to honor your father and mother travels back through the family line to the founder of the family. This always places the father above the son—the ancestor above the descendant. Now Jacob is greater than Levi because he is Levi's father, but Jacob is less than Isaac and Abraham.

Now that we understand the hierarchy and how the honor/ respect starts at the beginning of the genetic line and decreases as it goes down each generation, the author of the Book of Hebrews is noting that Levi is less than Abraham. Levi is technically in Abraham's loins since the DNA and genetic material that will one day give birth to Levi were in Abraham at the time. This means that Melchizedek is greater than Levi is because Melchizedek was greater than Abraham was. Therefore, if we were to list the two priesthoods in order of greatness or authority, Melchizedek would come first; and Levi [Aaron] would come last.

***

Keep in mind that the Melchizedek priesthood existed four hundred years before the Levitical/Aaronic priesthood.

Now following the logic from above [there are several legal arguments made above] we have Hebrews 10:9–10:

"Then said He, 'Lo, I come to do Your will, O God.' [God] *takes away* the first [the Aaronic priesthood], that He may establish the second [Melchizedek priesthood through Jesus]. [Emphasis added.]

By the [Melchizedek priesthood of Jesus]…we are sanctified through the offering of the body of Jesus Christ once for all."

God had made an oath, and so He cannot change or alter the priesthood of Melchizedek. But the priesthood of Levi/Aaron was not made with an oath. God gave it. God assigned it to the Tribe of Levi and specifically to the line of Aaron; but God did not make an oath. Therefore, this priesthood can be changed. In fact, God always intended to change it because it was imperfect. It could not do what God needed it to do—it could not remove sins forever.

So God sets aside the Aaronic Priesthood. He makes it null and void. It comes to an end because it was not working, and God no longer needed it. When the permanent procedure takes place, there is no need for the temporary procedure. Hebrews 7:18:

"For there is verily a *disannulling* of the commandment going before for the weakness and unprofitableness thereof." [Emphasis added]

In layman terms, God cancelled the Aaronic Priesthood. He made it null and void because it was imperfect. It was weak and it could not complete the job. It was only good to oversee the picture of God's Plan of Salvation, but not the actual Plan of Salvation itself. If the Latter Day Church wants to claim that they have the Aaronic Priesthood, then they are laying claim to a system that God set aside and shut down. In other words, if they do have the Aaronic Priesthood, it is worthless. It has no power or authority left in it. It is an empty shell. It is a title that has no authority attached to it.

***

As further proof that God is no longer recognizing the Aaronic Priesthood, consider the following: there is an interesting account in the Talmud.

Each year, during the Day of Atonement, two goats were selected for the ceremony. The High Priest would cast lots, and one goat would be selected as the Lord's goat. This is the goat that would be sacrificed, and its blood sprinkled on the Ark of the Covenant. The other goat is the scapegoat.

The High Priest transfers the sins of Israel onto this scapegoat by placing his hands on the head of the scapegoat and confessing the sins. This scapegoat is then led out into the Wilderness where it is released. It is a picture of God taking our sins away. As Psalm 103:12 puts it:

"As far as the east is from the west, so far has He removed our sins."

The question needs to be asked, "How do you know when the sins have been taken away?" "When do you let the scapegoat loose in the Wilderness and return to Jerusalem?" Well the Jews had a way of telling. A red ribbon was tied around the scapegoat's head—maybe the neck or horns. The person leading the scapegoat into the Wilderness would keep leading the scapegoat until the red ribbon turned white. When the red ribbon turned white, the man would release the scapegoat, and return to Jerusalem. This practice is documented in the Talmud [Tractate Shabbat Folio 86a].

However, about forty years before the destruction of the Temple—this would put it around the time of Jesus' Crucifixion—the red ribbon on the scapegoat did not change. It remained red. All of the scapegoats after that time had the ribbon remain red. God was no longer accepting the sacrifices offered by the High Priest. Why? God was not accepting their sacrifices or honoring their offerings because God had declared the Levitical/Aaronic Priesthood null and void. It had no authority with God. God had set aside the Jews and was now working through the Church [Deuteronomy 32:21]. The account of the red ribbon not changing colors is also in the Talmud [Tractate Yoma 39b].

***

So what about the Melchizedek Priesthood? They claim to have this priesthood, and it is the greater of the two. Well, there is a problem with their claim to the Melchizedek Priesthood. This priesthood was given to Jesus. It was given to Him by God with an unchangeable [irrevocable] oath. It was given to Him forever. There will never be an end to Jesus being the priest after the order of Melchizedek. Hebrews 7:24:

"But this man [Jesus], because He continues forever, has an unchangeable priesthood."

What does it mean for Jesus to have an *unchangeable priesthood*? It literally means that it is nontransferable. Jesus cannot transfer it to anyone else. This also means that no one else can claim it. The concept of the priesthood is that the person who is the priest continues in that office until He dies or becomes so old he can no longer perform the duties. Well, Jesus did die, but He is still performing the duties of the Melchizedek priest up in Heaven. Hebrews 4:14:

"Seeing then that we have a great high priest, who is passed into the heavens, Jesus the Son of God, let us hold fast our profession."

The Temple [or Tabernacle] where Jesus is performing His priestly duties and interceding on our behalf is located in Heaven, not on earth. Heaven is eternal and Jesus is eternal. Jesus will never die again, nor will He ever become so old or disabled that He will need to transfer the office to someone else. It is going to stay with Him forever.

If—by some great stretch of the imagination—the Melchizedek priesthood did pass to someone else; that person would need to be in Heaven as that is where the Temple and altar used by the priest of Melchizedek is located. It is not here on this earth, so no one on this earth could ever perform the office of the priest after the order of Melchizedek. There is no way that the Latter Day Church could ever obtain the Melchizedek priesthood. But let me take a moment and go back over the testimony of Joseph Smith and consider what he has said on the record.

"In May of 1829 Oliver Cowdery and Joseph Smith went into the woods to pray about baptism for the remission of sins. While they were praying, John the Baptist appeared and conferred the Aaronic Priesthood upon them and gave them instructions about how to baptize each other."

As an investigator, I will give them the appearing of John the Baptist and his teaching them how to baptize. It is possible for God to send messengers to us, and so if push comes to shove, I will say, "Okay. John taught you how to baptize." But there is no way that John could legally have given either of them the priesthood.

The Aaronic priesthood belonged to the line of Aaron. It was passed from father to son when the father was too old or ill to carry on the priestly duties. Now John the Baptist's father was of the line of Levi. He was serving in the Temple when Gabriel appeared to Zacharias to tell him that Zacharias' wife, Elizabeth, would bear a son and he would be used of God.

So while John the Baptist would be of the Tribe of Levi because his father was of that tribe; there is no evidence that John the Baptist was of the line of Aaron. There is no record of John ever serving as a priest in the Temple. He preached in the wilderness. His office was the office of a prophet; not a priest. However, let's give the Mormon's the benefit of the doubt. Even if John the Baptist may have been of the line of Aaron, John the Baptist never served as the High Priest. That is what the Aaronic Priesthood is. It is the High Priest who goes behind the Veil one day out of the year. The Bible identifies other people who were the High Priest when John was alive. John the Baptist was beheaded without ever being given the office of Aaron—the High Priest. So my question would be, "How can John the Baptist pass on an office that he never held?" Legally, he cannot.

We also have this observation by the author of the Book of Hebrews. Hebrews 5:4:

"And no man takes this honor [the priesthood] unto himself, but he that is called of God, as was Aaron."

The calling—and therefore the bestowing of the priesthood is not at the will of man. It is only given by God. So with one person laying hands upon another that is man conferring the office on another. Since it is not God conferring this office—if He would—it is not a valid transferal and the title is not valid.

Then we have this account of the Melchizedek priesthood:

"Later, Peter, James and John conferred the Melchizedek Priesthood upon them." [Joseph Smith, *History* 1:68–72]

Peter, James and John were not of the Tribe of Levi. They were working class fishermen. They were not priests under the Law of Moses. The Melchizedek priesthood was given to Jesus forever. If anyone could transfer this priesthood—which the Bible says cannot happen—it would have had to have been Jesus. According to Joseph Smith's testimony, Jesus had appeared to him before. But Jesus is not the one who gave him the Melchizedek priesthood. The priesthood is nontransferable by design. Jesus is still operating as the priest after the order of Melchizedek. There is no way that Peter, James and John could transfer this priesthood on to Joseph Smith and Oliver Cowdery.

As an investigator, I would question their statements. They are not credible. It is not convincing. It is not supported by the facts. Therefore, I must conclude that they never had either the Aaronic or the Melchizedek priesthoods. These ceremonies may have taken place and they were deceived into thinking that they had these priesthoods, but it is impossible for that to have happened. At best, they were deceived. More likely, they were doing the deception. They cannot transfer what they have never had.

Before moving on to the next discussion, let me just point out that God knew that centuries later Joseph Smith would make a claim to have both the Aaronic and Melchizedek priesthoods. It was no accident that the author of the Book of Hebrews was inspired to discuss both these priesthoods and their legal standing in such detail. God used the author of the Book of Hebrews to expose the deception two thousand years later and to provide the rebuttal we would need today.

***

There is one more observation concerning the priesthoods I would like to make. Both the Aaronic Priesthood—as the High Priest—and the Melchizedek Priesthood were held by a single person. There is only one person allowed to hold this title at a time. The concept of the Latter Day Church conveying this title to multiple people contradicts the structure and function of the offices.

So the Mormon who insists that the Scriptures can only be accepted when they are correctly interpreted does not have the legal or spiritual authority to interpret the Scriptures. Whatever their interpretation is will be wrong. The Aaronic Priesthood has been made null and void by God with the tearing of the Veil and the death of Jesus. It has no authority left in it. The Melchizedek Priesthood is still held by Jesus and operates only in Heaven. And, as noted above, they reject the Holy Spirit while we have been given power and authority directly from God through the Holy Spirit because of our acceptance of Jesus as our Savior. John 1:12–13:

"But as many as received Him [Jesus], to them He gave the power to become the sons of God, even to those who believe on His name:

"Which were born, not of blood, nor of the will of the flesh, nor of the will of man, but of God."

God gives us power through our accepting of Jesus as our Savior. When we have accepted Jesus as our Savior, we are given the Holy Spirit. This is a person. This is the Third Person of the Trinity. And the Holy Spirit teaches us concerning the Scriptures. He reveals things to us. The Latter Day Church does not have this Holy Spirit. According to their teaching, the Holy Spirit they have is not a person or God, but an impersonal force.

Now if you want to compare priesthoods, consider Revelation 1:5–6:

"And from Jesus Christ, who is the faithful witness, and the first begotten of the dead, and the prince of the kings of the earth. Unto Him who loved us, and washed us from our sins in His own blood,

"And has made us kings and priests unto God and His Father; to Him be glory and dominion for ever and ever. Amen."

The Mormons do not teach that Jesus has washed them from their sins. They teach that they have no sins; and if they do, they must atone for them personally. They teach that the death of Jesus only made a general resurrection possible. So they do not believe or accept the process that makes us priests before God. They had a defunct priesthood given by John the Baptist. They claim a priesthood they cannot have given by Peter, James and John. We have a different priesthood given to us by Jesus Christ Himself. In a court of law, I believe our authority and credentials would prevail over theirs.

When all is said and done, we have the priesthood and they do not. This gives us the spiritual authority to interpret Scriptures correctly and not them.

CHAPTER NINE

THE STRUCTURE OF THE UNIVERSE

I really cannot believe that I have to discuss this topic or even write this chapter. But to present my legal argument, I am forced to lay the foundation for my argument. Therefore, as part of my legal argument, I must establish by credible evidence how the universe came to be and how it works.

One of the nice things about reading a book versus writing a book is that you have the luxury of reading the finished product. You do not see all the drafts, revisions and rewrites the author sees. I had wanted to keep this simple. I was able to address the Jehovah's Witnesses doctrine regarding Jesus in just one chapter. I had planned to do that with the Jesus of the Latter Day Saints, but such is not the case. I had to add Chapter Eight to discuss the priesthood and spiritual authority because that would be a tactic of a Latter Day Saint to challenge the jurisdiction, and bar the evidence showing the flaws in their doctrine. They would argue that they had the jurisdiction [authority] to teach and interpret Scriptures, but I do not. So if this were to be a legal argument/analysis of the teachings of the Cults—which it is—then I would have to address that issue before the courts before I would be allowed to submit my evidence regarding the Latter Day Saints' Jesus. I need to make sure my evidence is not just credible. I must make sure my evidence is also admissible before the court.

Then there was a different Chapter Nine I was putting together on the Latter Day Saints' Jesus, and I realized that, unlike the Jehovah's Witnesses who challenged doctrine, Joseph Smith challenged the entire structure and nature of the entire universe, and this is the basis for his doctrines. Therefore, unfortunately, I will have to address this fictional universe that Joseph Smith and the founders/leaders of the Church of Jesus Christ of Latter Day Saints have created, and compare it to the true universe and world that the Bible teaches. [Hint: the Latter Day Church's universe and the real world are not the same thing.] So what I am going to do is to move some secondary issues to the end of the book and put them under Appendix. The two topics I am going to do this with is the claim of Joseph Smith and Church leaders to be prophets, and the manuscripts that Joseph Smith claims were given him by God and which he published and/or translated. I would like to address these now, but I need to keep on track and discuss the Jesus of the Latter Day Church.

***

When you change the history of the universe and the laws of physics, then you can rebuilt it any way you want. Unfortunately, a court of law and a legal analysis must deal with the reality that exists, not the reality others would like it to be. We need to understand the difference between fiction—where you can write what you want; and non-fiction where the information has to be true and grounded in reality.

This brings me to this new chapter dealing with the structure and nature of the universe. The non-fictional real universe we live in, and the fantasy/fictional universe Joseph Smith and his followers have created and adopted; are very different. It is so different that the two cannot coexist. One must prevail over the other. Unfortunately, for the Latter Day Church, like Don Quixote, the real universe has a way of making its truth known. And since we are trying to determine the truth of God and His contract with mankind, we will need to hold up many mirrors to the face of the Latter Day Church so that they can see what and who they really are, and not who they tell themselves who they are.

Before I begin this chapter, let me establish my legal basis for doing this. When introducing evidence or making a legal argument; the person trying to introduce the evidence must obtain the permission of the court/judge to do so. In some cases, you may also need to obtain the permission of the opposing party before introducing evidence. The opposing party will object. They will make all kinds of arguments so that, in the end, it will be the judge who makes the final decision as to whether or not your evidence is admissible; and if admissible, is your evidence credible.

In my situation, it seems that I have the permission of the opposing party to introduce the evidence and arguments I intend to introduce in these chapters. I was given this permission in writings by the founders and leaders of the Latter Day Church. Let me quote two leaders of the Church of Jesus Christ of Latter Day Saints. As they were the head or leader of the Latter Day Church at different periods in their history, what they say here should be considered as Mormon doctrine.

"Mormonism, as it is called, must stand or fall on the story of Joseph Smith. He was either a prophet of God, divinely called, properly appointed and commissioned, or he was one of the biggest frauds this world has ever seen. There is no middle ground.

"If Joseph Smith was a deceiver, who willfully attempted to mislead people, then he should be exposed; his claims should be refuted, and his doctrines shown to be false, for the doctrines of an imposter cannot be made to harmonize in all particulars with divine truth." [Joseph Fielding Smith, *Doctrines of Salvation* (1954) 1:188. Also:

"Take up the Bible, compare the religion of the Latter-Day Saints, and see if it will stand the test." [Brigham Young, Journal of Discourses (London: Latter-Day Saints Book Deposit 1854–1856) 16:46]

I am accepting both of these challenges, and in this chapter and throughout this book; I will be using the Bible to test the teachings of Joseph Smith and the Latter Day Church. The Latter Day Church would like to reverse this and test the teaching of the Bible against what their founders say. In other words, the Latter Day Saints will want their revelations to be considered the truth—the prima facie evidence, and all previous revelations tested by their new revelation. After all, in their theology,

God changes His mind. But that was not the challenge here. Both Joseph Fielding Smith and Brigham Young insisted that we take the Bible, and use the Bible to test the revelations of Joseph Smith and the Latter Day Saints. We will start with the Bible. We trust the Bible. The Bible will be our prima facie evidence. We test new revelations and teachings against what is in the Bible. If God is just, and God is fair; then He will reveal Himself to the first man and woman the same way He will reveal Himself to the last man and woman—and every man and woman in between. If, as Malachi 3:6 claims that God does not change; then we must start with the first revelation, and use the first revelation to test all later revelations. We are instructed by the Bible to do this. I Thessalonians 5:21:

"Prove all things; hold fast [to] that which is good."

We are required to put all doctrines to the test. We are to prove which teachings are true and correct. We are to hold fast to those teachings which prove to be good—from God. With these two statements from Mormon Leaders we have permission to add the teachings of the Latter Day Saints to this pool of testing.

If God is fair and God is just; and God does not change; then we start with God's first revelation of Himself to man and test any later revelations claiming to be from God by the first revelation.

The Latter Day Church will seek to use their more recent revelations from their source as the truth, and then test prior revelations against their truth. It does not work that way, and with both Joseph Fielding Smith and Brigham Young, they gave permission to use the Bible to test their revelations. Again, I accept this challenge.

***

If you confront a Mormon about being Christian, they will make a major point of letting you know that their Church actually bears the name of Jesus Christ in the Title. Their official title is *The Church of Jesus Christ of Latter Day Saints*. The fact that the name of Jesus Christ is in the title of their Church should end forever any question about their being Christian. That is their position. Unfortunately, I cannot accept that as the solution to the issue.

First of all, the *Church of Jesus Christ of Latter Day Saints* was not the first name of their Church. It was not even their second. What makes this even more of an issue is that the founder claimed that God was the one telling him what to call the Church. If God cannot lie, and God does not change; then why didn't God get the name correct the first time He named their Church?

For a time—and even today—it was referred to as the *One True Church*. According to the website for the LDS [Latter Day Saints] history, the Church was first named *The Church of Christ* on April 6, 1830. Its name was changed to *The Church of the Latter Day Saints* on May 3, 1834. It was finally named the *Church of Jesus Christ of Latter Day Saints* on April 26, 1838. In other words, it took God eight years to get the name right.

Again, as we consider whether or not an organization is a wolf in sheep's clothing we must not look at their appearance. They are trying to look like sheep. That is the issue. We must look at what they teach. In our analogy, the wolf has changed its appearance into that of a sheep. Our wolf is very good at looking and acting like a sheep. In other words, we cannot trust appearances.

The Mormons will want you to look at their appearance. They use the name of Jesus in the title of their Church. They focus on family. They have strong morals and good ethical teachings. They have wonderful programs to help their people. They have spread throughout the world teaching their doctrines and converting people to the Mormon faith. They look and act very much like a Christian Church. The sheep's clothing makes them look very much like a sheep. But we must examine what they teach, and not how they appear. We must also ignore signs and wonders or miracles their Church has performed because Jesus, Himself, warned that the false Christs and false prophets would have this ability. So let us limit our focus to what they teach, and how it lines up with the Bible.

***

Now, unfortunately, before I can get to the legal issue before us, I must lay the foundation for the issue I want to address. This means I must go back to what Joseph Smith and the Founders/ Leaders of the Latter Day Church teach about how the world came into being, and how legal jurisdiction was established. Please pay attention as this can get tricky, and in some cases, contradicts itself.

***

Just to clarify, the Latter Day Saints do not have a problem with John 1:1:

"In the beginning was the Word and the Word was with God and the Word was God."

In the Latter Day Theology, there are many Gods. The Latter Day Theology teaches that men can work their way to Godhood. There is, however, no doctrine at this time that allows women to work their way to Godhood. To be blunt, there is no personal Plan of Salvation in the Latter Day Church for women. In the Latter Day theology, a woman achieves her eternal status through her husband. If she has no husband, or her husband does not make it; then the woman cannot do anything on her own to fix that problem. She is helpless to secure her own salvation outside of her husband. There is no equality of the sexes in the Mormon faith. Women are second-class citizens in the Mormon structure.

Again, if God is just and God is fair; then He should also treat women the same way that He treats men. This is not the case here. God treats men one way; and He treats women completely different. This is not fair, nor is God being just if He does this. Men can control their eternal destiny in the Mormon faith; but women have no choice and have no control over their eternal destiny. How is that fair and just?

***

The Latter Day theology identifies several Gods. There is Elohem. There is Jehovah. And there is Jesus. [Now in a

148

footnote in the Latter Day Church publication of the King James Bible, it notes that Jesus is Jehovah. This can create some serious problems with the teachings of the Latter Day Church on other doctrines.] The Latter Day Church also recognizes the Holy Ghost as a God, but the Holy Spirit is described as an impersonal force like electricity. Rather than recognizing that there is only one God, and that He has many titles and names, they use the different titles and names to teach that there are many Gods. This becomes clear in the teachings of the Latter Day Church regarding the creation of our world.

***

It is obvious from a casual view that the doctrine regarding One God is not the doctrine of the Latter Day Church. The Latter Day Church teaches that there are multiple Gods. The Latter Day Church teaches where these Gods came from. And the Latter Day Church teaches how you, personally, can become one of these many Gods with a world of your own to rule over. This will be the first difference we will have to deal with.

The Latter Day Church's teaching on Gods is as follows:

"As we are, God once was…

…As God is, we may become."

Also, consider this passage from the Mormon's Book of Abraham:

"And I saw the stars, that they were very great, and that one of them was nearest the throne of God; and there were many great ones which were near unto it. And the Lord said unto me: These are the governing ones; and the name of the great one is Kolob, because it is near unto me, for I am the Lord thy God. I have set this one to govern all those which belong to the same order as that upon which thou standest." [Abraham 3:2–3]

[Now I need to clarify that this passage is from a document entitled, Abraham or the Book of Abraham. It is a Mormon document, produced by Joseph Smith in 1835. Joseph Smith allegedly translated this document from papyri he purchased from a traveling exhibition. It was adopted as Cannon by the

Latter Day Church in 1880. I will discuss this source in the Appendix of this book in more detail. But for now, let me just note that there is disagreement—even among the various sects of Mormonism—over what these papyri actually say.]

***

I noted that the Latter Day Church teaching on the creation of the world can become confusing. Let me take a moment here to ask some questions that are not answered.

In this passage of the Book of Abraham, there is one God talking. In other places in the Book of Abraham, the reference is to Gods [plural], not God [singular]. But here this is a single God speaking to Abraham. This one God does not appear to be named. But it seems to be the main God—the first God. Why do I suggest that?

There is what Abraham notes to be the "*throne of God*." This seems to be the highest God. It also notes that Kolob is great, not because of its size, but because it is near the throne of God. So logic suggests that this "*throne of God*" must be the throne of the God who made Kolob, and that is why Kolob is close to His throne. If this God is a different God—a later/lesser God, then Kolob would not be blessed to be close to that throne. The real blessing should be to be close to the greatest—or first—God. And please note that the God speaking to Abraham notes that these stars are "*close to me*." So the speaker is the God sitting on the Throne of God.

Let me deal with some confusion here—at least confusion for me, and so it is probably confusing you the reader. Kolob is referred to as a star in Abraham 3:2 above. But, according to Mormon Theology, Gods create worlds—not stars. Each God creates his own world. So question? Is Kolob a star; or is Kolob a planet; or is Kolob a star system? At this point, I have to introduce another teaching of the Founding Fathers relating to stars, moons and life on other planets.

"The Sun and Moon is inhabited and the stars and Jesus Christ is the light of the sun, etc. The stars are inhabited the

150

same as earth." [Hyrum Smith, "Concerning the plurality of gods and worlds" April 27th 1943]

"As far back as 1837, I know that he [Joseph Smith] said the moon was inhabited by men and women the same as this earth, and that they lived to a greater age than we do—that they live generally to near the age of 1,0000 years." [Oliver B. Huntington, Young Woman's Journal 1892 3:263]

So some sources teach that Kolob is a star. But other sources describe Kolob as if it were a planet. I guess in Mormon Theology that it does not really matter. According to Mormon Theology, there will still be life on it even if it were a star.

I would like to suggest that Kolob is a star system where both the sun and the planet are called Kolob. That would resolve so many issues; but I cannot find any Mormon Theology giving me that option, so I will refer to Kolob as a star from this point forward because that is how the God speaking to Abraham described it. Therefore, it seems that Kolob is the first star. It is closest to the throne of God [the first God], and it has life.

Here is my problem with this statement. Kolob is the first of all the stars. This means that this is the very first star created by a God. The wording here suggest that the throne of God and the God on this throne is the God who created Kolob. This would mean that this God who is speaking to Abraham is not the God of this world. That God, on the throne of God, would be the God of Kolob. So how can that God be the God of Abraham? Would not the God who created our world be the God of Abraham? Did more than one God make Abraham? Should Abraham worship and serve more than one God?

***

The founding fathers of the Latter Day Saints have introduced the concept of multiple Gods into their theology, and into their documents at the very beginning of the Bible. As we were invited by Brigham Young to "*take up the Bible*" and "*to test*" the theology of the Mormon Church, let me do so right here before going any further.

I had mentioned earlier that Joseph Smith contended that a different meaning of the Hebrew word "*bara*" was slipped into the Bible. The accepted and traditional translation of the word, "*bara*," is "*to call forth out of nothing*." This teaching is essential to the Jewish and Christian theology that God made the universe and the world out of nothing—another teaching Joseph Smith challenges. Joseph Smith has the Gods of Mormonism making the universe and world out of pre-existing materials.

Joseph Smith claims that a Jewish scholar changed the word without permission although there is no evidence to support such a claim. Joseph Smith claims that "*bara*" actually means, "*to call forth*"—as in calling forth a meeting of the Gods. Ignoring the true meaning of the word, "*bara*," Joseph Smith is able to teach that the Gods created all their worlds out of pre-existing materials.

Joseph Smith builds on this misrepresentation to create a Council of Gods, which is responsible for the creation of our world and to change how our world was made. These doctrines all trace back to this specific word and its mistranslation.

As I mentioned earlier, it is obvious that someone trained in the Bible and its theology and terminology was involved in Joseph Smith's writings and teachings. Statements by eyewitnesses, who knew Joseph Smith at that time, make it clear that there was no evidence of this level of theological training in his life when the Golden Plates were being translated.

I suggested at that time, that Smith's resource may have been an excommunicated minister named Sydney Rigdon. In the appendix dealing with the true origin of The Book of Mormon, the researchers noted he was teaching Mormon doctrine two years before he claims to have met Joseph Smith. The researchers further presented eyewitness statements that Sydney Rigdon lied, and that he was seen with Joseph Smith prior to and at the time of the translating process.

Putting all that aside, let's come back to the logic and the process of Biblical interpretation. There is just one problem with Joseph Smith's claim…it does not hold up when you follow proper procedures of Biblical interpretation. You cannot take one verse or one word out of context, and build doctrine on it. Joseph Smith misrepresented the meaning of the word "*bara*" and used that misrepresentation to change the entire Old Testament from a clearly Monotheistic Religion [One God, and only one God], and transformed it into a Polytheistic Religion [Many Gods]. The Jewish faith was reported to have been one of the earlier religions to hold that there was one God, and only one God. This is what made the Jewish faith different from all other religions.

Smith used this single word in the Hebrew text. He accepted only part of its meaning: "*to call forth*," and ignored the other part of its meaning: "*out of nothing*," to teach that the Supreme God was calling together a Council of Gods. Based upon this one mistranslation, he then altered the entire account of creation and attributed all creation—including Adam and Eve—to multiple Gods without any consideration as to how this affected God's legal authority over His Creation.

The entire Mormon Theology is built on multiple Gods. Refute the multiple Gods teaching; and the entire Mormon Theology comes crashing down. Yes, that teaching is that vital to everything else Joseph Smith teaches. Without multiple Gods, nothing else Joseph Smith taught works. His view of the universe collapses without a foundation to support it.

Here is Joseph Smith's problem: the rest of the Old Testament does not support his mistranslation of the word. His mistranslation of this word is the only "*Biblical*" evidence he can submit to support his doctrines and revelations. In fact, there are numerous verses that contradiction a concept of multiple Gods—several of these quotations are attributed to God, Himself.

The Mormon doctrine of multiple Gods clearly contradicts the teachings of the Old Testament. This is found in both the Septuagint [LXX] and the Dead Sea Scrolls. The Septuagint is the earliest translation of the Old Testament documents. They were translated 250 BC. The Dead Sea Scrolls were hidden away 200 BC. Both documents were created and preserved before the alleged corruption Joseph Smith claimed came into the Church.

According to Joseph Smith, the corruption came into the Church with the death of the last Apostle. These documents existed long before the first Apostle was even born—let alone before they died. Further, these documents were controlled by the Jews, not the Church; and the Jews would never have allowed these documents to have been altered. So this will be the teachings of the Bible before Joseph Smith, before Jesus Christ, and before the alleged corruption of the Church. Isaiah 46:9:

"Remember the former things of old, for I am God and *there is no one else*. I am God and *there is no one like me*." [Emphasis added]

God makes a similar declaration in Isaiah 44:8:

"Fear you not, neither be afraid: have not I told you from that time, and have declared it? You are even my witnesses. *Is there a God beside me*? yea, *there is no God*; *I know not any*." [Emphasis added]

As God dwells in the same plain of existence as Joseph Smith's Gods and Council of Gods, then God would know if He had any company or competition. God denies the existence of any other God. Also, consider Isaiah 44:10:

"'You are my witnesses,' says the Lord, 'and my servant whom I have chosen: that you may know and believe me, and understand that I am He: *before me there was no God formed, neither shall there be after me*.'" [Emphasis added]

This verse tells us God had three reasons for sharing this information with us: 1) that we would know, 2) that we would believe; and 3) so that we would understand. What were we to know, believe and understand? That there is only one God. And that no Gods were formed before He was formed, and no Gods were formed after He was formed. This pretty much shuts down all options for the existence of other Gods.

According to the Mormon Theology, there were many Gods formed before our God came to exist. According to Mormon Theology, new Gods are being formed all the time as Mormon men die and move onto the next step in their own Godhood.

Now with regards to the Christian faith and the teaching of the Trinity, this verse holds that God the Father, God the Son and God the Holy Spirit are One [Deuteronomy 6:4], and that They all came to exist at the same moment. None of Them came first. None of Them came after. This is the only way that this verse can be true.

Now, let's consider Isaiah 44:6:

"Thus says the Lord the King of Israel, and His redeemer the Lord of hosts; 'I am the first, and I am the last; and *beside me there is no God.*" [Emphasis added]

Notice that there are two people speaking here. There is the Lord, who is identified as the King of Israel; and there is the Redeemer, who bears the title of the Lord of Hosts. At first glance, it may seem that there are now two Gods; but the declaration is that there is only one God. They speak as one "*I am the first*" and "*I am the last.*" These two persons speaking are somehow joined so that even though separate, They are still one. This would be the doctrine of the Trinity.

According to this verse, God is the first God [there were no Gods before God came to be]; and God is the last God. There were no Gods who came to exist after our God came to be. Now this is important to consider because as noted above we have God the Father, God the Son and God the Holy Spirit. All three came to be at the exact same moment. None of Them came first or after the other. Add to this Isaiah 45:5—6:

"I am the Lord, and *there is no one else, there is no God beside me*: I girded you, though you have not known me;

"That they may know from the rising of the sun, and from the west, that *there is no one beside me*. I am the Lord, and *there is no one else.*" [Emphasis added]

How many different times or in how many different ways can God tells us that there is only one God and He is it?

Now let's consider this logically, as we would be forced to do if this were presented to a court of law. There are two possible interpretations of the Hebrew word, "*bara.*" There is the traditional interpretation that God called forth [the universe and earth] out of nothing. Then there is Joseph Smith's interpretation that "*bara*" means to call forth a Council of Gods to make the earth. Which translation is supported by the rest of the Old Testament? Which translation is refuted by the rest of the Old Testament? If we follow the procedures set down for interpreting the Bible, and accepted by scholars for thousands of years, Joseph Smith's interpretation is wrong. There is no evidence for his interpretation. There is no teaching in the Old Testament to support such an interpretation.

In fact, his interpretation cannot be neutral in light of the other teachings of the Old Testament. It challenges the basic teaching of the Jewish faith that there is only one God. We must go with the traditional interpretation of "*bara*," and reject the mistranslation suggested by Joseph Smith.

When you present these teaching to a Latter Day Saint, and prove that God is denouncing the worship of other gods, their traditional response states that they do not deal with other gods. They claim to only deal with the God of this world, and so they are not violating God's instructions. To be honest, this is *double-speak*. They are trying to teach both the statement and its opposite as truth. They cannot both be true. They contradict each other.

The Latter Day Saints worship a God who is one of many Gods. Whether you pray to these other Gods or worship these other Gods is irrelevant to the issue. You are teaching a doctrine that the Old Testament specifically refutes by God's own testimony.

These verses show that whichever God the Mormons claim to be the God of this world that they deal with; that God is NOT the God of the Bible. Even though they are using the names of God found in the Bible, their Gods are NOT the God of the Bible.

Their God is part of a multiple-Gods universe. God declares that there is no such universe where multiple Gods exist. The teaching of the Latter Day Church contradicts the clear teachings of the Bible. Again, if we do not live in a multiple-Gods universe, all other teachings of the Latter Day Church come crashing down.

As noted, the Latter Day Church side-steps this entire issue by claiming that the God of this world is the only God that they deal with. That does not resolve the issue. Let's take this argument one step further.

Their founder and prophet, Joseph Smith, declared his version of the universe to be from God, and he declared that his version was the true version. It was his status of Prophet that required others to accept what he said since he was speaking for God.

Let's respond to this claim. Consider another Old Testament teaching. Deuteronomy 13:1–3:

"If there arise among you a *prophet*, or a dreamer of dreams, and gives you a sign or a wonder,

"And the sign or the wonder comes to pass, whereof he spoke unto you, saying, '*Let us go after other gods,* which you have not known, and let us serve them;'

"*You shall not [listen] unto the words of that prophet*, or that dreamer of dreams: for the Lord your God [is testing] you, to know whether you love the Lord your God with all your heart and with all your soul." [Emphasis added]

If the prophet predicts something and it does not come true, then that prophet is also declared to be a false prophet. Deuteronomy 18:21–22:

"And if you say in your heart, 'How shall we know the word which the Lord has not spoken?

"*When a prophet speaks in the name of the Lord, if the thing follows not, nor comes to pass, that is the thing which the Lord has not spoken, but the prophet has spoken it presumptuously: you shall not be afraid of him.*" [Emphasis added]

So there are two ways that a prophet can qualify as a false prophet. The first is to predict something and it comes to pass. The prophet then seeks to lead the people to follow after other Gods. The second way is to predict an event, and it does not come true. We will discuss prophecy and Joseph Smith's claim to being a prophet in the Appendix, but for now Joseph Smith meets the first qualification as a false prophet. He tries to lure people to follow after other Gods. The God of the Mormon Church is NOT the God of the Bible—even though they claim the names are the same.

Therefore, if Joseph Smith, Brigham Young and other leaders of the Latter Day Church claim to be a prophet, and they teach that there are multiple Gods, then they fit the Biblical definition of false prophets perfectly. They are trying to lure us away from the God of the Bible—who is the only God, and there are no other Gods besides Him. They should not be listened to. We should not pay attention to what they are saying and teaching. We need to reject them and their doctrines as the doctrines of false prophets trying to lure us away from God.

***

Now this was not an isolated case of teaching multiple Gods. Mormon Theology teaches a hierarchy of Gods in a different plain of existence. This seems to be a kind of spirit realm and here the various Gods exist. Mormon Theology teaches that there is one great God, which governs all the other Gods. He is the one who called for the Council of Gods.

According to Mormon Theology, there is a star in this alternate universe that is the greatest star. This star is called Kolob. It is not great because of its size. It is great because it is the star closest to God—which God it is close to is never clarified, but it is the God speaking to Abraham. Kolob is also believed to be the first creation, and all other creations are designed after this template. Some Mormon theologians suggest that Kolob is at the very center of the universe—or at the very least, it is at the very center of our galaxy.

There is a song sung in Mormon Temples inviting Mormons to "*hie to Kolob*." This is their concept of Heaven. Now according to Mormon Theology, Kolob seems to function very similar to Heaven. It has its own passage of time that matches the passage of time for God. Both the Psalmist and Peter mentions that one day to God is as a thousand years for us. Psalm 90:4:

"For a thousand years in Your sight are but as yesterday when it is past, and as a watch in the night."

II Peter 3:8:

"But, beloved, be not ignorant of this one thing, that one day is with the Lord as a thousand years, and a thousand years as one day."

For this reason, the Last Days, which began with the resurrection of Jesus, has only been about two days by God's timetable.

If you are on Kolob or in the same universe as Kolob, time there passes a thousand years for a single day on Kolob. According to the Mormon documents, The Book of Abraham 3:4: "And the Lord said unto me, by the Urim and Thummim, that Kolob was after the manner of the Lord, according to its times and seasons in the revolutions thereof; that one revolution was a day unto the Lord, after his manner of reckoning, it being one thousand years according to the time appointed unto that whereon thou standest. This is the reckoning of the Lord's time, according to the reckoning of Kolob."

Again, whoever put this teaching together knew the Bible, and clearly drew from the King James Bible. This was not an accidental mistranslation—it is an intentional attempt to deceive.

Let me just point out in passing that this God spoke to Abraham through the Urim and Thummim in this passage. This is interesting because Abraham lived four hundred years before the Urim and Thummim were created. God instructed Moses four hundred years later to create the Urim and Thummim for the High Priest as part of his garments. How did Abraham get the Urim and Thummim four hundred years before God gave the design to Moses? [Ooops!]

It seems that there are different names, per the Book of Abraham, for our sun, and our moon and our stars. "And he said unto me: 'This is Shinehah, which is the sun.' And he said unto me: 'Kokob, which is star.' And he said unto me: 'Olea, which is the moon.' And he said unto me: 'Kokaubeam, which signifies stars, or all the great lights, which were in the firmament of heaven.'" [Abraham 3:13]

"... [T]herefore Kolob is the greatest of all the Kokaubeam that thou hast seen, because it is nearest unto me." [Abraham 3:16b]

***

Let me return to the passage from the Book of Mormon. The Mormon theologians claim that it is the God who created earth that is the only God that they have any dealings with. However, as noted, the God who is speaking to Abraham speaks as if He is the first God, the original God because Kolob is closest to Him. The very fact that Abraham's days are not a thousand years long is proof that we are not on Kolob. We are not near the throne of this God. Neither are we close to Kolob.

Yet this God speaking to Abraham claims that He is the *"Lord thy God"* when speaking to Abraham. This raises a serious issue concerning the Chain of Command among the Gods. Does the communication go through the God of this world; or can other Gods step in and deal directly with Earth? This appears to be the case with Abraham. If other Gods deal directly with Earth, and bypass the God of this world, how can we know which standards of performance apply to us, and which standards are given by our "God?" If this other God is trying to impose standards upon us, does this other God have the legal right to do so? This multiple-Gods system creates a lot of problems for the Creation.

Or to boil all this confusion down into a simple question: "If multiple Gods keep contacting us; how can we deal only with the God of this world?" The Book of Abraham suggests that Abraham—and probably other Old Testament saints—dealt with these other Gods. Mormon doctrines do not support their claim to only deal with the God of this world.

***

Many years ago, during my college days, I took a class in Ethics. I was required to present a paper on Ethics. I chose to use the teachings of the Greek philosophers. To summarize my paper, according to the Greek—and even the Romans—there were wars and battles among the gods. What was the basis for these wars and battles? These wars and battles were fought over what one god felt was right versus what other gods felt was right. In short, it appeared that there was no standard concept of right and wrong among the gods. Right and wrong differed from god to god. With multiple gods, and multiple standards of right and wrong, how can you hold the subject accountable to a standard that is not final—that keeps changing?

***

Let me discuss what seems to be another violation of the Chain of Command clearly documented by Joseph Smith's teachings. Joseph Smith taught that the Angel Moroni appeared to him. However, Moroni—if we believe the reports—had lived a good life, and he had died many years ago. Shouldn't he be on his way to Godhood? Shouldn't he be creating his own world, and watching over it? But he appears to be an angel now, not a God. Where do angels fit into all of this? Are they Pre-Mortal Estates? Are they Post-Mortal Estates? The Bible claims that they are created beings, and that God created them. That is not the same thing as spirit children. Where do they fit into the hierarchy?

I also have to ask what gives Moroni the jurisdiction to enter the world that some other God created, and start giving instructions to one of this other God's creations? Moroni is not the God of this world. He was an inhabitant of this world who died and moved on. By what right does he claim to come back into this world? By what right does he claim authority to intervene with one of the other God's humans, and give him information and assignments? Is there even a Chain of Command for all these worlds or is there just chaos of everyone doing what they want to do whenever they want to do it?

And there is more. According to Joseph Smith's sources, Jesus came back into this world. Rather than going to His own Disciples who were in danger of falling into corruption back in Israel, He chooses to visit America. Rather than saving the system He established, He lets it fall into corruption. He chooses to set up new Disciples in America and abandons Christians in Israel. This is in violation of His promise that He would be with them until the end of the world [Matthew 28:19–20]. Do His promises mean nothing now that He is dead? Why start over somewhere else, rather than fixing the problem in Israel?

Again, Jesus has died. He should be working His way to Godhood and creating His own planet. That should be His focus and not the world He has left. By what authority does He come back into this world and interfere with this other God's world? He may be the Son of God, but all humans in this world are sons and daughters of God according to Mormon Theology.

Toss in Joseph Smith's claims that John the Baptist came back. He claims Peter, James and John came back. Doesn't anyone move on and start their own worlds? Why is everybody and their brother coming back and interfering and usurping the authority of the God of this world? If all these manifestations are Gods or wanna-be Gods, Joseph Smith dealt with more than the God of this world.

If we believe the teachings of Joseph Smith that Jesus returned not once, but twice: once to select new Disciples and give the Gospel to America, and the second time to tell Joseph Smith not to join a church; then this suggests that Jesus can return to this world whenever He wants, wherever He wants; and as often as He wants. Why does Jesus come back and visit America, and then come back another time to meet with Joseph Smith? He could have avoided this entire problem if He had just come back sooner and prevented the corruption Joseph Smith claims took over the Church. Or, was Jesus just not smart enough to figure this out?

Jesus could have prevented all of this if He had just come back and gone to Israel instead of America. If the Church that He created was becoming corrupt, it's His fault for not coming back and protecting it. He came back twice and started it over. Why not do it right, and keep it on track? Jesus promised that He would be with His followers until the end of the world. Did He lie? Did He not keep His word? Why let everything get so corrupt if He can come into this world and speak directly with humans? Why not make a regular appearance and stop the corruption from happening? This does not make sense.

Now let's take this one step further. Suppose the Mormon fathers tell us that Moroni and Jesus were authorized to enter this world, and get involved with inhabitants of this world. What if they quote some new revelation that the God of this world pulls back his spirit children to do missions for him in this world? If this is the case, then shouldn't Joseph Smith come back into this world and get involved with Mormons to encourage them, lead them and guide them? Imagine the effect an appearance by the Angel Joseph Smith would have to wake up the entire world to the truth of the Mormon Doctrine. An appearance by the Angel Joseph Smith would fix all these problems with his lack of evidence. Question: Has anyone had a visitation from an angel of Joseph Smith in this world since he died?

There is no consistency in how these spirit beings, Gods and dead people operate in this world. If God is fair, and God is just, then God should work the same way with each person. In the Mormon scheme of the universe, God is not fair. He is not just. He is not even consistent.

***

Now with regards to the Mormon universe and its Multiple Gods, if there were one standard of right and wrong, then the God of this world would be the only one to contact us and speak to us. Yet Mormon Theology has changed over the years—take for an example, the truth as to whether or not a man of African descent can attain Godhood. This changed in 1978. I, personally, heard the announcement of the change. Given the Multiple-Gods Universe, I have to ask—and I have the right to ask this—who made the decision to change that concept of truth? Did the one who made that decision have the approval of all the Gods to do so? Are there other Gods still out there who do not agree with this change in the truth? If the truth changes; was it ever truth to begin with? Can other Gods now come back after-the-fact, and repeal this change and block men of African descent from being gods? What about men of African descent who died before this change was made? Do they get a "*do over*"?

***

The Book of Abraham raises a very interesting question as Abraham literally quotes from the first two chapters of Genesis, but changes a very important fact in the account. Abraham 5:11–13:

"11 And the Gods took the man and put him in the Garden of Eden, to dress it and to keep it.

"12 And the Gods commanded the man, saying: Of every tree of the garden thou mayest freely eat,

"13 But of the tree of knowledge of good and evil, thou shalt not eat of it; for in the time that thou eatest thereof, thou shalt surely die. Now I, Abraham, saw that it was after the Lord's time, which was after the time of Kolob; for as yet the Gods had not appointed unto Adam his reckoning."

Notice the subtle but very important change in this description of earth and the creation of man. It was not God who did this. Here Abraham declares that it was *the Gods*—plural. Now we have to ask, "Who is in charge here?" Who is creating this restriction upon the human race? Which one of these Gods has the jurisdiction to place this restriction upon Adam? Under what legal system do the Gods claim the jurisdiction to do this?

We see the same problem created with Abraham's account of the creation of woman. Abraham 5:14–16:

"14 And the Gods said: Let us make an help meet for the man, for it is not good that the man should be alone, therefore we will form an help meet for him.

"15 And the Gods caused a deep sleep to fall upon Adam; and he slept, and they took one of his ribs, and closed up the flesh in the stead thereof;

"16 And of the rib which the Gods had taken from man, formed they a woman, and brought her unto the man."

Again, Eve was the creation of multiple Gods. These Gods are not identified. The authority over woman is not identified nor established in this account. Who has the right to set standards for this woman? Were these standards ever properly relayed to the woman directly or even indirectly by the Gods? Did the God who relayed this restriction have the jurisdiction and legal authority over the woman to do so? Could the restriction of not eating the fruit apply just to the man and not the woman since different Gods made her?

This multiple-Gods Doctrine creates more problems that it resolves.

***

Now let me raise another question concerning these passages. We see the Gods making man. We see the Gods making woman. Yet nowhere in this account does it mention the Gods taking a Pre-Mortal State spirit baby and placing it in either Adam or Eve.

Not to confuse the issue further, but what determined male and female? When spirit babies are born in their Pre-Mortal State as Joseph Smith claims, are they all born male, or are some born male and some born female? If they are determined to be male and female in their Pre-Mortal State, what determined the male spirit babies and the female spirit babies? Since females cannot become Gods, what sin or crime did these female spirit babies commit that Godhood is blocked to them forever?

Now if all spirit babies are born male, then we have a more serious issue on our hands. Brigham Young noted that spirit babies are sinless when they enter the body of flesh and bone. If that is the case, what determines which male spirit babies are placed in female bodies and which male spirit babies are placed in male bodies? Are the Mormon founding fathers suggesting that there is truth to being a male born into a female body? I have not yet come across any Mormon doctrines that explain the male and female bodies and why females cannot become Gods like the males. After all, God is fair and God is just. He cannot force some spirit babies to never attain Godhood without a reason, can He?

But when we consider the Biblical account, males and females are personally responsible for their own salvation. Men and women choose on their own to accept Jesus as their Savior. Both male and female are treated as equals in the Bible when coming before God. The Biblical account maintains the teaching that the God of the Bible is fair and He is just. The Biblical account does not have the issues and problems created by the Mormon doctrines.

***

This same passage from The Book of Abraham raises another issue. It sounds almost as if "the Gods" in this narrative were all the Gods and specifically the First God who created Kolob. We can assume this because Earth was close to Kolob before it fell. Again, Abraham 5:12–13:

"12 And the Gods commanded the man, saying: Of every tree of the garden thou mayest freely eat,

"13 But of the tree of knowledge of good and evil, thou shalt not eat of it; for in the time that thou eatest thereof, thou shalt surely die. Now I, Abraham, saw that it was after the Lord's time, which was after the time of Kolob; for as yet the Gods had not appointed unto Adam his reckoning."

Adam and Eve—and the Earth—kept time after the order of Kolob's time. This time was in force up until the time that Adam and Eve fell, and the Earth fell with them. From the description of Kolob and its location, this involved the Earth being physically moved from its location near Kolob, and falling into our solar system where time was measured in a different manner. Brigham Young once explained that Earth was created near God and Kolob, but that it physically fell out of God's presence when mankind did:

"When the earth was framed and brought into existence and man was placed upon it, it was near the throne of our Father in Heaven. And when man fell . . . the earth fell into space, and took up its abode in this planetary system, and the sun became our light . . . This is the glory the earth came from, and when it is glorified it will return again unto the presence of the Father" [*Journal of Discourses Volume 17*, pg. 143].

Again, Brigham Young mentions Kolob and the "*throne of our Father in Heaven*." Is this the First God who created Kolob and that is why earth was near it, or was this the God of this world? I have a question which I did not find the answer to in the Mormon Theology: If the planet the "*God*" creates falls and is cast out away from Kolob and the Celestial worlds—as was the earth; does the God who created them—who created this imperfection—get removed from the Celestial plane until he can fix the problem with his world?

As the casual observer can see, there is information missing from the testimony of Abraham and Brigham Young. Further, the identity of the first witness, Abraham, is called into question by the Mormon Church itself and so any testimony of this witness can be barred based on credibility of the witness.

I would also like to point out that the references made by Brigham Young and others to the God speaking to Abraham keep mirroring the references others make to the God of this world. Are they equal? Are they the same?

***

There is also an issue of conflicting testimony. Notice how the God of the Bible describes the creation of the sun, moon and stars. Genesis 1:14–19:

"And God said, Let there be lights in the [skies] of the heaven to divide the day from the night; and let them be for signs, and for seasons, and for days, and years:

"And let them be for lights in the [skies] of the heaven to give light upon the earth: and it was so.

"And God made two great lights; the greater light to rule the day, and the lesser light to rule the night: He made the stars also.

"And God set them in the [skies] of the heaven to give light upon the earth,

"And to rule over the day and over the night, and to divide the light from the darkness: and God saw that it was good.

"And the evening and the morning were the fourth day."

Now this passage from the King James Bible claims that the creation of our sun, moon and stars took place before the Fall of man. It claims that the earth was made in the location where it currently is. It was not made somewhere else and brought here.

This is not describing an alternate universe. This is not describing Kolob. This is our universe. This is the Milky Way Galaxy. This is our solar system. The sun—our sun—was created to provide light during the day to our planet. The moon was created to give light at night to our earth.

Now with regards to the sun, moon and stars, they were created to be for signs and for seasons. They were created to help us measure days and years. This sun and this moon and these stars establish our sense of time, our days and our years. They are not measured by "*Kolob time.*" They were measured based upon our relation in space to the sun, moon and stars.

This account clearly contradicts the account of the Latter Day Church. This account was written and preserved prior to the corruption Joseph Smith claims came upon the Church. This is the first revelation. This is the earliest revelation. That makes this revelation the *prima facie evidence* by which all other revelations must be tested. In this case, the Latter Day Church's revelation fails to meet the test of the Bible, and it must be rejected.

***

Now let us move on and discuss other doctrines that apply to the pre-earth doctrines. This would be the Latter Day teaching that each one of us existed in a Pre-Mortal estate before we were born into this world. From several sources, we are told that when the God of this world has relations with his celestial wives, a spirit baby is produced. Our existence prior to birth is referred to in Mormon Theology as our Pre-Mortal Estate. Brigham Young had this to say about our souls:

"We understand, for it has long been told us, that we had an existence before we came into the world... Our religion teaches us that there was never a time when they were not, and there will never be a time when they cease to be..." [Brigham Young, Journal of Discourse 3:367]

This pre-existence of the soul is a Mormon doctrine. It is not taught in the Bible. In other words, it has not "long been told to us." In fact, the Bible makes it clear that only Jesus existed before He was born in Bethlehem. The reason He existed before His birth is because He is God. He has no beginning. He has no end. Brigham Young seeks to take this quality that is unique to God the Father, God the Son and God the Holy Spirit and apply it to our souls. John 3:13:

"And no man has ascended up to Heaven, but He who came down from heaven, even the Son of man which is in Heaven."

Also, John 17:5:

"And now, O Father, glorify You me with Your own self with the glory which I had with You before the world was."

Jesus is teaching that He was a glorified being before He was born into this world. In Mormon Theology, glorified beings are the state of Godhood that Mormon males strive to reach. Jesus is declaring that He is not striving for this glorified status. He claims that He had it before He was born, and that He set aside this glorified status to become human and live among us. There is also John 6:38:

"For I came down from Heaven, not to do my own will, but the will of Him who sent me."

Consider the description in the Bible of the Creation of man. Genesis 2:7:

"And the Lord God formed man of the dust of the ground, and breathed into his nostrils the breath of life; and man became a living soul."

God formed the body first. God did not take a Pre-Mortal soul and insert it into Adam. God breathed the breath of life into Adam, and this is when Adam became a living soul, not before.

Paul discussed the order of life. There was flesh [physical life] first, and then spirit or soul after. This contradicts the soul existing before the body was formed. I Corinthians 15:46:

"Howbeit that was not first which is spiritual, but that which is natural [physical]; and afterward that which is spiritual."

Before His birth, Jesus was not a Pre-Mortal Being. He was God, and He shared the glory of God the Father. This is not what Mormon Theology teaches.

***

Mormon Theology teaches that all of us existed before we were born. When Mormon doctrine refers to Pre-Mortal Estate, it is referring to our souls before we were born into this world. According to Mormon Theology, the actions and attitudes while in our Pre-Mortal Estate determine where it will be placed in this world when it is given a physical body.

"Is there reason then why the type of birth we receive in this life is not a reflection of our worthiness or lack of it in the pre-existent life? . . . Can we account in any other way for the birth of some of the children of God in darkest Africa, or in flood-ridden China, or among the starving hordes of India, while some of the rest of us are born here in the United States?" [Mark E. Peters, Former Apostle of the Mormon Church]

According to this theology, if the Pre-Mortal soul is obedient and makes good decisions prior to birth, then it will be placed in a Mormon home, which will ensure it a head start on becoming a God himself. If the Pre-Mortal soul is not obedient and does not make good decisions, it will be placed in a different home, culture, country or even a race that will limit or hinder the Pre-Mortal soul's chances of obtaining Godhood.

Now let me bring up my former series of questions because all these teachings deal with the male Pre-Mortal Estate. Is the sex determined in the Pre-Mortal Estate? When and how is the sex of the Pre-Mortal Estate determined? Are all the spiritual babies male? Is every Pre-Mortal being male; and then the female status is determined at birth?

I have to ask this because the female does not have the option of becoming a glorified being. She cannot attain Godhood. The best she can do is to be the wife of a God. In other words, being born female forever bars that Pre-Mortal being from being exalted and becoming a God of her own world. It is only the male who has this option.

So, if spirit babies are born male and female; then these female babies are forever doomed to remain female and will be forever barred from being exalted. Their fate would be sealed the moment they were born. If the sex is determined when the Pre-Mortal Being is born into this world, then I would have to follow the logic of the above statement of doctrine, and assume those Pre-Mortal Beings who were born into this world, as females must have done something very bad in their Pre-Mortal Estate to justify this kind of punishment. And in the Mormon Theology, this would be considered a punishment. Barring any Pre-Mortal Being from even the chance to be exalted was a special punishment reserved for Lucifer and his followers.

Per Mormon Theology, Lucifer led a rebellion in this spirit world [more on this in our next chapter] and was defeated. As a consequence of his defeat, he—and all of his followers in the rebellion—are barred from ever receiving a physical body [being born into our world] and, therefore, are barred forever from moving forward to become a God of his own.

There was even a teaching in the Mormon Church prior to 1978 that members of the Negro race were cursed before they were even born into this world, and could never become God. The black skin was taught to be the Mark of Cain that God placed upon Cain, and this would forever disqualify them from attaining Godhood.

"The whole house of Israel was chosen to come to mortality as children of Jacob. Those who were less valiant in the pre-existence and who thereby had certain restrictions imposed upon them during mortality are known to us as negroes." [Bruce McConkie Mormon Doctrine 1966 edition]

Fortunately for those of African descent, the Mormon Theology does not hold that God does not change. Their God, and the doctrines of their God, seem to change despite Malachi 3:6:

"For I am the Lord, I change not; therefore you sons of Jacob are not consumed."

Mormon Theology allows God to change, even on very important doctrinal issues. Therefore, on June 9, 1978, the late Spencer W. Kimball—then President of the Mormon Church—received a convenient *"revelation"* from God that said all worthy male church members were eligible for the priesthood, regardless of race. I wonder when they will receive a convenient revelation that all humans—male and female—are eligible for the priesthood regardless of their sex.

Allowing females to become Gods would forever change the structure of the Mormon afterlife. It would change the Celestial Kingdom forever. How would it be for the Goddess to give birth? Would her husband in the Celestial Kingdom be an exalted being, or could she choose a lesser male to father her spirit babies?

At some point, Mormon women are going to start asking, "What did we do that was so wrong that we cannot become exalted like men?" I hope for the sake of the Mormon leaders that they have a really good answer.

***

There are two problems with the theology of a soul pre-existing birth and being punished or rewarded for actions and attitudes in the Pre-Mortal Estate. One problem is created by Mormon Theology itself; and the other is created by Jesus, Himself. According to Brigham Young:

"Our spirits were pure and holy when they entered our tabernacles;"

[Brigham Young, Journal of Discourse 8:138]

If our spirits are pure and holy when we enter our *"tabernacles"* [bodies], then how can the actions or attitudes in our Pre-Mortal estate have any affect on us as we enter our bodies? Such things, if they existed, would have to be removed, atoned or resolved before entering a human body in order for the Pre-Mortal soul to be pure and holy [i.e. sinless] when it is born into a physical body.

Now Jesus was asked about birth defects by His Disciples. John 9:1–3:

"And as Jesus passed by, He saw a man who was blind from his birth.

"And His disciples asked Him, saying, 'Master, who did sin, this man, or his parents, that he was born blind?'

Jesus answered, 'Neither has this man sinned, nor his parents: but that the works of God should be made manifest in him.'"

We are born the way that we are because God has a plan for each one of us. God wants to work through us. God wants to reveal Himself through us. We all have those things in us that we must come to God for the strength to overcome. Who we are and what we are were all designed to bring us to God to allow God to work in us and through us. None of us is being punished at birth.

So this structure of the pre-birth world described by Leaders of the Mormon Church does not line up with what the Bible teaches. The Mormon Church got the pre-birth world wrong. Now let's look at their teaching as to how the heavens and the earth came to be—the physical universe that we live in.

***

Now as a follow up to this concept of Pre-Mortal Estates, this is based upon the Mormon Theology that marriage is mandatory for a male to move forward into Godhood. Before I present the Mormon position, let me just note that Jesus taught that there was no place for marriage in the afterlife. This is where a Mormon male would be with his celestial wives and produce souls in their Pre-Mortal State.

There were two main schools of Jewish doctrine at the time of Jesus. There were the Pharisees, and then there were the Sadducees. The main difference between the two groups dealt with the resurrection and the afterlife. The Pharisees taught that there was a resurrection and an afterlife. The Sadducees did not believe in a resurrection or afterlife. [This is why they were Sad...you see? (Sorry!)] They did not believe in the spiritual or the supernatural.

So the Sadducees confront Jesus with one of their favorite stumpers. According to the Law of Moses, if a man dies and leaves a widow, but no children, his brother is required to marry the widow and raise up children for the deceased brother. In their scenario, a woman ends up marrying five brothers and none of them can give her any children. Then she dies. They ask Jesus whose wife she will be in the Resurrection or the afterlife. Jesus begins by pointing out that they are making a mistake because they do not know the Scriptures. We can say the same thing concerning the Latter Day Church. They have made mistakes, and they continue to make mistakes because they do not know what the Bible says. Matthew 22:30:

"For in the resurrection they neither marry, nor are given in marriage, but are as the angels of God in Heaven."

Jesus also teaches on this in Luke 20:34–36:

"And Jesus answering said unto them, 'The children of this world marry, and are given in marriage:

"But they which shall be accounted worthy to obtain that world, and the resurrection from the dead, neither marry, nor are given in marriage:

Neither can they die any more: for they are equal unto the angels; and are the children of God, being the children of the resurrection.'"

Jesus should know about the Resurrection. According to Mormon Theology, Jesus' Plan created the Resurrection, and how it works. According to Mormon Theology Jesus' death secures a resurrection for all of us. So if anyone should know how the Resurrection should work, it should be Jesus.

Marriage is only for this world. In this world, we are mortal. We live and we die. And so God has given us marriage, and through marriage, we procreate—we have children.

If marriage is essential for our afterlife, why would Paul remain single and encourage others to remain single in this life? I Corinthians 7:7 - 8:

"For I would [prefer] that all men were even as I myself. But every man has his proper gift of God, one after this manner, and another after that.

"I say therefore to the unmarried and widows, 'It is good for them if they abide even as I.'"

Paul discouraged marriage as he felt that this distracted believers from serving God more fully. I Corinthians 7:32–33:

"But I would have you without carefulness. He that is unmarried cares for the things that belong to the Lord, how he may please the Lord:

"But he that is married cares for the things that are of the world, how he may please his wife."

If marriage were essential to salvation and our status in the afterlife, then it is reasonable to believe Paul would have provided different counsel concerning the need to marry. If marriage were part of the afterlife, then Jesus would have said so.

But here is what the Bible teaches. When we have died and been resurrected as immortal—on the same plane as angelic beings—then there is no need to be married or to get married. You are not procreating. You are not creating new life. That is just for this world only. This contradicts what the Latter Day Church teaches about the afterlife and marriage.

The Mormon concept of marriage in the afterlife is for the purpose of generating life to populate new worlds for new Gods. The Bible does not teach this kind of an afterlife. As we have already seen, there were no Gods that existed before God; and there are not going to be any Gods created after God. There will not be new Gods, so there will not be new worlds. There is no need for procreation after death and there is no need for marriage. Marriage, here on earth, is a picture of the relationship we will have in Heaven where Jesus will be the groom, and the Church will be His Bride. There is the Marriage Supper of the Lamb mentioned in Revelation; but there is no other reference to marriage in the afterlife.

In Mormon Theology, marriage is an essential part of salvation and becoming exalted [Godhood]. "...no one can attain exaltation to the fullness of the blessings of the celestial kingdom outside of the marriage relationship." [*Doctrines of Salvation*, 2:65]

Salvation has several requirements in the Latter Day Church. As mentioned before, a male Pre-Mortal Estate soul must meet requirements in his Pre-Mortal Estate to establish when and where he will be born into the human race—and what he will be born. Then there are the requirements to meet in this life to move forward toward exaltation [Godhood]. Then even in the afterlife, it is possible to blow it and to fail to attain an exalted status.

Then there is individual salvation and is "that which man merits through his own acts through life and by obedience of the Gospel." [Joseph Fielding Smith, Doctrines of Salvation, 1:134]

"…[S]alvation in its true and full meaning is synonymous with exaltation or eternal life and consists in gaining an inheritance in the highest of the three heavens within the celestial kingdom. . . .

"This full salvation is obtained in and through the continuation of the family unit in eternity, and those who obtain it are gods." [Bruce McConkie, Mormon Doctrine page 670]

Now as an investigator, I just need to stop the person who is giving the statement here. He has just slipped in a comment and a doctrine that is not supported by the Bible. He is now discussing something called *"full salvation"* and *"true and full salvation."* The Bible offers salvation. You are either saved, or you are not saved. You cannot be saved just a little. My salvation is not greater or more effective than your salvation. Salvation is a free gift of God [Romans 6:23]. It is the same gift for each person. This is because God is fair and just. He does not offer one kind of salvation to one person, and another kind of salvation to someone else. If I accept this person's statement that there is something called *"full salvation"* or *"true and full salvation,"* then I will have to accept his statement that there is *"partial or incomplete salvation."* I have to accept that there is a *"false salvation."* Salvation is something God offers. Salvation is something that Jesus has obtained for each of us. It is complete. There is nothing false or counterfeit about it. There is nothing that needs to be added to it. It is a package deal. Jesus did not buy us a *"Salvation*

Starter Pack," and then we have to track down, earn or buy the rest of the program. Jesus' salvation is all-inclusive, complete and needs no assembly or additional parts. The only choice is whether we accept this gift or not.

According to Mormon Theology, once a person has entered mortality and gained a physical body, he must fulfill a list of requirements in his endeavor to make progress toward exaltation, or godhood.

"This includes repentance, baptism, membership in the LDS church, innumerable good works, abiding by the Mormon 'Word of Wisdom'…marriage and other temple rituals…and 'keeping all the Lord's commandments until the end of [one's] life on earth'" [Gospel Principles pages 292–293]

There are seven elements dealing with salvation for those men in the Mormon faith:

1. Repentance,
2. Baptism,
3. Membership in the LDS church,
4. Innumerable good works,
5. Abiding by the Mormon "Word of Wisdom"
6. Marriage and other temple rituals
7. Keeping all the Lord's commandments

"It will be borne in mind that…there was a marriage in Cana…and on a careful reading of that transaction, it will be discovered that…Jesus Christ was married on that occasion. If he was never married, his intimacy with Mary and Martha, and the other Mary also whom Jesus loved, must have been highly unbecoming and improper to say the best of it." [Orson Hyde, Journal and Discourses, 13:259]

It is not the official position of the modern Mormon Church that Jesus was married or a polygamist, but the founding fathers taught that not only was Jesus married, but that He was a polygamist. Some current Mormon teachers continue to teach this doctrine.

Brigham Young, second prophet of the Latter Day Saints had this to say:

"The Scripture says that He, the Lord, came walking in the Temple, with "HIS TRAIN; I do not know who they were, unless his wives and children;" (Journal of Discourses, Vol. 13 page 309).

Here, Brigham Young is describing Isaiah 6:1:

"In the year that king Uzziah died, I saw the Lord sitting upon a throne, high and lifted up, and His train filled the temple."

This was a vision that the prophet Isaiah had, and the train in this case was not a collection of people, but part of His garments, like a long cape that flowed behind Him and filled the temple area. But the Mormon fathers were so determined to prove that God the Father was a polygamist that they mistranslated this passed to suit their own purposes.

Brigham Young further declared that Jesus was a polygamist in one of his sermons:

""Jesus Christ was a practical polygamist; Mary and Martha, the sisters of Lazarus, were his plural wives, and Mary Magdalene was another. Also, the bridal feast at Cana of Galilee, where Jesus turned the water into wine, was on the occasion of one of his own marriages." ["Wife No. 19 or The Story of A Life In Bondage... by Anna Eliza Young 1876 (Former wife of Brigham Young)]

The Mormon Jesus was a polygamist. He was married to at least four wives. There was the marriage in Cana to an unidentified woman, to Mary—sister of Martha, to Martha—the sister of Mary, and to Mary Magdalene.

The Mormons teach Jesus was married not because of any Biblical passage, but based upon their own doctrines: "... no one can attain exaltation to the fullness of the blessings of the celestial kingdom outside of the marriage relationship." [*Doctrines of Salvation,* 2:65]

Now it should be pointed out that there is NOTHING in any of the legal requirements or prophecies concerning the Messiah that He could not be married. In other words, there would be no need to hide the fact that Jesus was married if He had, in fact, been married. It is not a shame. It is not a scandal. It does not disqualify Him as Messiah. Therefore, there is no basis to conceal a marriage IF Jesus had married while He was here.

But the Bible does not mention Jesus being married. It does not discuss any wife that Jesus might have had. The Bible does mention Peter's wife and his mother-in-law. If Scriptures will mention Peter's wife and identify her as such; then why does the Bible not mention and identify a wife for Jesus? It does not identify a wife for Jesus because He never got married. It is that simple.

This *careful reading of the text* concerning the marriage in Cana is based upon the fact that Jesus provided the wine when they ran out. Those saying it was Jesus' wedding will claim that it was His place to provide the wine. The bridegroom is responsible to provide for the wedding feast.

So let's do *a careful reading of the text*. First of all, John 2:2 makes it clear that Jesus and His Disciples were called to the wedding. This means that they were invited. It does not mean that they were the one hosting the wedding. Also, in John 2:9, the governor of the wedding feast calls the bridegroom to praise the wine. If you want a careful reading of the text, then the governor [and it appears that the bridegroom] did not know where the good wine came from, but the servants did. If the bridegroom knew where the good wine came from, there would be no reason to point out that the servants knew where it came from. The reference to the servants knowing about where the good wine came from appears to be an inside secret for them. If Jesus was the bridegroom, then it would not be an inside secret, and there would be no reason to reference the servants' knowledge.

Finally, if Jesus were the bridegroom, then when the governor of the Wedding Feast called the bridegroom over to praise the new wine, he would have been calling Jesus over, and the passage should have identified Him by name.

We see that Jesus is a close friend of Lazarus and his two sisters. They were like family to Him, and He would visit and stay with them from time to time. This does not mean that He was married to them. There was nothing in how Jesus reacted to/

with Mary and Martha that would suggest it was inappropriate unless He was married to them. He came to visit Lazarus. He only came to see Mary and Martha apart from Lazarus when Lazarus was dead. There is nothing inappropriate about their relationship. There is no need to make Jesus married to them to explain such actions. The idea of Jesus marrying two sisters would be much more inappropriate for that culture than how Jesus reacted to them when He came to visit their brother.

Probably the closest thing that could even suggest a marriage would be Mary Magdalene as she followed Jesus after He delivered her of her demons. She was among His followers, and she traveled with the group. That might appear to be inappropriate. She was, however, not the only woman who did so. She was just the most visible.

Dan Brown, in his fictional book—and I stress the word *"fictional"*—suggested that Jesus and Mary Magdalene had been secretly married and had a daughter. His book, *The DaVinci Code* claimed that this was the secret that the Catholic Church had lied and killed for over the centuries to cover it up. As I said earlier, nothing in the prophecies concerning the Messiah forbade His being married. Jesus would not be disqualified from being the Messiah if He did marry. As a Jewish Rabbi, it was expected that He marry. There would be no logical reason to hide a marriage if Jesus chose to marry. The reality is, He did not marry; and any teaching of the Mormon Church to the contrary is grounded in fantasy and ignorance of the Scriptures.

In the Mormon Theology, marriage is so essential to salvation and Godhood, that marriages are arranged in the Mormon Church for those who die without being married. That practice is never even mentioned in the Bible.

It was a Mormon Theologian who was desperate to prove that Jesus was married to fulfill Mormon Theology that he suggested that the Marriage Feast in Cana was the wedding of Jesus. He tells us that if we examine the text closely we will discover this. We have done a careful reading of the text and it disproves his statement, not confirms it.

To conclude this section I will just note that nothing in the Bible even hints at marriage as a basis for salvation. Let me repeat once more the advice of Paul in I Corinthians 7:8:

"I say therefore to the unmarried and widows, 'It is good for them if they abide even as I.'"

The Apostle Paul was not married, and he encouraged believers—who were able to bear it—to be single so that they could give greater attention to serving God. Why would the Bible have this teaching if marriage were essential for salvation? It would not.

***

Let me take a moment to raise another question about this sexual relation with the God of this world and his Celestial Wife. I hate to raise this issue here as it becomes a kind of "*Spoiler Alert*" to issues raised later in this book; but this is the place where it fits.

According to Mormon Theology, God has a physical body. They describe this as a body of "*flesh and bones.*" I suspect that Joseph Smith was coached on this description of God's body by someone well-versed in the Bible. A resurrected body would have to be made of flesh and bones because Scripture says that "flesh and blood shall not inherit the Kingdom of God." I Corinthians 15:50:

"Now this I say, brethren, that *flesh and blood* cannot inherit the kingdom of God; neither does corruption inherit incorruption." [Emphasis added]

When we cross-reference this with how Jesus described His resurrected body, we find the answer to this problem. Luke 24:39:

"'Behold my hands and my feet, that it is I myself: handle me, and see; for a spirit has not *flesh and bones,* as you see me have." [Emphasis added]

The Resurrected Body of Jesus is made up of flesh and bone. But it did not have any blood in it. All of Jesus' blood had been poured out on the cross.

So according to Mormon Theology, God has a body of flesh and bone. When Latter Day Saints and others are resurrected into the Post-Mortal Estate, everyone has flesh and bone bodies. This means, according to Mormon Theology, that both the God of this world and his Celestial Wife who are having sexual relations to procreate for our world both have physical bodies of flesh and bone.

So, I just have to ask. If like begets like, and God and his Celestial Wife are begetting babies for the Pre-Mortal Estate; why are these begotten babies spirit babies? If like begets like, then these Pre-Mortal Estate babies should be flesh and bone like their parents. After all, according to Mormon Theology, when God had sex with Mary, and God's seed was placed into her [the same seed he places in his Celestial Wives], she produced a physical baby, not a spiritual baby.

I have not found where Mormon theologians have been able to answer this problem.

***

Now let me continue with the topic of salvation under the Latter Day Church teachings since we have already discussed one part of the Plan of Salvation: marriage.

Before the world was created, according to Mormon Theology, there were two Plans of Salvation presented to the Council of Gods. Lucifer offered a Plan of Salvation in which he would do everything and everyone would be saved. Jesus introduced a Plan of Salvation in which a person had to work for salvation and prove that he was worthy of salvation. Again, notice that there is no discussion of a Plan of Salvation for Mormon women. Mormon Theology ignores the direct teaching of the Bible that seeking to keep the Law or to live up to a moral standard will never produce acceptance with God. Romans 3:20:

"Therefore by the deeds of the law there shall no flesh be justified in His sight: for by the law is the knowledge of sin."

What does this mean in simple terminology? We can never live a life free of sin. No matter what efforts we make, we can never earn salvation. This means that we can never be worthy of salvation. Paul teaches over and over again in his letters that salvation is a gift that we receive, not a goal that we achieve. The standard of God is physically impossible for anyone to meet other than Jesus. The best the Law can do is to find us guilty and worthy of death.

It has never been God's plan or intention for us to live a good life and be worthy of salvation. God knew such a goal was impossible for us, and this is why He sent Jesus to offer us an alternative—a Plan of Salvation not based upon works, merit or being found worthy. The Mormon Plan excludes as many people as possible. God's true Plan through Jesus is to include as many people as possible.

Here is the harsh truth. There were no multiple Plans of Salvation suggested before the world was created. Let me comment on this for just a moment. If the Mormon Theology is true—but it is not—then we are talking about millions, maybe billions, of worlds that came before the earth. Each one of them would have had to select a Plan of Salvation. After that many attempts to build worlds, doesn't it make sense that this Council of Gods would have figured out the best Plan of Salvation millions of worlds ago and just keep using it. Why reinvent the wheel if you already have a good working model? There would be no basis for two people to make recommendations for the Council to choose between.

This is why the Mormon Theology does not make sense. It is not logical. In the real world, not the Mormon world, there was only one Plan of Salvation. It was the Plan of Salvation God the Father, Jesus the Son and God the Holy Spirit agreed on before They began the creation of our universe. Every action of God has been in the direction of providing salvation for His Creation. There has always been only one Plan of Salvation. Just as God does not change, neither does His Plan of Salvation change.

The true Plan of Salvation offered by the Bible is closer to the Mormon Plan of Lucifer than it is to the Mormon Plan of Jesus. Where the Mormon's claim Lucifer suggested that he does everything for everyone; that is the Plan Jesus is offering through the Bible. The only difference between the Plan of Salvation the Mormon's claim Lucifer was suggesting [and he never did suggest any Plan of Salvation in the real world] and the Bible's Plan of Salvation offered by Jesus is that the Mormon-rejected plan did not include free will. Everyone would be saved automatically. The Bible Plan of Salvation is where Jesus does everything to provide salvation and makes it available to us; but it does address free will and does require that we accept what Jesus is offering.

Does anyone else have an uncomfortable feeling that Mormon Theology takes the true Plan of Salvation that Jesus is offering, twists it slightly, and then attributes it to the devil to make it unacceptable for those in the Latter Day Church? Isn't this exactly what deception does?

Consider Paul's discussion of salvation in Ephesians 2:8–9:

"For by grace are you saved through faith; and that not of yourselves: it is the gift of God:

Not of works, lest any man should boast."

We are not saved of ourselves. We do not provide our salvation. It is not something that we control. We do not generate it. We do not make it. We are not responsible for how it works. All these concepts tell us that salvation is not something we make, earn or generate. It is there. It does exist. And through grace, God offers it to us free of charge. [Grace is unmerited favor—it is something we do not deserve.] It is there, and through faith, we accept it. Paul goes to great lengths in these verses to make it clear that works—or working for your salvation [or earning/being worthy] of your salvation is not an option. It is not even a possibility where God is concerned.

Paul also notes that salvation is a free gift that God gives. Romans 6:23:

"For the wages of sin is death; but the gift of God is eternal life through Jesus Christ our Lord."

Notice how Paul words this issue in Romans 4:13:

"For the promise, that he should be the heir of the world, was not to Abraham, or to his seed, through the law, but through the righteousness of faith."

The Law is another word for *"works."* Works is all about proving yourself worthy. Faith is about trusting God to do this for us because we are NOT worthy. Abraham did not become righteous before God because of the Law of Moses. The Law of Moses would not even be revealed for another four hundred years. Abraham was declared righteous because of his faith, not his works. Notice Genesis 15:6:

"And [Abraham] believed in the Lord; and [God] counted it to [Abraham] for righteousness."

This was part of documents preserved by the Jews, not the Christian Church. This was part of the Dead Sea Scrolls buried 200 years before Jesus was born. No one had the opportunity to alter this teaching. Paul repeats this teaching in Romans 4:3:

"For what says the scripture? 'Abraham believed God, and it was counted unto him for righteousness.'"

Even Jesus spoke of salvation as being based upon belief and not of works. Salvation is free and something that we accept and receive, not earn and deserve. John 3:16:

"For God so loved the world that He gave His Only Begotten Son, that whosoever believes on Him should not perish but have everlasting life."

Add to this that Jesus died for us not after we have proven ourselves worthy of His sacrifice; but Jesus died for us while we were unworthy and even considered to be enemies of God. Romans 5:8–10:

"But God commended His love toward us, in that, while we were yet sinners, Christ died for us.

"Much more then, being now justified by His blood, we shall be saved from wrath through Him.

"For if, when we were enemies, we were reconciled to God by the death of His Son, much more, being reconciled, we shall be saved by His life."

There is nothing in these passages about us being worthy of salvation. In fact, just the opposite is taught by the Bible. We do not deserve salvation. We cannot earn salvation. We will never attain salvation through our own efforts. It is only because Jesus fulfilled all the legal requirements that He is able to offer salvation to us. He offers salvation not as an incentive or as a wage. It is a free gift. It is ours for the asking. And once we have received this free gift from God, it will never be taken away. Romans 11:29:

"For the gifts and calling of God are without repentance."

However, Mormon Theology ignores the Plan of Salvation offered by the Bible and offers a counterfeit Plan of Salvation—something God never offered or even suggested. The Latter Day Church teaches that a male must be worthy of salvation and must work for his own salvation. Once a person has entered mortality and gained a physical body [been born into this world], he must fulfill a list of requirements in his endeavor to make progress toward exaltation, or Godhood. This includes repentance, baptism, membership in the LDS church, innumerable good works, abiding by the Mormon "Word of Wisdom"…marriage and other temple rituals…and "keeping all the Lord's commandments until the end of [one's] life on earth" [Gospel Principles pages 292–293] We have discussed the issues earlier.

***

Now let me go back to this list of items required to be saved in the Latter Day Church. This list is misleading. It tells the Mormon male that he must keep all the Lord's Commandments until he dies. But that suggests that he is not obligated to keep the Lord's Commandments after death and in the afterlife. However, according to Mormon Theology, this process of proving yourself worthy does not end with death. In the afterlife, Mormon Theology teaches that there are three kingdoms. There is the *Celestial Kingdom* this is where Mormons become Gods and bear spirit babies. Then there is the *Terrestrial Kingdom*. This Kingdom involves a general salvation [resurrection] but no Godhood. We would probably find non-Mormons in this area. Then there is the *Telestial Kingdom*—where those with sins go to be punished. However, this is not a permanent place. People come and go to this level as they struggle to atone for their own sins.

The need for three separate kingdoms suggests that once you die your fate is not final in the Mormon Theology. You can atone for sins and move up to the Terrestrial Kingdom. This way, those who end up in the Telestial Kingdom will only stay long enough to atone for their sins and move on. If you sin in the other kingdoms, there is a suggestion that you might end up in the Telestial Kingdom and have to work your way out.

If we follow this logic, then we must conclude that our eternal fate is never final and even in the afterlife we must continue to prove ourselves worthy of salvation.

Now I would have to ask that if we are proving ourselves worthy of salvation; then what part did the death of Jesus on the cross play in our salvation? According to Mormon Theology, the death of Jesus secured a general resurrection from the dead. Everyone will be resurrected into one of the three Kingdoms. Jesus does not offer salvation—He only offers resurrection into the afterlife. The rest falls on us to work and prove that we are worthy.

So far, we have looked at several teachings of the Latter Day Church and not one of these teachings is supported by the Bible—the contract that God is offering us. In many cases, not only does the Bible not support and teach the Mormon doctrine, the Bible refutes that teaching. Is this really a religion that you want to trust with your salvation and afterlife?

**

I have been stressing that the Bible is a legally-binding contract God wrote and has offered to the human race. It is a contract of salvation. In this contract of salvation, God does all the work, and all that we need to do is to accept His offer. We enter into the contract with Him through faith not works.

Looking at the structure of the universe as taught by the Latter Day Church there is no clear line of jurisdiction. There are multiple Gods, and the God of this world who wrote and offered this contract is not the one who created us and our world. The Book of Abraham makes it clear that multiple Gods made the world and created both man and woman. Therefore, there is no clear ownership in the Mormon Universe. As a result, the God of this world would not have clear jurisdiction. If there were no clear jurisdiction, then the God of this world would lack the legal right to set standards for us. If He has no jurisdiction or legal right to set standards for us, then He would not have the right to hold us accountable or to judge us should we fail to keep those standard. So I have to ask, "Who will judge us?" And I also have to ask, "Which standards will this judge use?"

***

As a closing thought to this chapter, let me just note that the Latter Day Church does not see eating the forbidden fruit as a sin. They suggest that the God of this world gave Adam two conflicting commands. In other words, the God of this world set both Adam and Eve up to fail. There was no way that they could complete the standards given to them. This is not the description of a fair and just God.

Adam was told to be fruitful and to multiply. He was also told to not eat the fruit of the Tree of Good and Evil. However, without eating this fruit, Adam and Eve would have never become mortal, and therefore their children could not be mortal. If they were not mortal; then they could not die. If they could not die, then they could not move forward to their own Godhood. Therefore, in order to fulfill the first command to be fruitful and to multiply, Adam and Eve had no choice but to disobey the command not to eat the forbidden fruit.

Let me be honest. There is a character in a movie we watch. He is the villain. He is always making mistakes. His stupidity becomes more obvious with each thing he does. He comments over and over, "Wow! I guess I didn't think this through." The more I look at the Mormon Universe; the more I would have to observe that obviously, someone did not think this through.

Let me add just one more thought about this needing to become mortal in order to die, and the need to fall in order to cease being mortal. If all the Gods created their worlds the same way, which is suggested by the fact that a council of Gods came together under the Head God to make our world, then this problem with Adam and Eve and earth would have been present on every previously created world. If the Adam and Eve of this world were created just like the First Father and First Mother on all the previous worlds, that would mean every other world in creation would have encountered this problem.

That means that every other world would have had to have fallen before the children of the First Father and First Mother on that world could become mortal and die in order to move forward to exaltation. That would also mean that Kolob would have had to have fallen as well. But Kolob did not fall. If Kolob did it right the first time so that it did not fall, then why didn't all the new Gods starting their own world follow the example and template of Kolob so they could get it right the first time?

There seems to be something lacking from this structure of the universe. Why give conflicting commands to make the planet fall? Why create a new plan of salvation every time you make a new planet? If Kolob is the template, and Kolob is the first, and Kolob did it right the first time and never fell; why not do what the God who made Kolob did? It would solve so many problems.

Again, I am not a God. I am not even a Mormon, but I can figure this out without being exalted. Why can't the Gods figure this one out on their own?

Now into this universe created by the founding fathers of the Mormon Church we find Jesus; but this Jesus is nothing like the Jesus the Bible teaches us. He does not die for our sins. We are responsible for our own sins. We must atone for our own sins by shedding our own blood. But if we are sinful; then how can our blood qualify legally as a sacrifice for sin? It can't. Again, it's obvious that someone really did not think this through.

The God of the Bible's Plan makes sense. It is carefully thought out. It is logical. It builds on the structure of the universe that actually exists. The Plan of Salvation fits perfectly with our world and our structure because the same God made them. God the Father, Jesus the Son and God the Holy Spirit designed, implemented and created our universe and our world. It was a package deal. God the Father, God the Son and God the Holy Spirit created the Plan of Salvation, and each detail of how it would work before God the Father said, *"Let there be light."* The Plan of Salvation and our universe are compatible.

There is physical evidence that God has provided of His existence through prophecies that He makes and that come true. He gave us three physical, historical events that we can point to in history and say, "This is God fulfilling His part of the contract."

So with the Mormon Universe presented and discussed, we can now move on, and examine the Jesus of the Mormon Church, and see if this Jesus is the true Jesus, or is He nothing more than another lie and deception?

CHAPTER TEN

"WHICH JESUS?"
PART TWO

L et me begin this chapter with an important observation. There will be those who honestly believe that they are saved and that they are serving Jesus Christ; but when it comes time for the Day of Judgment, they will have the frightening realization that they missed what the Bible was teaching completely, and that they are heading for Hell. This is why this book is entitled Damned Deceptions. Look at what Jesus tells people. Matthew 7:21–23:

"Not every one who says unto me, 'Lord, Lord,' shall enter into the kingdom of Heaven; but he who does the Will of my Father who is in Heaven.

"Many will say to me in that day, 'Lord, Lord, have we not prophesied in your name? And in your name have cast out devils? And in your name done many wonderful works?'

And then will I profess unto them, 'I never knew you: depart from me, you who work iniquity.'"

There are some important things to realize from these verses. Some will suggest that this is about working your way to Heaven. As we saw in the last chapter, we are saved by faith. We receive grace. God's salvation is a free gift that He offers and we accept. It is not something we work for. It is not a payment that God gives us. It is not something we are worthy of or deserve. Keep that thought in mind here. It will help you to understand what Jesus is telling us here.

How can it be possible for people to call Jesus Lord and not get saved? The Scriptures clearly state in Romans 10:13:

"For whosoever shall call upon the name of the Lord shall be saved."

That *whosoever* is an all-inclusive term. It offers salvation to everyone and anyone. Jesus put it this way in John 6:37:

"All that the Father gives me shall come to me; and he who comes to me I will in no wise cast out."

So there are some protections, promises and guarantees in place for the believer. If you call upon Jesus, He will save you. No matter who you are, or what you have done; Jesus will never turn you away. So how can we find people who did things in Jesus' name; but He did not save them?

I would just go back to the contract and the Plan of Salvation as it was first presented in the Book of Job. Job 33:27–28:

"[God] looks upon men, and if any say, 'I have sinned, and perverted that which was right, and it [did not profit me];

[God] will deliver his soul from going into the pit [Hell], and his life shall see the light."

Salvation is a simple two-step process. You confess your sins to God. And then you repent of those sins. You want to stop sinning. You want to change.

So how is God going to make this work? Job 33:22–24:

"Yea, his soul draws near unto the grave, and his life to the destroyers.

"If there be a messenger with him, an interpreter, one among a thousand, to show unto man [God's] uprightness:

"Then [God] is gracious unto him, and says, 'Deliver him from going down to the pit: I have found a ransom.'"

When we come before God at the end of our life, if there is someone with us to represent us before God—this is what a messenger or interpreter can be [someone to interpret the Law on our behalf (an attorney, if you will)]; then God is able to deal with us based upon grace. This person who has come with us would be Jesus; and He has become our ransom. He will pay to redeem us.

Now there are some key points we need to focus on here. If we confess our sins, but do not repent of our sins; then we are not saved. A lot of people are even proud of their sins and will brag about them. But we must confess. We must admit that we have committed sins. Then we must be willing to let God change us so that we stop sinning or that we sin less than we did before.

When we come before God, we have asked Jesus to be our Savior, and He will come with us before God and represent us before God.

Now here are some possible scenarios for why Jesus does not know us. The first is that we may not believe that we have sin in our life. The Latter Day Church does not recognize original sin, and so original sin is never dealt with. The Latter Day Church teaches that we must atone for [pay for] our own sins by shedding our blood. In other words, we are rejecting the legal procedure that God is offering us.

If you accept a different Jesus other than the Jesus of the Bible; then Jesus will not know who you are. In this scenario, you have created a fictional person that does not exist. You have trusted this fictional person to do what you want, the way that you think it should be handled. If you are wrong, you will go to Hell.

Remember our discussion of how the Bible is a legally-binding contract between God and mankind? We have even identified it as an insurance policy. Here's the truth about insurance policies. First of all, you must purchase it from either an agent of or from the actual insurance company. If you do, then the insurance company will provide the forms and outline how the policy works, what is covered, and how you obtain this coverage.

Now in the world of insurance, this would mean that you pay a premium to the agent/insurance company. The agent/insurance company would enter into a written agreement with you, and issue a physical insurance policy signed by the insurance company. This is how you know that you are covered.

Now I worked as part of the Special Investigation Unit dealing with various kinds of insurance fraud. One kind of insurance fraud is when the person you meet with lies to you. They claim to be an insurance agent for a specific insurance company; and they are not. They have fake documents that look like the real thing. But they are not authorized by that insurance company to sell policies. The agent has no authority to represent the insurance company. He takes your money, but never sends it to the insurance company, and he gives you a bogus paper that will not protect you.

Another form of insurance fraud deals with fake insurance companies. Many times these companies have their main office *"off shore"* on some island. You think that they are a real insurance company; but they are not. In order for an insurance company to be a real insurance company, they must file an application with the Department of Insurance in your state, and the Department of Insurance approves that company to issue specific kinds of insurance policies.

Even there you might get taken in. If an insurance company starts to sell you workers' compensation insurance, but the Department of Insurance has not approved them to sell workers' compensation insurance policies; you might be making payments, and your forms may look like the real deal; but you are giving your money to a company that cannot protect you.

This is why God administers His insurance policy personally. He writes everything down in His Bible. He lays out how you can be protected from sin [see above]. God makes several promises as to how He will deal with sin in your life. There are physical historic events that have taken place: the Virgin Birth of God into the human race, the death of Jesus on the cross; and the Resurrection of Jesus from the grave in the same body He died in is God's proof that God can save you.

Now, fortunately, the premium we would normally pay for coverage is not physical. It is not financial. It is an act of faith once we have accepted the terms of the contract and asked God to cover us.

If you have a fake insurance agent who is not giving you a real insurance policy; too bad/so sad—you are not covered. If you are going to a Church that offers to cover you and they are not authorized by God to make these kinds of promises on His behalf; too bad/so sad—you are not covered.

God wants to cover you. God WANTS to remove your sin and make you part of His family. But we need to confess our sins. We need to repent of our sins. And we need to accept the offer of Jesus Christ to represent us before God and to be our Savior.

If your policy does not have God—the true God backing it, then you are dealing with a fake insurance company. If your policy uses a different Jesus and denies the Jesus of the Bible, you have a fake policy and you are not covered. If your policy requires you to work to be saved, or pay to be saved or to use anything other than faith to activate the insurance policy; you have a fake insurance policy. You are not covered.

This is how you find yourself standing before God and waving a fake insurance policy in front of Jesus. You have his business card. You know His name; but you have never actually conducted any business with this Jesus. You fell for the fakes. You got scammed in the fraud. You are not covered; and Jesus will say, "I'm sorry. I don't know who you are. You were never one of my clients. Go away, I can't help you."

This was a very harsh lesson I had to learn when I started working in the insurance industry. Everything is controlled by the insurance policy. Everything has to be in writing. Everything has to be signed by the insurance company. If you buy a fake policy, or if you alter your insurance policy; it becomes null and void. It is not worth the paper it is written on.

So with this concept clearly in place, let us look at the Pre-Mortal State of Jesus per the Latter Day Church. Let's look at the transition of how Jesus became mortal and entered the human race; and then what kind of insurance policy do you have. What does it cover? How does it work? Is it authorized by the Bible to cover you?

***

We have discussed the Mormon concept of the Pre-Mortal Estate. According to Mormon Theology, each person existed in a Pre-Mortal estate as a soul. These souls were the by-product of the God of a specific world having sexual relations with a celestial wife. According to Mormon Theology, both Jesus and Lucifer were equals and both were created this way.

According to official Mormon teaching, Jesus Christ was *"begotten"* as the first spirit-child of the Father (Elohim) and one of his unnamed wives (often referred to as "Heavenly Mother"). Jesus, as a spirit-son, then progressed in the spirit world until He became a God. [Robert M. Bowman, *"How Mormons Are Defending Mormon Doctrine,* Christian Research Journal, Fall 1989, page 24]

There is confusion in the Mormon Theology concerning the Pre-Mortal Jesus. Some sources claim that He is Jesus; however, another Mormon source moves Jesus up to the level of Godhood in His Pre-Mortal State.

"Prior to his incarnation, Jesus was the Jehovah of the Old Testament." [*The Holy Bible, The Authorized King James Version with Explanatory Notes and Cross References to the Standard Works of The Church of Jesus Christ of Latter-Day Saints*, Salt Lake City Utah, The Church of Jesus Christ of Latter-Day Saints, 1990] "Jehovah is the premortal Jesus Christ and came to earth being born of Mary."

We will have a more extensive discussion on this part of the Mormon Theology later on.

"As for the Devil and his fellow spirits, they are brothers to man and also to Jesus and sons and daughters of God in the same sense that we are." [John Henry Evans, *An American Prophet,* Macmillan, 1933 page 241] This places Jesus on the same level as Lucifer.

Now before we go further on this topic, we need to clearly understand that there are two classifications of *"sons of God"* in the Bible. There is the only begotten Son of God. John 3:16:

"For God so loved the world that He gave His *only begotten* Son that whosoever believes in Him should not perish but have everlasting life." [Emphasis added]

The only begotten Son of God is God the Son. He is divine. He is God. Like begets like, and so since God the Father begot Jesus the Son, Jesus is also God.

There is, however, a lesser rank in the heavenly hosts below God. They are not God. They are not divine. But they were created directly by God; therefore, this group of created beings shares the title, "*Sons of God*" in the plural. This is not the same as the Begotten Son of God.

We see in the opening chapter of the Book of Job that there were certain ranks of angelic hosts who were referred to as "the sons of God." Job 1:6:

"Now there was a day when *the sons of God* came to present themselves before the Lord, and Satan came also among them." [Emphasis added]

If we do not take the time to study the Scriptures, then this verse might mislead us into thinking that both Jesus and Lucifer [Satan] were equal in bearing the title, "*the sons of God*." But a closer look reveals several things. In the Hebrew, the word for "*sons*" can refer to a son or grandson related by birth; but it can also refer to a member of a group. This reference is to the sons of God. So we are not specifically speaking of a genetic family relationship here where the sons of God were actually begotten by God. John 3:16 makes it clear that there is only one person to bear the title of the begotten Son of God. That person is Jesus.

We see in Genesis that there was a group of angels who also bore the title of the sons of God. Genesis 6:2:

"That *the sons of God* saw the daughters of men that they were fair; and they took them wives of all which they chose." [Emphasis added]

In this verse, the word used for "*sons*" still has the same applications and besides being related by birth, it can refer to a group or order.

Now John and Paul gives us insight into this group called the "*sons of God*." In the Old Testament, it appears to be a title for angelic beings. Some sources suggest that the sons of God are the same position as the "*Watchers*" mentioned in Daniel 4:13:

"I saw in the visions of my head upon my bed, and, behold, *a watcher* and a holy one came down from heaven;" [Emphasis added]

These Watchers had the task of watching over the earth and the human race. This would explain the response of Satan when God asked him where he had been. Job 1:7:

"And the Lord said unto Satan, '[Where are you coming from?]' Then Satan answered the Lord and said, 'From going to and fro in the earth, and from walking up and down in it.'"

This would be the job description of a Watcher, or of the sons of God. They were to patrol the earth, and keep watch over the human race.

Chuck Missler explains it this way. These *"sons of God"* are considered sons because they were directly created by God. Notice that they were created, not begotten. Consider the difference between your son and a bookcase you built. You made both of them, but how you made them is very different. What the end result is, is also very different. The son you begot is like you. He is alive. He is human as you are human. Like begets like. The bookcase you made is not like you. It is made of something else. It is something else.

When Luke gave the genealogy of Jesus in Luke 3:38, Luke identifies Adam as a son of God:

"Which was the son of Enos, which was the son of Seth, which was the son of Adam, which was *the son of God*." [Emphasis added]

Adam was directly created by God, just as the angelic hosts were directly created by God. However, the human race does not bear the title of *"sons of God."* We are called, the *"sons of Adam."* This is because we were created through Adam, and not directly by God. Our physical beings were begotten by Adam and his descendants. Again, like begets like.

Now John reveals that God is replacing the *"sons of God"*— that rank of angelic beings. John 1:12:

"But as many as received Him [Jesus], to them [He gave] power to become the *sons of God*, even to those who believe on His name…" [Emphasis added]

What is happening here is that our physical bodies were begotten by Adam and his descendants. But the souls within us are created by God. God brings them to life. This is how we are born again. Since God gave life to our souls, Christians are now created directly by God and deserve the title "*sons of God.*" We are still created. We are not begotten. Only Jesus is begotten. But through Jesus, we are adopted into God's family. This is not something God did with the angelic hosts.

Paul puts it this way in Romans 8:4:

"For as many as are led by the Spirit of God, they are *the sons of God*." [Emphasis added]

John also adds in I John 3:1–2:

"Behold, what manner of love the Father has bestowed upon us, that we should be called *the sons of God*: therefore the world knows us not, because it knew Him not.

"Beloved, now are we *the sons of God*, and it does not yet appear what we shall be: but we know that, when He shall appear, we shall be like Him; for we shall see Him as He is." [Emphasis added]

At this time, once we have accepted Jesus as our Savior, we are the sons of God. This is a position of power. God has brought our spirits within us to life. God has directly given us this eternal life. It is based upon adoption into the family of God. And we are in a transformation as we go through this life. We will transform from what we currently are into something so much more as we will eventually be given spirit bodies identical to the resurrected Jesus. Paul gives us some additional insight into this transformation. I Corinthians 6:3:

"Know you not that we shall judge angels? How much more [will we be able to judge the] things that pertain to this life?"

As we pass from this world into the next, our status—both physically and politically shall be above the angels. We will replace this class of angels referred to as the sons of God. We will rule over angels, and even judge angels.

In the Garden, God made the declaration to the serpent [Satan]: "I will put hostility between you and the woman…" [Genesis 3:15]. Satan knew that this Seed of the Woman would defeat Him and undo all that He had done. He also knew that the human race he was trying to destroy would replace Him in his position as a son of God.

So the reference to Satan [Lucifer] as a son of God does not elevate him to the same level as the Only Begotten Son of God. That title is for Jesus and Jesus alone.

However, in the Mormon Theology, Jesus is demoted from God the Son to "*a son of God*." He drops from being the Creator to becoming part of creation. This teaching ignores the teaching of the Bible. John 1:1–3:

"In the beginning was the Word, and the Word was with God, and the Word was God.

"The same was in the beginning with God.

"*All things were made by Him and without Him was not anything made that was made.*" [Emphasis added]

John identifies this Word as being Jesus who is born into the human race. John 1:14:

"And the Word was made flesh and lived among us, (and we beheld His glory, the glory as of *the only begotten of the Father*), full of grace and truth." [Emphasis added]

Again, John makes it clear that Jesus is the only one who is begotten of the Father. Jesus is the begotten Son of God. As such, He is equal to God, and with God. Like begets like. If God begot Jesus, Jesus is the same as God the Father.

Paul notes this in Colossians 1:16:

"For *by Him were all things created*, that are *in heaven*, and that are in earth, visible and *invisible*, whether they are thrones, or *dominions, or principalities, or powers: all things were created by Him*, and for Him:" [Emphasis added]

Notice that Jesus created all things. Paul specifically notes that Jesus created all the things in Heaven. That would include Satan and all the angels. The angels are created beings. Jesus is not created—He is begotten. This places Him above all created beings. He is the Creator. There is no way that He and Lucifer can be equal in the Pre-Mortal world [if such a world even exists]. Even though one is called a son of God, and the other is the Son of God [God the Son]; Lucifer and Jesus are not brothers.

***

The Latter Day Church produces its own edition of the King James Bible. They have edited it with commentary and footnotes to help their believers keep track of their truth should they take the time to read it. I mentioned previously a certain footnote from their publication.

"Prior to his incarnation, Jesus was the Jehovah of the Old Testament." [*The Holy Bible, The Authorized King James Version with Explanatory Notes and Cross References to the Standard Works of The Church of Jesus Christ of Latter-Day Saints*, Salt Lake City Utah, The Church of Jesus Christ of Latter-Day Saints, 1990] "Jehovah is the premortal Jesus Christ and came to earth being born of Mary."

Now let me take a moment to discuss the name Jehovah. This will also have an application with the Jehovah's Witnesses. As I noted at the beginning of this discussion on the Mormon Theology, there were several names and titles used for God in the Old Testament. There was the name Elohem [Elohim in Mormon translations]. Keep in mind that we are taking a word in a completely different alphabet and transferring it phonetically into English. This will result in a variation of spellings depending on who is doing the converting.

This word is actually evidence of the Trinity. In the Hebrew, there is a Hebrew word for a single God. That would be "*El.*" There is another Hebrew word referring to a duality of God— two Gods. It was so rare that even their High Priest and the Tribe of Levi did not recognize it when Jesus used it upon the cross. If anyone should have known their Hebrew, it should have been them. However, they did not recognize it because it does not appear in the Hebrew text. Matthew 27:46:

"And about the ninth hour Jesus cried with a loud voice, saying, '*Eli, Eli*, lama sabachthani?' that is to say, 'My God, my God, why have You forsaken me?'" [Emphasis added]

When Jesus called this out, those around the cross were sure that He was calling for Elijah [Eli]. They were wrong. Jesus was calling out to God. However, Jesus is the only human who could have used this variation of the title for God correctly. It is God as a duality—two Gods. Jesus was calling out to God the Father, and He was calling out to God the Holy Spirit as He hung on the cross. This is why He did not use "*El*" to call out to God. There is a reason that He did not use "*Elohem*" (more on this in a moment).

Jesus was the third member of the Trinity, and He was calling out to the other two members of the Trinity when He was on the cross. He cried twice—"My God, my God"—because He was calling out to the other two members of the Trinity.

Now I had mentioned the Hebrew word, Elohem. In the Hebrew, you make a single word into a plural form of the word by adding "*Hem*" to the word the same way we add an "*S*" to the end of the word in English. The example would be a reference to an angelic being: *seraph*. If we are talking of multiple angelic beings, we use the form "*seraphim*." (Again the use of an "i" versus and "e" is a choice by whoever is converting from Hebrew letters to English alphabet.) This title for God is first used in Genesis 1:1:

"In the beginning God [*Elohem*] created the heavens and the earth."

Time for a little grammar here. The name "*Elohem*" is for three or more Gods. It is used throughout the Bible to refer to God, but it is always used with the singular verb. Example: God is one versus Gods are one. To do this correctly means that these three Gods are somehow joined in such a way that they are still only one God. This would be the Trinity.

***

Now I hate to interrupt this train of thought at this point, but I really feel that I must. When Joseph Smith spoke of the creation of the world, he spoke of a Council of Gods. The term, Elohem, is not referring to a Council of Gods. It is not referring to multiple different Gods. It is speaking of three Gods who are joined in such a way that They are one. It is used with a singular verb so this is a reference to the Trinity.

Also, in Genesis 1:1 we have the statement: "In the beginning God [*Elohem*] created ["*bara*"] the heavens and the earth."

I've discussed in a previous chapter how Joseph Smith made a major point of pulling up the word "bara" from this verse, but giving it a completely different definition. As noted, the Hebrew word, "bara" means, "to call forth out of nothing." This teaches that when God made the heavens and the earth, He did not use pre-existing material—as Joseph Smith claims. God started with nothing, and He called forth matter. He made the matter that He used to create the Heavens and the earth. This was to ensure that God was the sole Creator, and that God has sole jurisdiction over His Creation.

Joseph Smith alters this definition. He insists that "*he is wise*," and he insists that "*bara*" means "*to call forth*" as in calling together the Council of Gods who will make the earth. He points to "*Elohem*" and its multiple Gods meaning, and misrepresents the meaning of "*bara*" and limits it to just "*to call forth*." This is how he translated Genesis 1:1 into "*calling forth Gods*" as in a Council of God.

As I noted, someone trained and versed in the Bible coached him in his doctrines and arguments. But, although they understood the meaning of the words, they missed the grammar. Pay attention to who is performing the action of calling, and to what is being called. "*Elohem*" is doing the calling. "*Elohem*" is calling the heavens and the earth. "*Elohem*" is used with a singular verb. When you put the proper grammar back into the verse, the meaning is clear. "The Trinity called the heavens and earth forth out of nothing."

Joseph Smith insists that an old Hebrew translator got the word wrong, and he is setting the record straight. He is the one getting the word wrong and like so many Biblical terms, he is giving it a new definition to suit his doctrine in order to deceive others.

***

Now let me get back on track here. Another name for God is YHWH. This is the most holy of all names for God. There are no consonants in this word so a Jew will not accidentally speak the word aloud. There is also a ritual involved in writing the word. According to some sources, the writer must bathe, change clothes, use a new quill, and then break the quill after the word is written. It is that holy. [Some other sources may use variations of this ritual; but you get the point. This word is given very special treatment.]

If we were to write this name for God in the Paleo-Hebrew alphabet [the alphabet used by the Children of Israel before the Babylonian Captivity] it would form a pictograph. The Paleo-Hebrew letters were not just sounds, but they represented concepts and images. The YHWH in Paleo-Hebrew are four letters: Yod, Heh, Vav, Heh. Yod can refer to the hand. Heh is a call to look upon or pay attention. Vav is a nail or a peg. Put these four Paleo-Hebrew letters together, and it creates the message: Behold the Hands! Behold the Nails! YHWH is the message of the Messiah who will come and be crucified to save us.

So how did YHWH become Jehovah? Let me give you a little history of the English Language. There was an event called The Great Vowel Shift. It took place from around 1350 AD through the 1600's and, in some cases, the 1700's. It began in the Middle English Period and finished in the Modern English Period. The reason for the shift is still unclear, but the most accepted theory had to do with the Black Death and the quick movement of populations in Europe to avoid the Plague.

As a result, some letters began to change how they were pronounced. Where this is most obvious is in the German language. We see that the "J" now sounds like a "Y" in German. We see the "W" now sounds like a "V" in German. When these words are written, they are written as a "J" or a "V", but in German, they are still pronounced as a "Y" or a "W." If we apply this vowel shift to YHWH, we get JHVH. Those who do not read German would give them the "J" and "V" sounds. With the addition of a few vowels for the Gentiles in the audience, it becomes Jehovah. This is how YHWH came to be Jehovah.

Some Mormon theologians try to suggest that Jehovah and YHWH are separate Gods in their hierarchy; but they are just the Hebrew and the English for the same title. The King James translators used the vowel shift to convert YHWH into Jehovah for the Old Testament. In reality, this would be an inaccurate translation.

There is a third term used to refer to God. This is the term "*Adoni.*" It can more correctly be translated into "*Lord.*" Depending upon the hierarchy of this Lord, it can refer to God or it can refer to a lesser ruler.

Now, with their footnote in their edition of the King James Bible, the Latter Day Church equates Jesus with Jehovah. As YHWH is the more correct translation for Jehovah, the Latter Day Church has just made Jesus—the Pre-Mortal estate of Jesus—to be YHWH.

This would make Jesus a God in His Pre-Mortal Estate. For Christian believers, the Bible does teach that Jesus is God, and so there is no problem with such a translation. For the Latter Day Saints, who insist you must become mortal before you can become a God; this throws a wrench into everything. It contradicts one of their most basic teachings.

***

Now the Mormon Church instructs their followers to not worship Jesus. Although He is the "*Savior*" [more of that in a few moments], he is not God in their theology, and therefore should not be worshiped. This, however contradictions the teaching and practices of the Bible. They also teach that we should not pray to Jesus. [McConkie, *Mormon Doctrine,* page 587]

***

I am going to offer evidence to refute these teachings of the Latter Day Church in a minute, but before I do, I want to discuss something that has become so obvious I am surprised no one has asked this question before. If the Jesus—the real Jesus—is exactly as the Mormons describe Him; then I have to ask, "What good is He?" In other words, "Why did Jesus come and die on the cross for us?" According to the Mormon theologians, His death on the cross did not address sin. It does not even address inherited sin—i.e. the original sin of Adam and Eve—because Mormon theologians teach that eating the forbidden fruit was not a sin.

If you want to attain your way to Godhood, then it is all upon you. You have to obey and do everything in your Pre-Mortal Estate. You have to obey and do everything in your mortal state. You have to obey and do everything in your Post-Mortal state. It's all about you. According to Mormon Theology, all that the death of Jesus did was to secure the resurrection of your physical body into the Post-Mortal estate. But there are three Kingdoms in the Post-Moral world, and Jesus has nothing to do with which one you end up in. You are responsible for where you end up. As the Math of the Cults states: "They subtract from Jesus." In this case, they have subtracted so much from Jesus that He serves no importance, and makes no difference in the world. Therefore, if this is who Jesus truly is; then I have to ask from a legal standpoint: "Why Jesus?" "What good is He?"

If all He did was ensure that there would be a resurrection of our physical bodies into the afterlife, and there is no sin involved with this; then what would hinder us from resurrecting without Him? Especially when all the other worlds created before our world was created had this same resurrection available to all of its inhabitants. It should have been possible to remove Jesus completely from the equation and still achieve the same result. The Latter Day Church has subtracted so much from Jesus that there is no need for Him at all.

Consider this: if our world is only one of countless worlds that came before ours; then doesn't logic suggest that someone on one of those other worlds would have created the perfect Plan of Salvation? If they did; then why are the Gods not using it on all the new worlds? Why are the Gods reinventing the wheel each time? It makes no sense. If these Gods that Joseph Smith keeps referring to and claims to hear; made our world, then are they not intelligent enough to see which Plan of Salvation did the best job—because it seems everyone else in the afterlife is following this plan—and just use it in each new world.

***

Now, what does the Bible tell us about Jehovah [YHWH] and Jesus? Here's a little clue that the translators of the King James Bible slipped in. There were some places where they used the word Jehovah. But if they were dealing with YHWH, they translated this word as "LORD" with all capital letters. When you see "LORD," it is a reference to YHWH.

There are many references in the Old Testament to worshiping and praising Jehovah:

1. Deuteronomy 4:7;
2. 2 Chronicles 7:14;
3. Psalm 5:2;
4. Psalm 32:6; and
5. Jeremiah 29:7, 12

But let me use one reference that is very specific: Psalm 7:17:

"I will praise the LORD according to His righteousness: and will sing praise to the name of the LORD most high."

Now the Strong's Exhaustive Concordance translates "*LORD*" in these cases as "*Jehovah*" but the reference in the Strong's Exhaustive Concordance is to the Hebrew word "*YHWH*." So both of these names for God are connected to this "*LORD*."

The Psalmist called for the people to praise this "*LORD*" [Jehovah/YHWH], and that they were to sing praise to the name of this "*LORD*" [Jehovah/YHWH]. Based on this, I can declare that the Old Testament does specifically instruct us to worship and praise Jehovah.

Now in this case, both the Biblical and the Mormon Theology are calling upon us to worship and praise Jesus. Mormon Theology, combined with this verse, calls for us to worship and praise Jesus. This would be based upon their own information about who Jesus was in His Pre-Mortal Estate. Therefore, what is the basis for Mormon theologians to tell people not to worship and praise Jesus? It contradicts this teaching.

There are accounts in the New Testament where Jesus [who is Jehovah/YHWH] in physical form was praised and worshiped, and He accepted the praise and worship.

1. A leper worshiped Him (Matthew 8:2);
2. A ruler bowed before Him in worship (Matthew 9:18);
3. A blind man worshiped Him (John 9:38);
4. A woman worshiped Him (Matthew 15:25);
5. Mary Magdalene worshiped Him (Matthew 28:9);
6. The disciples worshiped Him (Matthew 28:17).

We even find evidence that the Post-Mortal Jesus is to be praised and worshiped. Revelation 4:10–11:

"The twenty-four elders fall down before Him who sat on the throne, and worshiped Him who lives for ever and ever, and cast their crowns before the throne, saying, 'You are worthy, O Lord, to receive glory and honor and power: for You have created all things, and for Your pleasure they are and were created.'"

Also in Revelation 5:11–14:

"And I beheld, and I heard the voice of many angels round about the throne and the beasts and the elders: and the number of them was ten thousand times ten thousand, and thousands of thousands saying with a loud voice, 'Worthy is the Lamb that was slain to receive power, and riches, and wisdom, and strength, and honor, and glory, and blessing.' And every creature which is in heaven, and on the earth, and under the earth, and such as are in the sea, and all that are in them, [I heard them] saying, 'Blessing, and honor, and glory, and power, be unto Him who sits upon the throne, and unto the Lamb forever and ever.' And the four beasts said, 'Amen.' And the twenty-four elders fell down and worshipped Him that lives forever and ever."

So the Bible makes it clear that this Jehovah [YHWH] and that this Jesus is to be praised and worshiped. There is evidence before Jesus was born into this world. There is evidence of this while He was in this world. And there is evidence of this after

He left this world. There is no instruction from the Bible to not worship or give praise to Jesus. To the contrary, there is specific instruction from Jesus and through His Disciples that we are to pray to Jesus or to ask things of the Father in His name. John 16:23:

"And in that day you shall ask me nothing. Verily, verily, I say unto you, Whatsoever you shall ask the Father in my name, He will give it you."

We are told to call upon Jesus in order to be saved. Romans 10:13:

"For whosoever shall call upon the name of the Lord shall be saved."

***

There is a problem with this concept of Jesus being Jehovah in His Pre-Mortal state. Jehovah is clearly identified as a God in the Old Testament in Mormon Theology. He is deserving of worship. He is deserving of praise—even though the Mormon theologians try to block this worship and praise to Him. His title, Jehovah, is used interchangeably throughout the Old Testament with Elohem and God.

This creates a serious problem for Mormon Theology, because if Jehovah is Jesus in His Pre-Mortal state, and Jehovah is clearly a God per the Old Testament use of His name; that would mean that Jesus was a God in His Pre-Mortal state. Mormon Theology teaches that it is impossible to achieve Godhood prior to obtaining a physical body or without getting married.

""In the pre-existence we dwelt in the presence of God our Father. When the time arrived for us to be advanced in the scale of our existence and pass through this mundane probation, councils were held and the spirit children were instructed in matters pertaining to conditions in mortal life, and the reason for such an existence. In the former life we were spirits. In order that we should advance and eventually gain the goal of perfection, it was made known that we would receive tabernacles of flesh and bones and have to pass through mortality where we would be tried and proved to see if we, by trial, would prepare ourselves for exaltation. We were made to realize, in the presence of our glorious Father, who had a tangible body of flesh and bones which shone like the sun, that we were, as spirits, far inferior in our station to him" (Joseph Fielding Smith, *Doctrines of Salvation,* 1:57)."

The reference to *"exaltation"* is the Latter Day Church terminology for achieving Godhood. In the Pre-Mortal state [pre-existence], as noted, we begin this process of moving toward an exalted estate in the Pre-Mortal world. The mortal world becomes the actual testing to see if we are worthy of exaltation [Godhood]. The Post-Mortal world is where we complete the process, and achieve exaltation because we are worthy.

"Under such conditions it was natural for our Father to discern and choose those who were most worthy and evaluate the talents of each individual. He knew not only what each of us *could* do, but what each of us *would* do when put to the test and when responsibility was given us. Then, when the time came for our habitation on mortal earth, all things were prepared and the servants of the Lord chosen and ordained to their respective missions" (Joseph Fielding Smith, *The Way to Perfection,* 50–51).

So if Jesus is Jehovah [YHWH] in His Pre-Mortal state, and documents teach that Jehovah [YHWH] is a God, how did this happen if Jesus had not yet been born into the mortal world with a flesh and bone body?

Per Mormon Theology, there is no way that Jesus could have been a God in His Pre-Mortal state. This teaching of the Latter Day Church contradicts its own teaching for other Pre-Mortal souls.

***

We now want to take a few minutes and discuss the process whereby the Pre-Mortal Jesus became mortal and received a body of flesh and bones. In the Christian Church, this is referred to as the Virgin Birth. The technical name is the Incarnation—God becoming flesh.

Let's examine the first promise God made to send a Messiah to save the human race from sin and death. Genesis 3:15:

"And I will put enmity between you and the woman, and between your seed and her seed; it shall bruise your head, and you shall bruise His heel."

There are some things that we need to be aware of here. Although God is speaking to the serpent, God is speaking to the power behind the serpent. The serpent was only a pawn used by Satan. So this is a discussion of Eve and Satan. There is going to be hostility between Satan and the woman. God is revealing to Satan that this Seed of the Woman is going to defeat Satan and undo all of his work and efforts to destroy the human race. So this is the first thing we need to point out.

The second thing is regarding the seeds. The seed of the serpent, or the seeds that Satan gave life to, were sin and death. With the eating of the forbidden fruit, sin entered the world. Adam and Eve came to understand right from wrong. They experienced wrong first-hand, and committed a sin in order to understand from experience the difference between right and wrong.

Would Adam and Eve have ever understood right from wrong without committing wrong? Yes, they would. Otherwise, God would have placed them in a no-win scenario. The decision-making process reveals both good and evil through experiencing one or the other. If Adam and Eve would have chosen not to eat the fruit, they would have obtained an understanding of good [right] by experience. They chose to do right. At that point, they would have understood evil without having to commit evil. But Adam and Eve chose to do wrong, and not only did they understand evil [wrong], they now understood the concept of good [right], and were required to choose good from that point on.

The Temptation would teach Adam and Eve the difference between right and wrong—good and evil—no matter which decision they made. It is just unfortunate that they made the wrong decision.

211

Up to this point, Adam and Eve had continually done what was right: they did not eat the fruit. But this is not the same thing as temptation. They did not eat the fruit because they did not desire the fruit. The discussion with the serpent changed that. Notice that after speaking with the serpent, Eve saw the fruit was desirable. Now desire was involved. Now there was temptation. Now it became a test of their character. Would the spiritual side prevail or would the flesh prevail? This is why the tree was the tree of knowledge [personal experience] and it was knowledge of both right and wrong—good and evil. You could learn—obtain that knowledge—of both from a single experience.

Doing what was wrong created sin. It made Adam and Eve sinners. They had failed to keep God's commandment. They had missed the mark of perfection that God has set for them.

The second thing that was created that day, and which entered the world, was death. "In the day that you eat of it, you shall surely die." Now the first thing that died was Adam and Eve's spirit. They experienced spiritual death. As of that day, they were separated from God. That is the definition of spiritual death; we are separated from God.

So the seeds of the serpent are sin and death. Now let's discuss this concept of the woman's seed. We need to understand that the Bible clearly teaches that the seed is always from the man. The Bible identifies the *SEED* of Abraham. There is the *SEED* of Isaac. There is the *SEED* of Jacob. Man provides the seed; woman provides the egg. When the seed [sperm] and the egg unite, life is formed in the woman's womb. God did not refer to the *EGG* of the woman. He referred to the *SEED* of the woman. This is something that the female of the species does not have.

Now given the theology of the Latter Day Church, I need to stress this point right here. This passage does not say the *SEED OF GOD*. My need to mention this will become clear in a short while. It is clearly the woman's seed.

So this concept of the Seed of the Woman is a reference to a virgin birth. A woman will give birth without the aid or genetic material of a man/male. The woman will produce the genetic material needed to produce a male embryo on her own. No other genetic material needed to be added.

Now theoretically it is possible for a woman to have a virgin birth. Theoretically, it is possible for a woman to become pregnant on her own without any genetic material from any man. How does this theory work? The woman provides one-half of the set of the chromosomes needed to produce life. The seed [sperm] contains the other half of the set of chromosomes to produce life. When these two partial sets of chromosomes connect and line up, they produce a complete set of chromosomes, and this complete set produces life. It becomes the first cell that grows and splits into the embryo, then the fetus and finally the baby. Also, with this joining of the partial sets of chromosomes, a new soul is created, and this becomes the soul of the baby who will be born.

According to this theory, a woman could release two eggs at the same time. According to this theory, both eggs contain one-half of the set of chromosomes needed to produce life. Given the right set of circumstances, the two eggs join, and both sets of the partial chromosomes join creating a complete set of chromosomes, that produces life; and which can grow into a full-size baby. Again, this is a theory.

There is just one problem with this theory. We are talking about the "X" and "Y" chromosomes. These are the chromosomes that determine male or female babies. The woman, obviously, has the female chromosome. She has it because she is female. The male is the one who must introduce the male chromosomes into the genetic mix. The male has the male chromosome because he is male. Remove the male genetic makeup and there is no way that the baby can be a male. A virgin-birth baby created by two eggs joining in the mother's womb would have to be female.

Here is the problem: God identifies this Seed of the Woman as a male offspring. It is not the seed of the man. It is not the seed of God. It is the seed of woman. Somewhere down the long genetic line leading to the coming Messiah, a woman will generate a seed—a sperm, and that seed will be her seed. It will not be the seed of anyone else. And that seed will somehow have the male chromosome to generate a male child. That is what this prophecy is telling Adam and Eve.

That child will engage the seed of the serpent: sin and death. Sin and death will wound this Seed of the Woman. That wound will not be a fatal wound. Even though sin and death are inflicting the wound upon the Seed of the Woman, they cannot produce a permanent death. Sin will allow the Seed of the Woman to die; but death will not be able to hold Him in the grave. This is implied by the wounding of the heel.

However, this Seed of the Woman will wound the head of both sin and death. Now this is not a fatal wound, either. Sin and death are weakened. They are wounded, but they continue to exist. Those who do not accept Jesus as their Savior will still fall under the power of sin and death. But it is a wound to the head. It will eventually destroy sin and death. When the last person dies without Christ, sin and death can claim him/her. But from that point on, everyone else has accepted Jesus as Savior. Sin and death are completely powerless and are no longer important. It will be as if they had died.

God's Law gave both sin and death power. Romans 6:23:

"For the wages of sin is death…"

Here in the Greek, the word for sin is singular. A single sin has the power to produce death. Death becomes a wage. If there is a single sin in your life, you have earned death. That is the power of sin and death. Adam and Eve died spiritually that day in the Garden; but sin and death continued to infect Adam and Eve until they died physically.

Notice that the wound to the head of sin and death is referred to as a bruise. It does not crush the head. It bruises the head. Why does God describe it like that? God is describing the power of sin and death being broken; but it is not an automatic protection. Remember that we are talking about a contract. For the terms of the contract to apply; then the other party must enter into the agreement. For those who do not enter into this agreement, sin and death still have power. This is why they were only bruised and not crushed. But the ultimate victory will be when all life has passed through death and either continued to die spiritually, or is delivered into spiritual life. At that point, sin and death will have claimed their last victim and have no further power.

Now let us look at three other prophecies relating to the Incarnation of Jesus. Isaiah 7:14:

"Therefore the Lord Himself shall give you a sign; 'Behold, a virgin shall conceive, and bear a son, and shall call his name "Immanuel."'"

There will be those who point to the Hebrew here and claim that "*virgin*" simply refers to a young girl of marrying age. That is true, but not correct. The word is "*almah*." It means: 1) a virgin, young woman, 2) who is of marrying age; and 3) maid or newly married. This creates an even greater restriction on this virgin. She is a young girl of marrying age who is recently married; but is still a virgin. How is that possible? [I will come back to this.]

Now this child shall be a male and shall be identified as "*Immanuel*" ["*Emmanuel*" in the Greek]. Matthew 1:23 gives us the definition for this word, "*Emmanuel*." It means that "*God is with us*." This is not a reference to God being on your side: "God is with us. We can win this battle!" No! It is saying that God will physically come into our world and live among us. God will be here physically with us.

Now this is God who is already God who has come into our world. He is God while He is in this world. This is NOT the Mormon Jesus because the Mormon Jesus cannot be God until after He dies and proves Himself to be worthy. Isaiah 9:6:

"For unto us a child is born, unto us a son is given: and the government shall be upon His shoulder: and His name shall be called Wonderful Counsellor, The Mighty God, The Everlasting Father, The Prince of Peace."

Notice the titles that belong to this child. These are titles that can only belong to God. We can pass over the Wonderful Counselor and the Prince of Peace. They are nice titles, but they could also apply to someone who is not God. But the title of the Mighty God and the Everlasting Father apply to God and only to God. In fact, they apply to God the Father. But remember what Jesus said in John 10:30:

"I and my Father are one."

Again, Jesus is God. He is God the Son. He is equal to God the Father. Now we have one more prophecy to consider. Micah 5:2:

"But you, Bethlehem Ephratah, though you be little among the thousands of Judah, yet out of you shall He come forth unto me [the one] who is to be ruler in Israel; whose goings forth have been from of old, from everlasting."

This is identifying the city of Bethlehem [part of the province of Ephratah] will be where this future King of Israel is to be born. Now the reference to "*going forth*" is speaking of this King and noting this is what He is and has done. He has existed in olden times. In other words, He existed before He was born into Bethlehem. The reference to "*from everlasting*" is an interesting poetic term in Hebrew. It refers us all the way back in time as far as we can go. This would be to the beginning. Then go further. Go back before everything began. Then do the same thing heading into the future. Move your mind as far as you can in the future. Go toward the end of time and then go a little further.

The Palmist used this term to describe God in Psalm 93:2:

"Your throne is established of old: You *are from everlasting*." [Emphasis added]

This person who shall become the King of Israel, and who will be born in Bethlehem will have always existed. He will have no beginning. He will exist forever. He will have no end. He will be God. Notice how Psalm 49:15 put it—just in case there was any doubt:

"But God will redeem my soul from the power of the grave; for He shall receive me. Selah."

Whoever is coming to save us, is coming to redeem our soul from the grave. Whomever that must be, must also be God in order to fulfill this prophecy. This is the Biblical Jesus. He is God. And just like God, He has no beginning and He has no end. As noted in other passages, He created all things.

He was existing before Creation even began—any creation. This would move Him all the way back before Kolob existed in the Mormon Theology. Obviously, this Jesus is not the Jesus taught in Mormon Theology because that Jesus had a beginning and was created after many other worlds and Gods had been created.

***

Now, let me come back to the definition of *"virgin"* in Isaiah 7:14. How can you have a young girl, have her be recently married; and still have her be a virgin and not to have had sex? That is where a Jewish custom called *"betrothal"* comes in. In the Jewish culture—especially with arranged marriages, there is the Betrothal Ceremony. The parents of the bride and groom come together. They draw up the marriage contract. The parties enter into this agreement and in the eyes of the Jewish community; the couple is now married. To break this contract, the man and woman must divorce. It is that binding.

However, during the betrothal period, the bride continues to live with her father's family. The groom is required to go off and prepare a place for them to live. Did you know that the promise Jesus made to His Disciples the night of the Last Supper [John 14:2] was actually part of the marriage contract? "I go to prepare a place for you. And if I go and prepare a place for you, I will come again, and receive you unto myself; that where I am, there you may be also."

Jesus was entering into a marriage contract with His Bride, the Church. He made an oral contract with those who made up the Church prior to His death. The following day, He will pay the dowery to purchase His Bride. That would be His blood shed upon the cross.

In the case of Mary and Joseph, they had entered into the marriage contract. He and Mary were considered married in the eyes of the law. They could have sex and they could move in together without a wedding ceremony. It was frowned upon in the culture. It was improper; but they would still be married, and it would not be considered to be adultery. It would not constitute a sin.

Per this betrothal agreement, Mary would stay with her father's family and he would continue to provide for her. Joseph would go off, and build a house or place where they could move into as part of the Wedding Feast. When the place had been prepared for Mary, Joseph would form a parade with his friends going to Mary's home to claim her as his bride. She was to have friends watching for Joseph to start this wedding procession and be ready when he arrived. They would form a parade back to where the Wedding Feast was to be held, close the door and only those inside would be part of the Wedding Feast. During this Wedding Feast—which normally began on Tuesdays in Jewish cultures and could last up to a week—the Bride and Groom would move in together and have sexual relations.

Again, this betrothal status is as binding as the marriage contract. When Joseph discovered that Mary was pregnant, he was considering *"putting her away privately"* [Matthew 1:19]:

"Then Joseph her husband, being a just man, and not willing to make her a public example, was minded to put her away privately."

I cannot stress enough that this betrothal is as binding as a marriage contract; and is part of the Jewish marriage contract. God needed to wait until after Mary and Joseph were betrothed, but before they came together to consummate their marriage so that this *"Seed of the Woman"* would not be considered a bastard—conceived out of wedlock. If Jesus was conceived/born out of wedlock; He would be barred from entering the Temple, and He would not qualify as the Messiah. This would be a sin upon Him. He had to be sinless to be God's Passover Lamb.

Here is the actual description from the Bible as to how Mary became pregnant. Luke 1:35:

"And the angel answered and said unto her, 'The Holy Ghost [Holy Spirit] shall come upon you, and the power of the Highest shall overshadow you: therefore also that holy thing which shall be born of you shall be called the Son of God.'"

Now pay careful attention to the description. I added the Holy Spirit in brackets. The Christian Church believes that the Holy Spirit and the Holy Ghost are one-in-the-same. The Mormon theologians teach that they are different. So I wanted to deal with that issue right away. The Holy Spirit comes UPON Mary. He does not come into Mary. The Holy Spirit is a spirit. He comes upon her the way the Holy Spirit came upon people throughout the Old Testament. Even though Mary was blessed and chosen to give birth to the Messiah, there was still sin in her, and sin was still an unresolved issue. Therefore the Holy Spirit could not come into her or inside of her. He came upon—like a robe or garment covering her. If you need a visual illustration, consider the Holy Spirit being a spotlight, and Mary steps into the spotlight. It may have been like that.

It was not God that overshadowed her. [Mormon theologians use this description of God overshadowing her to suggest God having sex with her. So I need to keep the process very clear here in Biblical terms.] It was the POWER of God. There is a difference. [Again, every word, every phrase and every provision must be accounted for] The Holy Spirit gives us access to the power of God. The Holy Spirit, by coming upon her was able to give her the power to produce a male seed out of her own genetic make up. Nothing was placed into her. If something was placed in her, it invalidates the prophecy. The Holy Spirit transformed what was already in her—her own genetic material. That transformation created a male sperm—the Seed of the Woman.

The point that needs to be stressed is that Mary's womb became a self-contained reproducive system. It had everything it needed within her and of her. Nothing was added from outside of her and her womb. When the Power of God worked within her, it was taking what was already there. Nothing outside was added. It had to be Mary's seed, and it had to be Mary's egg in order for the prophecy to be fulfilled as it was given back in Genesis 3:15.

Now Mary's own genetic material was compatible and would join with one of her eggs and produce the Messiah.

Again, it is the seed of Mary. It was not the seed of man. It was not the seed of God. It was not the seed of the Holy Spirit. Any of those scenarios would have invalidated the prophecy, and disqualified Jesus as the Seed of the Woman.

Now you know the Biblical account of the incarnation. Let's look at what the Latter Day Church teaches on this subject.

***

As we begin our discussion into the Mormon Theology regarding the birth of Jesus, we need to discuss the nature of God. When Jesus met the woman at the well, she asked Him about the worship of God. John 4:24:

"'God is a Spirit: and they who worship Him must worship Him in spirit and in truth.'"

Now whether we accept the teaching of the Latter Day Church that Jesus was Jehovah in His Pre-Mortal state, or if we adhere to the Biblical teaching that Jesus is God and existed in Heaven prior to His birth in Jerusalem; we must both accept the conclusion that Jesus knew what God was like since He had been with God before His birth. Therefore, if anyone were an actual eyewitness to God; it would be Jesus. John 1:18:

"No man has seen God at any time; the only begotten Son, who is in the bosom of the Father, He has declared [revealed] Him."

Luke 10:22:

"'All things are delivered to me [by] my Father: and no man knows who the Son is, but the Father; and who the Father is, but the Son, and He to whom the Son will reveal Him.'"

Jesus declared that He knew who God the Father was. He is the only one who knows who God the Father is. He knows this from first-hand experience. So if Jesus tells us that God the Father is a spirit; then Jesus is the only one who would know the truth of that statement.

Now Doctrine and Covenants Section 130 identifies the source of the information in this section. It states: "Items of instruction given by Joseph Smith the Prophet, at Ramus,

Illinois, April 2, 1843." At verse 22, Joseph Smith, acting as a prophet of God, makes this declaration:

"The Father has a body of flesh and bones as tangible as man's; the Son also; but the Holy Ghost has not a body of flesh and bones, but is a personage of Spirit. Were it not so, the Holy Ghost could not dwell in us."

Mormon Theology has God beginning in a Pre-Mortal state on some other world. Per Mormon Theology, the God of our world lived as a mortal in a physical body on some other world, and proved Himself to be worthy of Godhood. After His death, per Mormon Theology, the God of this world was resurrected into the Celestial Kingdom. Mormon Theology teaches that the God of our world has a physical body of flesh and bones [Doctrine and Covenant 130:22]. To support this teaching, which clearly contradicts the teaching of Jesus who is an eyewitness of God, they cite several Bible verses that speak of physical parts of a body belonging to God.

1. Isaiah 5:25: "Therefore is the anger of the Lord kindled against His people, and He has stretched forth His hand against them…" The Latter Day Church holds that this verse proves that God has a physical hand.
2. Psalm 33:18: "Behold, the eye of the Lord is upon those who fear Him, upon those who hope in His mercy;" The Latter Day Church holds that this verse teaches that God has physical eyes.
3. Psalm 89:13: (Speaking of God) "You have a mighty arm: strong is your hand, and high is your right hand" The Latter Day Church teaches that this verse proves that God has an arm and a hand. In fact, it suggests two hands as this verse identifies God's right hand specifically. This would mean that God has more than one hand.
4. Psalm 18:8 (Speaking of God): "There went up a smoke out of His nostrils, and fire out of His mouth devoured: coals were kindled by it." The Latter Day Church uses this verse to teach that God has a face and that God has both a nose [nostrils] and that God has a mouth. It

is strange that they do not suggest that God is a fire-breathing dragon since smoke comes out of His nostrils and He breathes fire. This is closer to a description of a dragon than a man.

5. Psalm 18:9 (Speaking of God): "He bowed the heavens also, and came down: and darkness was under His feet." The Latter Day Church uses this verse to teach that God has feet.

They put all of these verses together, along with many other verses, in which there is a reference to a body part to contradict the clear teaching of Jesus that God is a spirit. They hold that God has a physical body based upon these references. Now I have to ask: "Who are you going to believe?" Are you going to believe Jesus who is His Son and lived with Him prior to the Incarnation; or are you going to believe a man who seems to have been wrong about many teachings in the Bible?

The Latter Day Church has a difficult time understanding figurative language. It is a simple process of common sense and logic that those who wrote the Bible used figurative—not literal—language to describe God's attributes, actions and character. If we follow this logic of the Latter Day Church, we would have to make the following assumptions:

1. God is either a chicken or a bird because Psalm 91:4 makes reference to God having both feathers and wings: "He shall cover you with His feathers, and under His wings shall you trust…"

2. We would have to assume that God is food that we can physically eat. John 6:35: "And Jesus said unto them, 'I am the bread of life: he who comes to me shall never hunger; and he who believes on me shall never thirst."

3. We would have to assume that Jesus is a building that we can come into and leave. John 10:9: "I am the door: by me if any man enters in, he shall be saved, and shall go in and out, and find pasture." Following the logic of the Mormon theologians, we must assume that Jesus is made of wood, has a doorknob and He also has hinges.

4. If we follow this logic, we would have to teach that Jesus is, in fact, a plant. John 15:5: "I am the vine, you are the branches: He who abides in me, and I in him, the same brings forth much fruit: for without me you can do nothing."

This is the concept of figurative language. We can compare or describe someone or something in an abstract way. There is something we want to illustrate, and in order to save time and words we compare this with that. Jesus was standing before the crowd as a physical man. No one in the crowd believed for a second that He suddenly became wood and was now a physical door. In fact, if we do further research—something that seems to be lacking in Mormon Theology—we would learn that when a shepherd brought his flock into the fold for the evening he would lie down across the opening to the fold and sleep there. The shepherd became the actual physical door that blocked the sheep from going in or coming out of the fold.

But the Mormon theologians took what was figurative language designed by the writers to give us the concept that God could see us, hear us, respond to our needs, and speak to us; and ignored the clear teaching of the only eyewitness to God and what God was like. So where does this lack of common sense lead the Mormon theologians?

"Jesus was begotten by an Immortal Father in the same way that mortal men are begotten by mortal fathers." [Bruce McConkie *Mormon Doctrine* page 546–547]

Compare the Mormon Theology with the Bible—the Word of God. Isaiah 7:14:

"Therefore the Lord Himself shall give you a sign; 'Behold, a virgin shall conceive, and bear a son, and shall call His name Immanuel.'"

Notice three important points that Isaiah is making in this verse:

1. God is the one who created this sign. The reality is that God created this sign all the way back in the Garden of Eden when He spoke of the Seed of the Woman [Genesis 3:15].

2. This woman is a virgin when she conceives.
3. This woman is still a virgin when she gives birth to this male child.

So what is the Mormon response to this?

"There is nothing figurative about his paternity; he was begotten, conceived, and born in the normal and natural course of events, for he is the Son of God, and that designation means what it says." [Bruce R. McConkie, *Mormon Doctrine*, Salt Lake City Utah, Bookcraft 1966, page 742]

"The man Joseph, the husband of Mary, did not, that we know of, have more than one wife, but Mary, the wife of Joseph, had another husband—that is, God the Father." [Brigham Young, Deseret News, October 10, 1866]

Bruce McConkie claims *"virgin"* refers to someone who has not had sexual relations with a mortal man. In other words, he gave *"virgin"* a new definition to support their teachings. Again, this is the SEED OF THE WOMAN [Emphasis added]. It is not just that she is a virgin. It is that God used her own genetic material to have her become pregnant. It was HER SEED and HER EGG. If God impregnated her, then it was not her SEED. It was God's SEED. That does not fulfill the prophecy.

So let's take these various quotes and connect the dots. Mormon Theology teaches that God has a physical body. They claim that God, in His physical flesh and bone body, had physical sexual relations with Mary, and that is how she conceived Jesus. They specifically deny the account that the Holy Spirit caused her pregnancy.

"Christ is not the Son of the Holy Ghost, but of the Father." [Joseph Fielding Smith, *Doctrines of Salvation*, Salt Lake City, UT, Bookcraft, 1975, 1:18–20]

The way the Mormon Theology gets around Mary having sex with a physical body is to redefine the term: *"virgin."* In their teaching *"virgin"* does not refer to a woman who has never had sex, but as a woman who has never had sex with a *"mortal"* man. Since God is no longer mortal, He can have sex with women, and they all remain virgins. To be blunt, *"virgin"* does not refer to the person who performed the sex, but to the person having the sex.

Let me go back and discuss the initial prophecy of the Virgin Birth. Genesis 3:15:

"And I will put enmity between you and the woman, and between your seed and her seed; it shall bruise your head, and you shall bruise His heel."

Let's focus on this word: "*seed.*" As noted in the Bible, reference to a person's seed has always been referring to the male. There was the Seed of Abraham. There was the Seed of Isaac. There was the Seed of Jacob. The only place where the seed is attributed to a woman is here in Genesis 3:15.

Now since the woman supplies the egg for conception, and the man supplies the sperm for the conception; then it is logical to assume that "*Seed*" refers to sperm and not eggs. So to fulfill this prophecy, Mary will produce and provide her own egg, and she will also provide her own sperm. If any man provided the sperm—even God—it would not be her seed. It would be the seed of the male sperm donor. So if the Mormon God provided his sperm to Mary through sexual relations [or any other means]; then Jesus is not and cannot be the Seed of the woman. The prophecy of Genesis 3:15 remains unfulfilled. If God failed to fulfill His promise [prophecy] He has failed to live up to His part of the agreement in the contract He wrote. The contract becomes null and void.

When the Bible tells us that the Holy Spirit came upon her; and the Holy Spirit overshadowed her; this is not a description of Mary having sex with the Holy Spirit. First of all, the Holy Spirit is a spirit and does not have a body. [This is why Mormon theologians insist it was not the Holy Spirit/Ghost; but it was God who had a physical body.]

If we follow the logic here, the Holy Spirit overshadowed Mary causing her body to somehow produce sperm from her own genetic makeup. The Holy Spirit did not put anything into her. There was no sexual relation involved. The only difference is that this sperm—even though made from her genetic makeup had the male chromosome to determine the child would be male. It was her own sperm. It was her own genetic material. No other genetic material could be used in the process; otherwise, this child would have been the seed of that other person.

Now there was another difference in this process that it appears that the Holy Spirit controlled. When two sets of chromosomes come together, they form life. This means a new soul is created and is part of the embryo. This soul will grow with the embryo and become the soul of the person who is born into the world. But the embryo in Mary's womb did not create a new soul. The embryo needed a soul for it to become life, so that it could grow into a person. The spirit that was Jesus joined with the embryo and became the soul for the life in her womb. Jesus became the person that would be born into the human race.

This is the only way that a sperm and an egg could be present in her womb without sexual intercourse or artificial insemination. Mary had to produce both halves of the chromosomes that joined to form Jesus.

***

Now let me follow the logic of the Mormon teaching. If their God came to Mary and had physical sexual relations, they have a very serious problem. Their God just committed adultery with another man's wife. [Does this realization cause problems for anyone else?] The other man would be Joseph. Joseph and Mary were contracted as husband and wife. They were betrothed, and that has the same legal binding relationship that required a divorce to end the contract.

Let me introduce the parable that Nathan the Prophet used on King David. David had slept with Uriah's wife and got her pregnant. He tried to hide this by having Uriah killed in battle. Nathan presented this case to King David. "There was a man who had only one sheep. It was his prized possession. It was like a family pet—a member of the family. His neighbor was wealthy and had many sheep.

"A guest came to visit the rich neighbor and instead of taking one of his own sheep and killing it for the meal, he killed the sheep that the neighbor loved. He killed his neighbor's sheep." David declared that the man should be put to death. In response, Nathan noted that David was that man. Nathan noted that God had given David several wives. Uriah only had one. Why did David take Uriah's wife away from him?

I would ask the same question here. If the Mormon theologians are correct, and the God of this world has many wives for his pleasure in Heaven, why did he come down to earth and take the only wife of a poor carpenter? He took the wife that this carpenter loved with all his heart, and had sex with her [not love—a one night stand]. He took her, used her and then left her. Isn't there a word for someone who would do that? Would you worship and serve a God who would do that?

How can you create a sinless person through such an act? If that is how Jesus was conceived, He would be disqualified to be our Savior. He would not qualify as our sacrifice for sin.

The God of the Mormons did not respect the sanctity of marriage. He came in and had sex with another man's wife. He committed adultery—something that the Bible lists as a sin. If we follow this logic, the Mormon God just committed sin, and that makes the Mormon God a sinner. How can God forbid us to do something that He has already done? He can't! You can't have two standards.

But let us assume that this is the case. Let us assume that the Mormon God came down and had sexual relations with Mary. He was not her husband. She was not married to Him. Where was the marriage contract? Where was the marriage ceremony? There was none. If there were, then we have the only instance where a wife had multiple husbands because Joseph was legally considered to be her husband. After the angel revealed to Joseph that Mary was pregnant "*of the Holy Spirit*," Joseph took her into his home and she was his wife. There was no further procedure needed for her to be his wife. She was his wife when she became pregnant. Does the Bible teach that a woman can have multiple husbands at the same time? Of course not.

Which leads to the ultimate conclusion that Mary was not married to the father of Jesus at the time of the birth of Jesus. This invokes part of the Law of Moses. Deuteronomy 23:2:

"A bastard shall not enter into the congregation of the Lord; even to his tenth generation shall he not enter into the congregation of the Lord."

This is a generational curse that God honored even before the Law was given. Judah had three sons. He married his first son to Tamar. The first son died without having any children. Judah had his second son marry Tamar to raise up children to the deceased son. The second son refused to do this, and God struck him dead. The third son was too young to marry, so Judah sent Tamar back to her father's home.

Time passed, and Judah did not send for Tamar to marry the third son. So Tamar disguised herself and set up a tent along the path where Judah would be traveling on business. He thought that she was a prostitute, and offered her a goat to sleep with her. She asked for a promise that he would pay her; and he gave her his signet, bracelets and staff. When he sent the goat through a friend, she was nowhere to be found and Judah let the matter drop.

A while later Judah received word that Tamar was pregnant. He ordered her brought before him to accuse her of adultery. [Apparently, the marriage vows were still in place.] He demanded to know who the father of her child was. She presented the signet, bracelets and staff and said, "The man who owns these is the father."

That shut everything down. It was not determined to be adultery as there was a duty owed to her by Judah to raise up children in the name of her deceased husband. But, they were not married. As a result, there was this ten-generation curse upon the line of Judah. God had to wait until David was born to select the Tribe of Judah to be the king of Israel. David was the first generation where this ten-generation curse did not apply.

Now even if we accept the arguments of the Latter Day Church that it was alright to have the Mormon God come in and have sex with a married woman; he and Mary were not married. She had been married to another. Therefore, Jesus would have been born outside of wedlock. If that was the case, Jesus was barred from the Temple; and He could not serve as our sacrifice for sin. In other words, we would still be lost in our sins.

Now let's slip in the last piece of information here.

According to official Mormon teaching, Jesus Christ was *"begotten"* as the first spirit-child of the Father (Elohem) and one of his unnamed wives (often referred to as "Heavenly Mother"). Jesus, as a spirit-son, then progressed in the spirit world until He became a God. [Robert M. Bowman, *"How Mormons Are Defending Mormon Doctrine,* Christian Research Journal, Fall 1989, page 24]

Let me refer to the Hebrew in Deuteronomy 6:4 with the Hebrew names inserted:

"Hear, O Israel: The LORD [YHWH or Jehovah] our God [Elohem] is one LORD [YHWH or Jehovah]"

In the Hebrew, this verse makes it clear that YHWH or Jehovah is the same God as Elohem. They are one. We are not talking about multiple Gods here. There is one God and He is known both as YHWH [Jehovah] and as Elohem. This means that Jehovah is the same God as Elohem. In the footnotes of the Mormon edition of the King James Bible it states that Jesus was Jehovah in His Pre-mortal state.

If Elohem is the God who came and had physical sexual relations with Mary; and Elohem and Jehovah are the same; then following the logic of the Latter Day Church, Jesus has sex with His mother to impregnate her with Himself. This is incest no matter how you try to twist things around.

Now Mary did not have sex with anyone. She was still a virgin. Mary was not unfaithful to Joseph. Mary did not commit adultery. Her body produced both the egg and the sperm that led to her pregnancy. The child was produced only by those within the marriage relationship and no one else—although in this case it was just the wife, not the husband and wife. Therefore, Jesus was conceived in marriage, and was born in marriage. There was no adultery. There was no sin. Jesus was not a bastard. She was married to Joseph when this happened. Jesus was protected by the marriage contract.

This is why God waited until after the marriage contract was in place before causing Mary's body to produce both the egg and the sperm in her womb. Jesus was not illegitimate. He was not a bastard. He was not barred from the Temple. She was a virgin when she conceived Him as required by the prophecy of Isaiah. Joseph did not have sexual relations with her until after Jesus was born. So she was still a virgin when she gave birth to Jesus just as the prophecy of Isaiah required.

Everything the Latter Day Church teaches concerning the pre-existence of the soul, the nature and identity of Jesus before His birth and all the information relating to His conception and birth not only contradicts the account of the Bible; it violates the Law of God.

CHAPTER ELEVEN

THE PLAN OF SALVATION

We have discussed that the Bible is a legally-binding contract between God and mankind. The basis of a contract is that one party agrees to provide something or do something for another party. It might even be that this party agrees to provide something or do something for multiple parties.

The party that is making this offer becomes Party One [the First party]. The First Party will then put this agreement into writing. 1) This is what the First Party will do. 2) This is how the First Party will do it. 3) This is when the First Party will do it. It then becomes the legal obligation for the First Party to make this agreement as clear and as easy to understand as possible. If there is any ambiguity or multiple interpretations in this agreement, the courts will rule against the First Party in favor of all the other parties who entered into the agreement.

In the case of the Bible, we have God who is the First Party. As the First Party, it falls to Him to write out the agreement. How did God do this? II Timothy 3:16:

"All scripture is given by inspiration of God, and is profitable for doctrine, for reproof, for correction, for instruction in righteousness:"

Hebrews 1:1–2:

"God, who at [various] times and in [different] manners spoke in time past unto the fathers by the prophets,

"Has in these last days spoken unto us by His Son, whom He has appointed heir of all things, by whom also He made the worlds;"

God used inspiration to inspire men to write what God was telling them to write. When Jesus came to be upon the earth,

God chose to speak and reveal Himself through Jesus. When Jesus returned to Heaven, God used His Holy Spirit to guide various people to speak for Him. All this came together as the Bible—God's Word.

God selected each person who wrote specific parts of the Bible. God inspired and guided each writer as to what to write and even how to write it. God oversaw the entire process. It is like God being the head of a law firm, and dictating various portions of the contract out to different legal secretaries. Each legal secretary wrote their assigned portion of the contract, and then God handed this off to another paralegal assistant to put together the final draft of the contract. Remember, if God made a mistake, it goes against Him, not us.

Now, each one of us becomes the other party to this agreement. Because there are billions of us, this could take forever to list each and every one of us. However, since we all enter into this agreement the exact same way, and each one of us receives the exact same benefit from entering into this agreement; I am going to make it easy and name each one of us as the Second Party [Party Two]. Since the contract is identical for all parties involved, then each one of us will qualify as the Second Party with regards to this contract.

There is the First Party [Party One] who is making the offer and writing out the contract. All of us become the Second Party [Party Two]—the party that is receiving what the First Party is offering. Hopefully, it will not get any more confusing than this. God is the First Party. God is making the offer. God is writing the contract. All of us are Party Two; the ones who received what God is offering.

With regards to the Bible, what God is offering is salvation—specifically salvation from Hell. How is God going to accomplish this? He will accomplish this by offering Himself in human form to die in our place, shed His own blood and atone for our sins. This will be done through a legal process outlined in the Law of Moses. An innocent will die in the place of the guilty. For this to work, the sins of the guilty will need to be transferred to the innocent. The innocent will then die and shed His blood in a very specific manner and following specific rules for this transfer to work.

When will God do this? He will do this during the Passover Meal. Which Passover Meal will God use? He will use the Passover Meal that will begin 173,880 days after the King of Persia signs a decree that will allow the Jews to return home from Babylon and rebuild the walls. If we count out the number of days, we will come to April 6, 32 AD by our calendar. [These calculations are based upon the research of Sir Robert Anderson in his book, "*The Coming Prince*."] This date in the Jewish calendar will be the Tenth of Nisan.

On the Tenth of Nisan, the lamb each person is going to offer as a sacrifice for the Passover Meal must be identified. On this specific Tenth of Nisan, Jesus identified Himself as the Messiah, God's Passover Lamb. He identified Himself by riding a donkey into the Temple area and fulfilling the prophecy of Zechariah 9:9. Four days later, the Passover Lamb is sacrificed. Four days later, while all the Passover Lambs were being sacrificed, Jesus died upon the cross.

Now there is more involved in this. Each time God provides a prophecy; this becomes what we call in the insurance industry an Addendum. "*Addendum*" is a legal term for something added to the agreement—to the insurance policy. An Addendum can add additional parties to the contract; or it can remove additional parties from the contract. An Addendum can increase the level of coverage. It can reduce the level of coverage. It can also increase or decrease the premium that you will pay for that coverage.

Now God has issued approximately 300 prophecies concerning the coming of the Messiah, who He will be and what He will do. With each prophecy, God expands information about the contract and how it will work. Each prophecy will become an Addendum. All of the prophecies become part of the promise of God. To simplify the contract at this point, God uses the contract to make a promise to do something. In order for this contract to be valid and enforceable before a court of law, God must fulfill each and every promise He makes in that contract. If additional promises are made via an Addendum, God has the same legal obligation to fulfill that promise as part of the contract. If God fails to fulfill even one small part of the promise; then the entire contract will become null and void.

Now in most contracts—especially insurance contracts—there is a clause that the insurance company will add to the policy to protect itself. This clause will identify the laws and which state controls this policy. "This policy shall comply with the laws of the State of California…" [as an example]. Now laws can change in a state. I cannot tell you how many times the Legislature of the State of California changed the laws regarding workers' compensation. There were about three new laws passed concerning workers' compensation every year. Then about every ten years, the Legislature would overhaul the entire system. Every time the Legislature did this, this clause would automatically change the terms of the contract so that the policy would now comply with the new laws.

However, there was another part of this protective clause. You see, whenever you write and pass a new law, there is always going to be an attorney somewhere who does not like it—or his/her client does not like it. This will result in a lawsuit filed with the courts. Let me give you an example. Let us say that the workers' compensation insurance policy has an Addendum added to it. This Addendum has a clause that bars coverage for people while they are taking a break for lunch. However, a union believes that the employer is still controlling employees by making them stay at work during their lunch break. They hire an attorney and file a lawsuit in civil court.

After much litigating, the court agrees with the union that since the employer is exerting control over the employees by making them stay at work during their lunch break; then the workers are still employees during their lunch break. As such, they are entitled to benefits if injured on their lunch break. This means that the Addendum that bars coverage during the lunch break is now null and void.

The smart insurance companies will add a clause to the basic policy that says, "If part of this policy is found by the courts to be null and void, then only that part of the contract declared to be null and void will be affected. The remainder of this contract will remain in force." This way a bad court decision does not invalidate the entire contract.

Let me point out something to you. God does not have this kind of protective clause in His contract. There is no Scripture or passage in the Bible that says, "If I fail to meet just one point of the contract; the rest of the contract remains in force." What does this mean from a legal standpoint? It means that God must perform all that He has promised to perform, and perform it in the manner He has promised to perform it. If God fails to perform even one small part of the contract—say a prophecy, such as "None of His bones shall be broken"—the entire agreement becomes null and void.

Let's say that one of the Roman soldiers is new at this. As he pounds the nail through the carpal tunnel of Jesus' wrist to nail Him to the cross, the nail is not in the correct position and it breaks one of the carpal bones. That mistake means God has not fulfilled the entire contract. One of the Addendums remains unfulfilled. The Bible becomes invalid. Yes! It is that delicate of an agreement.

Those who seek to change the Bible, do so at their own risk. If they change the Bible, so that the promises God made are not fulfilled; they invalidate the entire Bible. Now let me point out something else missing from God's contract. Many contracts will contain a clause that if this contract becomes null and void; then the entire process reverts to some other state system as a default.

When I dealt with workers' compensation in California and we were trying to control the costs of providing medical treatment, a fee schedule was created. The fee schedule would say: "This is the reasonable cost for performing this medical procedure." In the Labor Code, there was a clause that would say: "If a procedure is not listed in the Fee Schedule we will use the MediCal or MediCare Fee Schedules." In other words, there was a back up system in place.

God does not have a back up system in place. There is no default program that will step in and protect us. It is literally His promise and His agreement. If we reject this agreement or make that agreement null and void, there is no Plan B. We are all still lost. We are all guilty of sin. We are all going to Hell. Only this time there is no alternative system for us to turn to.

I really need to stress this concept as we investigate God's Plan of Salvation. There is one Plan of Salvation, and only one Plan of Salvation. No one—other than God who set the standard for perfection—can introduce an alternative Plan of Salvation. God had such confidence in His Plan of Salvation that He not only did not create a back up plan; but through His Son Jesus Christ's statement, God deliberately and intentionally invalidated any other plan out there.

Let me remind you of the Mathematics of the Cults. They ADD to the Bible. They SUBTRACT from Jesus. They MULTIPLY the ways of salvation. They DIVIDE the body of Christ. In this chapter, we are going to be looking at the action of Cults when they MULTIPLY the ways of salvation. They create multiple ways for each one of us to be saved. They did not like Plan A—God's Plan. Therefore, they pull information out of the contract and organize it out of context. They change the definitions and meanings of words. They ignore parts of the contract. They do this to create Plan B, Plan C, Plan D and so forth. This is like you ignoring what your insurance policy says, and writing your own policy after an auto accident, and then expecting your insurance company to honor it. That is not going to happen.

Here is the reality of their actions. If they invalidate or reject Plan A, there is no alternative plan. As I mentioned, God had Jesus issue a statement that invalidated any other plan anyone tried to introduce. This was deliberate on the part of God. This was intentional on the part of God. Jesus made this statement in John 14:6:

"Jesus said unto him, 'I am the Way, the Truth and the Life; *no man comes unto the Father but by me.*'" [Emphasis added]

Jesus is God on earth. He is God's representative. For lack of a better term, Jesus is God's attorney. He has just added to the contract the night before the contract is enacted. Hours before God performs what He has promised for thousands of years;

His attorney, Jesus, adds one last Addendum to the contract. As God's attorney, He has the legal right to do so. This piece of information is an Addendum to the Contract. Now we are not the ones writing the contract. We cannot make God promise to do something He does not want to agree to. Both parties have to agree to changes in the contract. God agrees by making the change and endorsing the agreement. We agree to the change by entering into the agreement.

I really am not trying to confuse you, or to make this more complicated than it is. But when you deal with a legal system, there is always an attorney out there who says, "I can get around that." Let me be very blunt here: not in this case. Not with this contract. Not in this court. And not before THIS Judge.

Let me take this declaration of Jesus as the example. I will use it to walk you through the legal process. This statement is an Addendum. Now it really is not new information. It really does not change the terms of the contract. It clarifies part of the contract. Back in Job Chapter Thirty-Three, God's Plan of Salvation is listed. We confess our sins. We repent of our sins. Then there is someone who will come with us when we stand before God. He is a translator or interpreter [of the law]. This would mean "an attorney" for us today. This attorney will stand with us and defend us before God. He will become the ransom. In other words, this attorney will pay the price to set us free. This information has always been in the contract.

Now all that Jesus did in John 14:16 is that He identified who the attorney representing us would be. He will represent us. He will go with us before God. If we go before God without Him, then there is no one to pay the ransom on our behalf. This is why no one can come before the Father unless they come before the Father with Jesus.

So, technically, nothing has changed. The Addendum clarified one point of the contract. But let me give you the big picture here of how this Addendum affects those who were already a party to the contract.

We have a group of people at the time that Jesus added this Addendum who were already relying upon the original contract with its ambiguity for their salvation. This would be every believer who had died before Jesus came. According to the Bible, prior to the death of Jesus, if a believer died, they would enter a separate waiting place in the afterlife called the Bosom of Abraham. They were sent here by God, and taken care of by God while they were waiting for the issue of sin between them and God to be resolved. Isaiah clarified the issue in Isaiah 59:2:

"But your iniquities have separated…you and your God, and your sins have hid His face from you, [so] that He will not hear [you]."

Until this issue of sin is resolved, we cannot come into God's Presence. Our sins build a barrier that makes it impossible for God to be with us. This is why God built this separate waiting place for those who died before sins were resolved. The contract had not yet been fulfilled. God had promised, but He had not yet delivered on His promise.

To put it into modern terminology, this was a holding cell where they waited until Jesus paid the ransom and resolved the sin. Jesus had to fulfill this part of the contract by dying on the cross.

Since He had not yet died on the cross, sin would still separate us from God. So God *"suspends"* the sentence. He withholds the punishment. He provides a wonderful place for everyone to wait until the contract is fulfilled.

Now the people in the Bosom of Abraham did not know the name of the defense attorney who would go with them when they stood before God. All that was required of them based upon the contract, as it was when they died, was that they trusted God to send the Messiah to save them—whoever that might be. The contract did not add any further obligation for this group of people.

God—through His representative, Jesus—has just revealed who their defense attorney will be. It is no longer enough to believe that God will send the Messiah to save you. God has identified who that Messiah will be. He will be Jesus.

Now in contract law, all those in the Bosom of Abraham have greater protection. They signed up when this new information was unknown. It was an ambiguity in the contract. The courts will protect them from any greater obligation. They did what the original version of the contract asked. The court will not add any other burden on them. So long as they believed God would send a Messiah—whomever that might be, they are still covered.

Now those who enter into the contract after Jesus has identified Himself as the Messiah will have to accept Jesus as their Messiah and Savior by name. They will fall under the amended contract. If someone comes along after this Addendum has been added and says, "I don't like this change. I don't want Jesus as my Messiah. I'm going to trust God to send a different Messiah." That is not the contract that God is offering. They are trying to change the contract. They are refusing to enter into the contract. They will not be covered. They will not be saved. That's how this works.

So let us look at this Plan of Salvation as God has outlined it in His Bible. Once we understand God's Plan of Salvation, we will look at the Plans of Salvation offered by the Jehovah's Witnesses and the Church of Jesus Christ of Latter Day Saints to see how they compare to the original.

***

As I begin to discuss God's Plan of Salvation, let me explore this concept from a legal standpoint. When we use the word "*saved*," or "*salvation*," this suggests that there is some kind of threat that we are in danger of. In the case of the Bible, Jesus speaks of Hell Fire. Matthew 5:22:

"'But I say unto you, "That whosoever is angry with his brother without a cause shall be in danger of the judgment: and whosoever shall say to his brother, 'Raca,' shall be in danger of the council: but whosoever shall say, 'You fool,' shall be in danger of hell fire.""'

In another place, Jesus warns us that there is the danger of being cast into hell fire. Matthew 10:28:

"And fear not those who can kill the body, but are not able to kill the soul: but rather fear Him who is able to destroy both soul and body in hell."

Jesus gives us this description of Hell. Mark 9:46:

"Where the worm dies not, and the fire is not quenched."

This is the fate of those who are judged and found guilty. Matthew 25:41:

"Then shall He say also unto those on the left hand, 'Depart from me, you cursed, into everlasting fire, prepared for the devil and his angels:'"

The judgment is to be sent into everlasting fire. It is an eternal judgment. The fire lasts forever. Now because we are in our spirit body, which is immortal, the fire cannot kill us or consume us. Since the fire lasts forever and our bodies last forever, we shall burn forever, and be fully aware of the heat and the flames and the pain.

Notice that God did not make these everlasting fires for us. He made these everlasting fires to punish Satan and his angels. If we reject Jesus' offer of salvation, then we will share the same fate as Satan. God does not want to send us there, but without our willingness to accept His Plan of Salvation, He must obey the Law, and sentence us along with Satan to the everlasting fire.

There will be an actual trial in which God will consider if you have accepted Jesus as your Savior or not. If not, then God will judge you based upon your works. Those who are judged based upon their works will not prevail, and will be cast into the Lake of Fire. Revelation 20:12–15:

"And I saw the dead, small and great, stand before God; and the books were opened: and another book was opened, which is the Book of Life: and the dead were judged out of those things which were written in the books, according to their works.

"And the sea gave up the dead who were in it; and death and hell delivered up the dead who were in them: and they were judged every man according to their works.

"And death and hell were cast into the Lake of Fire. This is the second death.

"And whosoever was not found written in the Book of Life was cast into the Lake of Fire."

Let me clarify the above passage. The Bible speaks of two Books of Life. There is The Book of Life [Revelation 20:12], and then there is what John describes as The Lamb's Book of Life [Revelation 21:27]. They are not the same thing.

Everyone who was ever born was listed in The Book of Life. If you die without accepting Jesus, your name is *"blotted out"* of that Book of Life. You did not accept God's offer of life. God will wait up until the moment you die to allow you the chance to accept. But when you die without accepting the offer of life, God then blots out your name. It is not blotted out before that moment. You will always have the chance to accept God's offer as long as you are in this world. If you have accepted Jesus' offer for eternal life, your name is not blotted out. It stays in that book.

If you have accepted Jesus as your Savior, your name is added to the Lamb's Book of Life. Once your name is added here, it is never blotted out or removed. The Lamb's Book of Life is used at the Bema Seat of Christ [I Corinthians 3:13–15] where believers are judged FOR their works. The Book of Life is used at the Great White Throne Judgment where non-believers are judged BY their works [Revelation 20:11 15].

So we now know the danger we face. If we die without accepting the offer of Jesus to save us, we will be judged based upon our works. No one will be exonerated based upon their works. Those judged based upon their works will be cast into the Lake of Fire for all eternity. The torment will never end.

Now this is how the Jehovah's Witnesses deal with this judgment. They have removed Hell and the Lake of Fire from their theology. They have removed the Great White Throne Judgment from their theology. They do not believe it; that solves the problem.

According to Jehovah's Witness' theology, if you die and are not worthy, your body will decay in the ground and your soul will be annihilated. That is nice because once you are annihilated you won't even be aware that you have been annihilated. It's fast and painless. It has no lasting bad side effects related to it.

What the Jehovah's Witnesses have done is to remove the danger waiting for the lost at the end of their lives. Technically, they are not being saved because there is no danger to be saved from. But we have to ask: "*What if they are wrong?*" If we are wrong, there is annihilation, and we are no longer aware. We won't have the chance to regret our decision. However, if they are wrong, they will suffer forever in the Lake of Fire. This is not a topic that you can afford to be wrong about.

The Latter Day Church notes that there is no original sin. They also add that even if you sin, but you were not intentionally trying to sin, it does not count as sin. Here they have changed the definition of sin so that it does not exist in their life. Since they insist the newer revelations through their prophets replaces older revelation in the Bible, then they are not in danger. There is nothing that they need to be saved from.

Without sin in your life, then you will not be found guilty when you are judged. Think about it. You drove fifty-five miles an hour through a twenty-five mile per hour zone. You got caught. You got a ticket. You have to go to court. The day before you go to court, the State Legislature decides to repeal the entire Vehicle Code. It no longer exists. The law you broke no longer exists. Since there was no law that you broke, the judge cannot find you guilty. You don't need to be saved.

For the Latter Day Saint, they live their life in such a way that their theology declares that there is no sin on them. Without sin, there is nothing to save them from. Again, if we are wrong, we end up in the mediocre Kingdom. Bummer! But that's it. Well, there is the Telestial Kingdom, which is bad, if we are bad. But we can even work to fix the problem. But if they are wrong, there is no escape. Again, this is a topic no one can afford to be wrong about.

What these Cults have done is to remove the Law that finds them guilty, or to remove the court that would judge them. They have changed the definitions relating to sin, judgment and Hell. So technically, they do not need salvation because there is nothing to save them from. I would suggest in that case, that there would be no need for a Savior. If there is no sin, or there is no judgment or there is no punishment, why did Jesus need to become human and die on the cross to save us if there is nothing threatening us or posing a danger to us?

There is just one problem with their solution. They lack the legal authority to repeal or rewrite the laws. They lack the legal authority to redefine terms. They lack the legal authority to remove truth from our reality. They can do whatever they want; but God will not honor their changes. They are going to be one of those standing before Jesus on Judgment Day waiving their *New World Translation* or *Book of Mormon* and shouting, "I'm on the Plan B program!" Jesus will look at them and say, "I never knew you." Ignoring and redefining reality is not a viable solution to the problem.

This is a contractual agreement. This falls under a court of law. This is not based upon what you believe. This is not based upon how you would like the program to work. It is based solely upon what the law and the contract says. The plain meaning of the law will prevail. What you believe or do not believe has no bearing on what God will do.

The reality is that there is sin in our lives. The reality is that we are in danger of being cast into the Lake of Fire. This is a very real danger. The reality is that there is a need for salvation in our lives. So how does this system God put together work?

***

I am going to use what has come to be called *The Romans Road to Salvation*. This is because each of the verses is found in the Book of Romans. But I also want to pull information from other parts of the Bible where I think it is relevant. What is nice about using the Romans Road to Salvation is that Paul put this together after all the Addendums were added. So there will be no more Addendums. No further clarification is needed or provided. I will make this as simple to understand as possible.

Let me start with a Bible verse that many people know by heart. It is a quotation from Jesus Christ, so if anyone knows how this system is supposed to work, it would be Him. John 3:16:

"For God so loved the world, that He gave His only begotten Son, that whosoever believes in Him should not perish, but have everlasting life."

There are some important points that were made in this verse. The first is that God's motive behind doing this was love. There was no ulterior motive. As John had noted, "we love Him because He first loved us." We are responding to His love. We do not have to win His love or earn His love. He already loves us.

Has this thought sunk in yet? The goal all the Cults are telling their members to strive for is to be worthy of God's love—to get God to love them. That goal has already been achieved. There is nothing else that we need to do to get God to love us. He already does.

Next, the salvation process is exclusive to Jesus Christ. Which Jesus Christ is this talking about? This is the Jesus Christ that is God's only begotten Son. It is not that Jesus is one of many begotten sons. He is the only begotten Son. There are no others like Him. This narrows down how many ways there are to get saved. We rely upon Jesus to save us and no one else.

This salvation is identified. It is everlasting life. It is not Godhood. It is not living on earth for a thousand years. It is a life that will begin through Jesus and it will last forever. It will never end.

I want to come back to this Third Chapter of John, but there is some other relevant information Jesus gives us further in this Gospel. John 14:2–3:

"'In my Father's house are many mansions: if it were not so, [then] I would have told you. I go to prepare a place for you.

"And if I go and prepare a place for you, I will come again, and receive you unto myself; that where I am, there you may be also.'"

It's not just that we are going to live forever. There are many scenarios where living forever is not a good thing. Here Jesus tells us that He has prepared a home for us in Heaven with Him.

Wherever He is going to be, we will be there with Him. This place would be Heaven, not here on earth.

Contrary to the teachings of the Jehovah's Witnesses, this is not limited to just 144,000 people. See how John described the number of people in Heaven. Revelation 7:9:

"After this I beheld, and, lo, a great multitude, which no man could number, of all nations, and kindreds, and people, and tongues, stood before the throne, and before the Lamb, clothed with white robes, and palms in their hands;"

It may take a while to count out 144,000 people; but you can do it. In fact, John identifies the 144,000 and how they are counted. There are 12,000 Jews from each of the twelve tribes of Israel. If you are not a Jew; then you cannot be part of the 144,000. The 144,000 are not the multitude without number. This is a gathering that is too great to be counted. This number would far exceed 144,000. Jesus has promised to prepare a place for each one of us. Jesus will make room for each and every believer in Heaven. He is not going to leave anyone out.

Okay, back to John. John 3:17:

"'For God sent not His Son into the world to condemn the world; but that the world through Him might be saved."

This is the mission of Jesus. He came to earth this time to save as many people as He can. John 3:18:

"He who believes on Him is not condemned: but He who believes not is condemned already, because he has not believed in the name of the only begotten Son of God.'"

The reason Jesus came into the world was to save us. He was not sent into the world this time to condemn us. If we believe on Him, we are saved [we will avoid the everlasting fires, we will live forever; and we will live in Heaven with Him]. Now this next comment is important to understand. We are not condemned because we refuse to accept Jesus as our Savior. God is not that petty. But many people will try to misrepresent this position. "So if I don't accept Jesus you are going to send me to Hell?" We are not condemned for not accepting Jesus as our Savior. Each and every person that has ever lived, is living and who will ever live in the future is already condemned.

Before we leave the womb, or stand in front of God, the verdict has already been handed down. And that verdict is that we are condemned. We start out being condemned. We would be sent to Hell whether Jesus came into the world or not.

This is the truth of the concept. If God really wanted to send anyone to Hell, He does not have to look for a reason. Each one of us is already condemned by the sin in our lives. All God has to do for us to go to Hell is…nothing. If God does nothing, we are going to Hell. But God does not want us to go to Hell, and so He did something. He sent His Son Jesus into the world so that we can have a choice. We can have an alternative to Hell. If we choose not to take the alternative; then nothing changes. God does not get mad at you. He respects your decision. But you are still heading for Hell. You have not changed your destiny. You will end up exactly where you would have ended up if Jesus had never come into the world.

This was not God's original plan. He kept things very simple for Adam and Eve: "Don't eat the forbidden fruit." At the end of the day, "Did you eat the forbidden fruit?" "No." "Good! No problem."

It was not that there were any magical chemicals in the forbidden fruit and it altered our DNA. No, the only way they came to know wrong from right was that they chose to do something that was wrong. Adam and Eve always did what was right. They always chose not to eat the forbidden fruit. Therefore, there was no need for a Savior or for salvation. There was nothing to save them from. But then Satan made the forbidden fruit appealing; and it became a test of character.

But when they ate the forbidden fruit, they now had knowledge from personal experience of the difference between wrong and right. They knew the difference between wrong and right. Now Adam and Eve, and their children became responsible to always make the right decision and to never, ever make the wrong decision. This was more than the human race was designed for. I would not call it a design flaw, but it was not what God intended.

Now there is sin because we know the difference between right and wrong. Now that there is sin, we are accountable for our choices, decisions and actions. Now that there is sin, there is the danger of the judgment. With the danger of the judgment, there is the danger of everlasting fires. There is now the need for a Savior because now there is something that we need to be saved from. This is why, before God judged Adam and Eve, He gave them the promise of the Seed of the Woman who could break the power of sin and death and save us. So the need for salvation and the process of salvation were laid out by Paul and others. Romans 3:23:

"For all have sinned and fallen short of the glory of God."

The glory of God is God's standard of righteousness. It is God's righteousness that is His glory. We cannot attain this because there is now sin in our lives. Paul adds to this in Romans 3:10:

"As it is written, There is none righteous, no, not one:"

Isaiah described our righteousness compared to God's righteousness in Isaiah 64:6:

"But we are all as an unclean thing, and all our righteousnesses are as filthy rags; and we all do fade as a leaf; and our iniquities, like the wind, have taken us away."

Even on your best day, as the best person you can be, you fail to come even close to God's righteousness. Unfortunately, God's righteousness became the standard that we have to attain when Adam and Eve ate the forbidden fruit. God's righteousness does not allow Him to grade on a curve. There is a standard we must meet. Each one of us fails to meet this standard. We are all in this situation. Paul noted that all of us are guilty of sin. It is in each and every one of us. So what does this mean for us? Romans 6:23:

"For the wages of sin is death; but the gift of God is eternal life through Jesus Christ our Lord."

Here Paul is giving us hope as he delivers the bad news. If there is a single sin in your life—if you have only blown it one time, you have earned death. When God pays you what you have earned for committing just one sin, it means that you will die. It is not just a physical death, but it will also involve a spiritual death. Yet with this unpleasant news, Paul notes that God is providing an alternative. It is not just eternal life. There is a structure in place. If it were just eternal life, then everyone would have it. But it is eternal life through Jesus Christ our Lord. Without Jesus Christ, this gift is not available. Romans 5:8:

"But God [demonstrated] His love for us, in that, while we were yet sinners, Christ died for us."

God did not wait for us to clean up our act and stop sinning. We did not have to improve what we were. God is accepting us just the way we are—sins and all. Romans 10:9–10:

"That if you shall confess with your mouth the Lord Jesus, and shall believe in your heart that God has raised Him from the dead, you shall be saved.

"For with the heart man believes unto righteousness; and with the mouth confession is made unto salvation."

This brings us back to the Plan of Salvation outlined in Job 33:27–30:

"[God] looks upon men, and if any say, 'I have sinned, and perverted that which was right right, and it [did not profit me];'

"[God] will deliver his soul from going into the pit [Hell], and his life shall see the light.

"Lo, all these things works God oftentimes with man,

"To bring back his soul from the pit, to be enlightened with the light of the living."

God is looking not just for an action. He is looking for an attitude. The confession of sin is from the heart. "I have sinned." God even gives us the definition of sin: "I have perverted that which was right." And there is repentance, "It did not profit me." In other words, it was not good for me to do this. This involves a realization. "Sin is not good for me. I need to stop sinning." There is a change in the attitude. We want to stop perverting that which is right. We want to do those things that are good for us.

God delivers that person from going down into the pit. The pit was the grave. It was also called Hell, and it will lead to the Lake of Fire and the everlasting fires. We will be enlightened.

We will come to understand God: who He is and what He is doing. We shall see the light of God. How is God going to do this? Job 33:22 -24:

"Yea, his soul draws near unto the grave, and his life to the destroyers.

"If there be a messenger with him, an interpreter, one among a thousand, to show unto man [God's] uprightness:

"Then [God] is gracious unto him, and says, 'Deliver him from going down to the pit: I have found a ransom.'"

This is a very important point here. Confession and repentance will not save you. It does not have the power in and of itself to save you. There is still a price that needs to be paid. Whether you are sorry for your sins or not, it does not matter. Whether you are trying to be better or not, it does not matter. The sin has been done. There is a price that must be paid. Death must claim the person who has sinned.

This is why this second part of Job Chapter Thirty-Three is so important. This is how the power of sin and death will be broken. Sin and death have laid claim to you and to your soul. You are their legal prey, and any court of law would have to allow sin to claim you, and that means that death will own you. But this interpreter, this messenger who comes with you will be Jesus. He will stand with you when you stand before God, and He will become the ransom. He will become the price that must be paid to break the power that sin and death have on you. He will be the innocent who dies in your place. I Corinthians 15:52–57:

"In a moment, in the twinkling of an eye, at the last trump: for the trumpet shall sound, and the dead shall be raised incorruptible, and we shall be changed.

"For this corruptible must put on incorruption, and this mortal must put on immortality.

"So when this corruptible shall have put on incorruption, and this mortal shall have put on immortality, then shall be brought to pass the saying that is written, 'Death is swallowed up in victory.'

"O death, where is your sting? O grave, where is your victory?

"The sting of death is sin; and the strength of sin is the law.

"But thanks be to God, who gives us the victory through our Lord Jesus Christ."

Let me shift over to a different kind of legal system for a moment to make this concept clear. Let's go to debtor's court. Let's discuss the concept of a *lien*. A lien is a debt. It is a bill that you owe, but cannot or will not pay. The person trying to collect will present this bill to the court, and ask the court to order you to pay the bill. If the court issues this order, the bill becomes a lien. You are ordered to pay the bill. The person you own this money to can file a legal document on your property. That property is now partly his. He controls it.

Let's talk about a *mechanic's lien* on your car. You hired this mechanic to fix your car. You were thinking it could be fixed for fifty dollars. Unfortunately, when the mechanic hands you the bill, it is for $200. Your car might be worth a lot more than $200. But if the mechanic files a lien against your car, that mechanic can take possession of your car, and he can sell it to get his $200 to settle his bill. The car becomes his property. He can sell it for $200, and whatever else the car was worth is lost. You get nothing.

There is a bill that you owe. Sin is the party that is owed payment. Sin has placed its lien on your life. The price you must pay for sin is that you must die. You must die both physically and spiritually. If it was just a physical death, then when you die, sin has lost its legal claim to you, and your soul is free and clear. But this death is both a physical death and a spiritual death. Your physical death would only be a partial payment.

Jesus steps up to represent you in this court of law. He pays the lien sin has placed on your life. With the bill satisfied, sin has no legal claim upon you. You are free. Sin cannot come back and seek any further payment.

Jesus is the ransom. He has paid the price that sin filed against you and your soul. In the court of law, sin is no longer a party recognized by the court. Any debt has been discharged. Sin has no legal claim, and is, therefore, powerless in this court of law. You are free.

The term we used in our legal system is that someone is *"no longer a party to the action."* In layman terms, they no longer have a dog in the race. Only those who are parties recognized by the court have a right to attend the hearings and trials. If you are not a party to the action being presented to the courts, you cannot come to the hearings. You cannot be present at the trial. It is not opened to the public. These parties will be barred from ever coming back. They lack the legal authority to do so. When Jesus paid the price, sin and death were dismissed. They are no longer a party to the action. There is nothing the courts can do for them. They have no legal right to appear—ever.

This is why it is not enough to admit that you have sinned. It is not enough that you are sorry that you sinned. It is not enough that you want to be a better person. Sin has filed its lien against your life, and sin now has legal ownership of you and your soul. Someone has to discharge the debt. Someone has to pay the price. You do not have the price. You do not have the resources to pay this lien. But Jesus does, and Jesus pays it. Sin's lien on your life and soul is cancelled and thrown out. The court refuses to recognize it. Now let's go back to the Romans Road of Salvation. Romans 10:13:

"For whosoever shall call upon the name of the Lord [Jesus] shall be saved."

You have to call upon Jesus to save you. You do not have the resources or ability to save yourself. If you think that you do, then you are mistaken. The Cults convince you that you can redeem yourself, or that there is no lien against your life and soul. They are deceiving you so that you do not take proper legal action to protect yourself. They are like the mechanic who wants your car, and has filed a mechanic's lien to get it because you forgot to pay $20 for that windshield wiper he replaced. You get notice of the court date. You get notice of the mechanic's lien. You go to him, and he tells you not to worry. He tells you that is already taken care of. You do not take proper legal action to protect your property, and it is now his. He owns it for $20.

Satan is the one filing the lien on behalf of sin against your life. You go to the Cults to fix the problem, and they tell you that there is no problem. They tell you that there is no lien. They tell you that there is no court of law. They convince you to not take the proper legal action to protect your soul. You die, and discover their deception; but you discover it too late. You cannot fix it. You are lost and going to Hell.

Now this salvation is an immediate thing. You are saved in this life, at this time. You do not have to wait until you are being called to court to stand trial for this sin lien on your life and soul. Romans 8:28:

"For there is NOW no condemnation to those who are in Christ Jesus, who walk not after the flesh, but after the spirit."

Now do not be deceived. There is NOW—at this time and at this moment, no condemnation upon you. No one has any claim upon your life or soul. No one is charging you with any crime. The lien has been discharged, and no longer has any authority over you. There is nothing that it can do.

Now there are those who take what Paul means as a *description* of a believer and try to misrepresent it as a *condition* of the believer. If you have been saved, you are now in Christ Jesus. You are now walking in the spirit. This is because the Holy Spirit is now inside of you and leading you and guiding you. You are not walking after the flesh. It has now become impossible for you to walk after the flesh. Romans 6:14:

"For sin shall not have dominion over you: for you are not under the law, but under grace."

There is a legal concept that applies to interpreting and applying laws. It is called a *"legal imperative."* In the workers' compensation Labor Code, Labor Code 15 gave us a working example of legal imperatives. It said, *"Shall* is mandatory, *may* is permissive."

What does that mean for us? When you see a law where it tells us that we shall do something, then it is mandatory to do this action. If that law does not list an exception to that requirement, then there is no exception, and you have no choice but to do what it is telling you to do. If you see the word *may* in a law, this is flexible. This is optional. You can choose to do this, or you can choose not to do this.

Now the negative of this is also true. If there is a negative legal imperative in a law, then this becomes a forbidden action. Where the laws says that you *shall not* do something, then you are forbidden to do it. If there are no exceptions listed in the law, then there are no exceptions. You cannot do it. It will not be allowed by law. No court would ever allow this action to take place.

That is what is happening in this verse. "Sin *SHALL NOT* have dominion over you…" [Emphasis added] Sin has forever lost any legal claim on you. There is not a court in the land that will ever give sin authority or control of your life. Why is this? It's called *Double Jeopardy*. What does that mean? It is a legal concept that states that you cannot be tried with the same crime twice. If you are tried and found innocent, you cannot be forced to stand trial for that crime ever again. If you go to court and are found guilty, and you have paid your debt; they cannot bring you back into court and try you again.

In this case, you were pulled into court. Sin was entitled to your life and to your soul. You were found guilty, but Jesus discharged the debt. The court has no authority to charge you a second time. Sin can only claim you once—only once, and then never again.

Now there is an added benefit from being represented and protected by Jesus. It is not just that the charges have been dropped. Because Jesus is your attorney, He has filed paperwork and obtained a court order that you are no longer under the law.

How is this possible? The price that had to be paid was death. Jesus died in your place. Jesus took His death certificate, and had it filed with the court on your case. In the court's records, you are now dead. The price has been paid. Once a person is dead, the law and the court have no jurisdiction over you. We do not dig up and exhume dead people and put them on trial. The most the law can do to you is kill you. According to the court records, you are now dead. There is nothing more the law can do. The maximum penalty has been paid.

This is a legal technicality. You, personally, are not dead. But the court records list you as "*deceased*." Every sin listed in your court record has been deleted. But then Jesus has deleted your court record, too. If sin shows back up in court to file a new lien over a new sin, too bad/so sad. The court has no file on you, and any new filing or legal actions cannot take place. The court cannot/will not file anything further against you.

Jesus has transferred your case out of the court system and it will never be transferred back into the court system. This is a legal standing in the court. Paul was describing your current legal status in Christ. Right now, there is no condemnation. Right now, you are in Christ. Right now, you are walking in the spirit and not in the flesh. And your legal status will never change.

Paul was not identifying a rehabilitation program you have to follow under a court order. You have not been placed on probation by God, and now have to behave yourself or the court will reactivate the charges against you. Whatever law was broken that gave the court authority over you, that charge has been dropped. That debt has been forever discharged. Sin's lien on your life is gone. Sin cannot take you back into court and try to reestablish its legal authority over you again.

Satan will try to play on your ignorance of law. He will lie to you and try to deceive you into thinking that somehow you lost your legal standing. But Jesus knows the judge. God is the judge, and Jesus had God drop the charges. In fact, Jesus had God transfer your case and file out of the legal court, and gave it to Jesus to keep. It's never going to show up in the legal court again. If someone wants to make any charge against you, then they must go through Jesus. This is why there is at this time and forever after, no condemnation—no charges—against you. Your record is clear and clean. It will remain clear and clean forever.

There is an important legal concept demonstrated in the sacrifice used for the Day of Atonement in the Law of Moses. A goat is selected by the priest. The priest lays his hands upon the goat and confesses all the sins of Israel over this goat. This process transfers every sin of every person in Israel onto this goat. This way, when this goat dies, its single death will cover the entire nation of Israel. It is possible for a single sacrifice to cover multiple offenses and people. The more sins that are transferred, the more sins are covered by that single death.

When Jesus hung on the cross, before He died, God confessed every sin that had ever been made, was being made and which would ever be made, and transferred that sin into Jesus. Isaiah 53:6:

"All we like sheep have gone astray, we have turned every one to his own way, and the Lord has laid on Him the iniquity [sins] of us all"

There was, for lack of a better description, a data dump. The file God kept all sins documented in was transferred to Jesus so that none of them would be missed. God downloaded every sin into Jesus. This is how He was able to pay for all sins for so many people with just His single death. There is legal precedence for this in God's court of law.

Now some will suggest that we need to work to pay off this debt to Jesus. It was not a debt. Jesus did not send you a bill for services rendered. Under the Law of the Kinsman Redeemer, the kinsman who redeemed his brother cannot turn around and now charge the brother the cost of the debt. The kinsman absorbs that debt, pays the debt, and it no longer exists. The brother who is redeemed is set free. Look at how Paul describes this in Ephesians 2:8–9:

"For by grace are you saved through faith; and that not of yourselves: it is the gift of God:

"Not of works, lest any man should boast."

We are saved by grace. Chuck Missler defined grace as *"God's Riches At Christ's Expense"* [G.R.A.C.E.]. Grace is unmerited favor. Look at that word in the description: *"unmerited."* That means you do not deserve it. You are not worthy of it. You cannot earn it. This is God's grace. God has chosen to give us this gift of salvation. He is offering it free of charge. There are no strings attached. We do not deserve it. We cannot earn it. We cannot buy it. There is no way that we can get it. It is beyond our ability to obtain. God is giving it to us just because we believe what He says and are accepting His offer.

The next verse makes this point very clear. It is not given to us because of any work we have done nor for any work that we are going to do. God does not want anyone coming into Heaven and bragging that they were saved because they deserved it. It is a free gift. It's ours for the asking. God is offering it. All we have to do is accept it.

Someone out there is going to quote James 2:20:

"But will you know, O vain man, that faith without works is dead?"

They will pull this out of context. They will try to make it say something that would clearly contradict the Bible. They will tell you that if you do not perform good works, then your faith is dead, and you are no longer saved. Again, the court lacks any jurisdiction over you. The court cannot file new charges against you. The court cannot reactivate charges or liens that have been resolved. It lacks the legal authority to do so. PERIOD! However, let me show you the true meaning and application of this verse.

A well-written contract will take the time to define the terms used in the contract. God has provided a well-written contract. He made sure to define the terms used in His contract. He gave us a definition to the term *"works of God."* This is Jesus' response to questions about works. Let me take you over to John 6:28–29

"Then said they unto Him, 'What shall we do, that we might work the works of God?'

"Jesus answered and said unto them, 'This is the work of God, that you believe on Him whom He has sent."

The works that God is looking for is that we will believe Jesus. We will trust Him and what He has promised. We will accept Jesus. Nothing more and nothing less.

I know that someone is now looking up Philippians 2:12:

"Wherefore, my beloved, as you have always obeyed, not as in my presence only, but now much more in my absence, *work out your own salvation* with fear and trembling." [Emphasis added]

They will pull out this one phrase: "*work out your own salvation*" and they will try to build an entire doctrine on it. That is not what it says in context. Look at Philippians 2:13:

"For it is God who works in you both to will and to do...His good pleasure."

God gives you the desire to become better. God gives you the ability to do better. This is not a teaching of works. It is about growing as a believer. You are a believer. You are saved. That is your legal status before God. That can never change. Jesus has secured that legal standing for us forever.

Salvation is our status. We are saved. Stamped on every court document with our name on it is the big rubber stamp on the cover of every file: SAVED!. That is our legal classification. But we are going through a transition now. Jesus has a plan to make us the best that we can be. Just as a parent desires their child to improve and do better, so God wants us to improve and do better. A parent does not disown the child or stop loving the child if they stumble and fall. God will never disown us or stop loving us if we fail. He will pick us up, dust us off and encourage us to try again. This process is called *sanctification*. This is different for each believer. My best is not your best. Your best is not someone else's best.

Look at it this way...salvation is your spiritual birth. Your spirit has been born within you. It can never be unborn. Sanctification is your growing up. Just as a baby is not all it can be at birth, and goes through life learning to reach that potential, sanctification is our growing up spiritually and maturing spiritually.

Salvation is immediate. Salvation is permanent. Sanctification is an on-going process. It does not affect our salvation. That is already assured. But Paul wants us to keep trying to do better. That is what "*working out your own salvation*" means here. The end result of salvation is for us to be all that God knows we can be. Salvation starts the sanctification process. It is just like birth starts the process of growing up and improving. Salvation is the birth. Sanctification is the growing up.

Jesus wants to turn us into a work of art for Him. He wants to present us before God without spot or blemish. Ephesians 5:27:

"That He might present [His Church] to Himself a glorious church, not having spot, or wrinkle, or any such thing; but that it should be holy and without blemish."

Jesus wants us to become all that we can be. This is not a prerequisite for salvation. This is a result of salvation. Jesus is going to work in your life to bring out the best in you. Now what may be best in you might be more than it is in someone else. What might be best in you might be less than it is in someone else. What Paul is speaking of here is the on-going process in a believer's life. We are saved. However, we are also becoming sanctified. Your mind and attitude will change. You will see things differently.

Now Philippians 2:13 makes it clear that God is the one doing the work here. Paul is not telling us that we now have to work for our salvation. In his letter to the Ephesians, Paul said that this was a free gift and it had nothing to do with works. So Paul is not changing his mind. He is not contradicting himself. He is encouraging believers to work with God—to allow God to makes these changes in their life.

What if you fall flat on your face? What if you don't do well? What if you mess things up? Doesn't matter. Your salvation is secure. You are not the person who is responsible for your salvation. You have entrusted your salvation into the care of Jesus Christ. Here's what Paul says about that. II Timothy 1:12:

"For [this] cause I also suffer these things: nevertheless I am not ashamed: for I know whom I have believed, and am persuaded that He is able to keep that which I have committed unto Him against that day."

We have placed our salvation into the hands of Jesus to take care of it, and to keep it safe so that when we stand before God at the end of our life, it will be there for us. Can anything keep this from happening? Never! Check our Romans 8:38–39:

"For I am persuaded, that neither death, nor life, nor angels, nor principalities, nor powers, nor things present, nor things to come,

"Nor height, nor depth, nor any other creature, shall be able to separate us from the love of God, which is in Christ Jesus our Lord."

Nothing can separate us from the love of God. And in case you ever wonder if you will blow it and God will change His mind about saving you, check out Roman 11:29:

"For the gifts and the calling of God are without repentance."

If I were to put this in legal terms for contract law, this is a clause in the insurance policy. It would be called a "non-cancellation" clause. The insurance company does not have the legal authority to cancel your insurance policy—ever!

Salvation is a gift. It is a free gift that God gave you. God called you to be saved. These are without repentance. That means that it is irrevocable. It can never be undone. That means that God will never, ever change His mind. You are that secure.

For God to change His mind about saving you would require that you are able to do something that God did not know about. It would require that you caught God off guard. God knew exactly what He was getting into when He saved you. You'll never surprise Him. He will never change His mind.

For those who keep making these statements, let me ask, "Why are you trying to bring a believer back into bondage?" "Why are you trying to place a burden on them that they could not bear when they were lost?" Salvation is a free gift. It is not a credit card purchase. You do not charge it on your Christ Card, and then have to perform so many good deeds each month until the account is paid off. It did not work that way before salvation. It does not work that way after salvation. It is a gift that Jesus gave you forever just because you asked for it.

Sin shall not have dominion over them. That is forbidden by law. The court of law that you keep trying to pull them into and put them in front of the judge, that court no longer has any file on them. They do not exist as far as that court is concerned. There are no charges pending. They are not on probation. Let me repeat that: THEY ARE NOT ON PROBATION. They do not have to report to anyone. They do not have to act a certain way. No one has any legal authority over them. No one can come back and pull them back into court for whatever brought them into court the first time. All the charges have been dropped. Let me repeat that: ALL THE CHARGES HAVE BEEN DROPPED. Sin and death have no claim on them. There is no lien or legal claim to their life or their soul.

Trying to make them work for something that God has given for free is bondage. There is no other name for it. They already have it. It is theirs. They already have possession of it. God is not going to change His mind. God is not going to take it back. It is in Jesus' custody. Nothing can get between us and God and His love. You cannot get any more secure than that. And that is what God's contract has promised in writing. And that is what God's contract through Jesus Christ has delivered.

Let me take a moment to remind you of an important concept in contract law. The person writing the contract has the burden to make the contract as clear as possible. If there is any ambiguity in how the contract reads, the court will accept the more liberal interpretation that is in favor of those signing the contract, not those who are writing the contract. Consider all that I have presented above. I have documented everything using the contract itself. Salvation is a free gift of God. Salvation is ours for the asking. God does everything, and all we have to do is to accept what He is offering. If, and again this is a VERY BIG IF, there is some verse in the Bible that suggests we have to work or pay for our salvation, or that we can lose our salvation, these portions of the contract will override it. The courts, that would be God, would have to reject any argument that adds any burden or obligation to the party receiving the salvation. When presented with two or more interpretations of a contract's intent, the courts will rule in favor of the more liberal interpretation and find in favor of the party signing the contract. That would be us. Now let's see what the Cults have to offer...

CHAPTER TWELVE

THE PLAN OF SALVATION PER THE JEHOVAH'S WITNESSES

As we discussed earlier in this book, the Jehovah's Witnesses do not believe that Jesus is God. They claim that He is "*a god*" but not "*THE God.*" In their theology, he is actually an angel. He is believed to be the Archangel Michael. This means that he is a created being and not a begotten son. This would disqualify him from ever being the Savior. According to Jehovah's Witnesses' Theology, there is no Trinity. There is God. There is the Holy Spirit; but the Holy Spirit is not a person. It is an invisible active impersonal force from God. They refuse to recognize the Holy Ghost.

Even though their Jesus [Michael] does not qualify to save them, they still add additional requirements to obtain salvation. Let me repeat, their Jesus [Michael] lacks the legal status and qualification to be our savior. They have no Savior to offer the world. So add all the requirements you want to your system, it will always be invalid. No Savior equals No Salvation!

But here are the other requirements they add to their system. In order to be saved, you must be baptized into the Jehovah's Witnesses church. You must prove yourself worthy of salvation and work for it by going door-to-door. You can also lose your salvation. So one of their requirements is that you can never blow it.

Now even the definition of being "*saved*" has been redefined by the Jehovah's Witnesses. The Jehovah's Witness Theology allows for only 144,000 people to be in Heaven. That number was reached in 1935. I am not sure how they kept count. If the Old Testament saints qualify as being saved, then that number would have been reached before Jesus was even born. So when they speak of being "*saved*" they are not speaking of dying and going to live in Heaven. According to Jehovah's Witness Theology, when you die you cease to exist. They call it "*annihilation.*" Your soul—with all its personality and memories, ceases to exist. Your body decays in the ground.

When the time comes for the return of Jesus to set up His Kingdom here on the earth, that is when your body will be recreated—not resurrected. You will get a new body, not the body you have now. It might look like this body; but it is not this body. Also, your original soul has been annihilated. It no longer exists. Therefore, a new one will have to be provided as well. Hopefully, this new soul will be programmed with the same memories and emotions your old soul had. In other words, nothing that was you gets to live on earth during the Kingdom Age. An imitation you gets to spend a thousand years on earth with Jesus. I hope that makes you feel good about yourself.

I would suggest that this is like an avatar we use in computer games, but this is not the same thing. An avatar is a little replica of you that moves about the computer screen, and does what you tell them to do. In the case of the Jehovah's Witnesses Theology, the avatar is there; but you are not. There is no control because the you that you were was annihilated at death. It no longer exists.

There are many problems with this doctrine. The first problem is that this Kingdom Age, per Revelation 20:6, will only last for one thousand years. At the end of these one thousand years, the earth and the rest of the universe come to a violent end Revelation 20:7–9:

"And when the thousand years are expired, Satan shall be [released] out of his prison,

"And shall go out to deceive the nations which are in the four quarters of the earth, Gog and Magog, to gather them together to battle: the number of whom is as the sand of the sea.

"And they went up on the breadth of the earth, and compassed the camp of the saints about, and the beloved city: and fire came down from God out of heaven, and devoured them."

Consider how Peter describes this event. II Peter 3:10:

"But the day of the Lord will come as a thief in the night; in…which the heavens shall pass away with a great noise, and the elements shall melt with fervent heat, the earth also and the works that are therein shall be burned up."

Not only will the earth cease to exist, the heavens [all the stars, planets, moons and galaxies] will also come to an end. The description is of an atomic explosion. The elements—the smallest piece of molecular matter creates a great noise and converts into fervent heat. Everything that is matter in this universe ceases to exist. Try surviving that.

So if the Kingdom Age only lasts for one thousand years, what happens to the inhabitants of earth at the end of those thousand years? If we follow the logic of Jehovah's Witnesses' Theology, when everything blows apart, so do you. Your body that is not really you ceases to exist. Your soul that is not really you is annihilated again. You no longer exist, and your replica has ceased to exist. Is there anything in Jehovah's Witnesses' Theology that lets God create another imitation of you to live on? How does any of this benefit you, personally? For that matter, how does this thousand-year kingdom benefit you? You won't be part of it. A copy of you will be enjoying it; but not you. You have been annihilated.

Here is another problem to think about… The Book of Revelation Chapter Twenty makes it clear that the Kingdom Age here on earth will only last for 1,000 years. This "salvation" offered by the Jehovah's Witnesses is temporary at best. It does not last. At the end of that thousand-year age, there will be a massive rebellion against Jesus Christ. As we saw in Revelation 20:7–9 above, Satan is released, he leads the earth in rebellion against Jesus, they surround the city of Jerusalem. There are more people rebelling than we can count, and then God destroys everyone and everything.

Now the question we need to answer is: "If only Jehovah's Witnesses will be in the Kingdom Age; does this mean that the majority of Jehovah's Witnesses will rebel and attack Jerusalem trying to overthrow Jesus?" If only Jehovah's Witnesses are there; then we have no choice but to conclude that many of the Jehovah's Witnesses will be so unhappy with the Kingdom Age that they will rebel against Jesus. That is not a very good endorsement for wanting to live in the Kingdom Age.

Now in the Jehovah's Witnesses Theology, it is possible to lose your salvation. It is based upon your works and that you are worthy. If you fail to prove yourself worthy, you lose your salvation. Even if you make it to the Kingdom Age, you can still be annihilated.

***

I want to pause here and discuss this concept of being worthy. You might get away with this demand to be worthy in the Latter Day Church's system. It does not seem to stress God's love and forgiveness because you have to atone for your own sins. God is not giving you anything. It has nothing to do with love. It has everything to do with work and entitlement. Such a system has no place for love. Therefore, I will give the Latter Day Church that demand to prove themselves worthy in their theology.

But the Jehovah's Witnesses speak about how much God loves them. When they come to my door, I can honestly believe that they think God loves them, and they really want to worship Him.

So here is the problem with having to prove yourself worthy. What are you proving yourself worthy of? Is it not that you are worthy of His love? Now stop and consider what that is actually saying. If you must prove yourself worthy in order for someone to love you, is that actually love? How would you react if you have to win your spouse's affection and prove yourself worthy enough for them to love you? How could you ever feel secure in such a relationship? Add to this that you can do something to prove you are not worthy—even by accident, and you have to start all over again.

How many people would put up with that treatment and marry this jerk? This proving yourself worthy is an on-going thing. You can never stop proving yourself worthy because if you do, your spouse will divorce you and kick you out without a moment of regret. Can we say: "dysfunctional relationship"? Love is supposed to make you feel safe and secure. Where is the security in such a relationship?

When we were first married, I told my wife that I loved her. She asked me, "Why?" I'm newly married. I haven't learned the game, and so I honestly thought about her question before answering. The more I thought about it, I could not come up with a single reason to love her. Don't panic, there is more to that conclusion. If I loved her because she was beautiful— which she is—then what happens if she does not age well, or if she has a horrible accident? Do I stop loving her then? If I love her because she is doing things for me, is that love; or have I turned my affection and emotions into a payment for services rendered relationship?

I finally came to my answer. There was no reason why I loved her. I had chosen to love her, and so I loved her.

So why is God loving you? Does He want anything other than to be with us? Do we have to prove ourselves worthy of God's love? Isn't that emotional blackmail? Isn't that what people do to try to manipulate people? They withhold love, or threaten to withhold love, if they do not get what they want. If that is the reason, then it is not truly love. If it is not truly love, then God does not deserve our love.

But John tells us in I John 4:19:

"We love Him, because He first loved us."

God started the process. He chose to love us. He extended His love toward us. Romans 5:8 tells us:

"But God [expressed] His love toward us, in that, while we were yet sinners, Christ died for us."

This was while we were not worthy. Romans 5:10 describes it this way:

"For if, when we were enemies, we were reconciled to God by the death of His Son, [how] much more, being reconciled, we shall be saved by His life."

Both God the Father and Jesus the Son demonstrated how much They loved us. They demonstrated that love to us when we were considered enemies of God. How much more unworthy can we be than to be an enemy of God? We can't. So why does God demonstrate His love for us when we are His enemies and do not deserve His love; but then when we respond to His love, He now demands that we prove ourselves worthy? The logic just is not there.

I can see from our part, as humans, that we want to do better. Our love for God wants us to be the best person we can be for God. I can see that. But that means the need to prove ourselves worthy is on us and it did not come from God. If God truly loves us, and gave His Son to save us when we were His enemies, why would He demand more of us after we respond to His love. Was the death of Jesus nothing more than a galactic "*bait and switch*"? Was the death of Jesus and His saying He loved us nothing more than a pretense to lure us in? Once we are lured in, does God change the rules and now He will not love us unless we do things for Him?

In this scenario, God becomes the ultimate manipulator. If this was all just manipulation to get us to serve Him; then He does not love us. If He does not love us, this makes God and Jesus liars. They claim to love us, but they do not. They are using emotional blackmail to get something from us.

Let me come back to this concept of "*sanctification*." Do not mistake "*sanctification*" for proving yourself worthy. They are two different things. God's love for us does not depend on how good we become. Sanctification is the maturing process of believers. We are learning to walk spiritually. If we stumble and fall, God picks us up, dusts us off, and encourages us to try again. If we are struggling or even if we give up, God does not stop loving us. God does not disown us. There is this non-cancellation clause in His contract: "the gifts [salvation] and callings of God are without repentance." They are irrevocable.

God's love and acceptance of us is based upon His decision to love us. Keep in mind Malachi 3:6: "...I change not..." God docs not change His mind. He will never decide to stop loving us. God's love for us is as constant as His decision to love us.

Again, one of the purposes for putting something in writing as a contract is to guarantee what you are promising in writing. If it must be earned, and it can be lost; then is God really guaranteeing anything with His contract?

***

I need to discuss the concept of the Resurrection as it relates to the Plan of Salvation. As Jesus hung on the cross, God transferred every sin ever committed: past, present or future into Jesus. Remember the Day of Atonement? The High Priest had to place his hands on the head of the scapegoat and confess the sins of Israel over the goat. This way the sin was transferred to the goat, and the sins could be taken away. The transferring of sins to the sacrifice is the only way that sins can be removed. If a sacrifice dies and no sin has been transferred to it, the death is meaningless. It serves no purpose. Therefore, God had to transfer every sin that is being atoned for into Jesus.

Now remember Romans 6:23:

"The wages of sin is death..."

This Greek word for sin is singular. A single sin can and will result in death. A single sin has the power to hold someone in the grave. Jesus took every sin that would ever exist into His body. He died because that sin was in His body. Now He has to prove to us that every sin has been resolved. Every sin has been removed. Every sin has been atoned for. How can He do that? The only way He can prove to us that there was not a single sin left unatoned in His body was for Him to come back from the dead. He had to bring His dead body that had held every sin in it back to life. If every sin is resolved, then death cannot hold Him. Sin results in death. If sin is gone, then death should have no power over Him. The sin was in His body. That body holding all that sin has to come back from the dead to prove the sacrifice worked.

While the Crucifixion is the action that the Law required to atone for every sin in the world, the Resurrection is the proof that the sacrifice of Jesus was accepted by God and that every sin was resolved. This is why the Resurrection is as important to us as the Crucifixion. The Crucifixion is the sacrifice Jesus offered to God. The Resurrection proves that God accepted the sacrifice of Jesus, and sin has been resolved forever.

So, with regards to the Resurrection, the Jehovah's Witness Theology teaches that Jesus resurrected as a spirit—not in the body He died in. And they teach that during the three days Jesus was in the tomb, He was annihilated—He ceased to exist. If He could not resurrect the body that held the sin, then how can we ever know if His sacrifice worked? We can't.

But Jesus knew that over a thousand years after His death and Resurrection, someone would come along and teach that His body did not resurrect. Jesus made this a sign that He was of God. John 2:18–21:

"Then answered the Jews and said unto Him, 'What sign [will you show] us, seeing that you do these things?'

"Jesus answered and said unto them, 'Destroy this temple, and in three days I will raise it up.'

"Then said the Jews, 'Forty and six years was this temple in [the] building [stage], and you will rear it up in three days?'

"But He spoke of the temple of His body."

The people asked for a sign. Jesus gave them the sign: "After you destroy the temple of my body, I will restore it in three days." This means bringing the body He was in when He made this claim back to life, and Him continuing to live in it. If Jesus cannot/did not do this, then He lied. If He lied, He was not sent by God. If He was not sent by God; then we are still lost in our sins. Yes, it is THAT serious.

This is why Jesus appeared to His Disciples. He appeared to those who knew Him best. When He came into the room, they were afraid. They had no doubt that it was Him. It was not someone looking like Him. They thought it was His ghost. Jesus submitted to testing to prove to them that He was not a ghost. In Luke 24:39 He invited them to physically examine the body He was in:

"'Behold my hands and my feet, that it is I myself: handle me, and see; for a spirit has not flesh and bones, as you see me have.'"

In fact, Jesus submitted to whatever test they could ask of Him to prove, beyond any shadow of doubt, that this was His physical body that had been resurrected from the death. You cannot touch a spirit. These tests disproved the teaching of the Jehovah's Witnesses concerning His coming back from the dead being nothing more than a spirit.

The Jehovah's Witnesses cite the fact that the two disciples on the road to Emmaus did not recognize Him when He joined them as proof it was not Jesus in His body. They do not pay attention to what the Bible says about this encounter. Luke 24:16:

"But their eyes were holden [blocked] that they should not know Him."

God kept them from recognizing Jesus on the road. When He prays over the meal in Luke 24:31, God stops blocking their eyes from recognizing Jesus. Luke 24:31:

"And their eyes were opened, and they knew Him, and He vanished out of His sight."

The fact that they did not recognize Him had nothing to do with His body. It had everything to do with how God allowed their eyes to function. This vanishing out of their midst is not a spirit; it is the resurrected glorified body we shall all have. It can function in this world and the spirit world. This is how Jesus stepped into the Upper Room when all the doors and windows were locked. He was in a glorified physical body—but it was still His original body.

When Thomas missed this meeting and demanded further proof, Jesus came back and submitted Himself to Thomas' tests. Whatever it would take to prove to His Disciples that He had resurrected from the dead in the body He had lived and died in was offered. His Disciples had to be 100% certain so they could convince us two thousand years later.

***

A 1950 issue of The Watchtower magazine "invites careful and critical examination of its contents in the light of the Scriptures."

In keeping with this, a 1973 issue of Awake! Magazine says that people should examine all the evidence, and that one arrives at the truth by examining both sides of a matter.

II Corinthians 13:5 in the New World Translation states:

"Keep testing whether you are in the faith, keep proving what you yourselves are."

I believe that we have done just that with regards to the teaching of the Watchtower Society and the teachings of the Jehovah's Witnesses. So what are the results of our comparison?

1. Their Messiah is not God. Therefore, their Messiah has not fulfilled Isaiah 9:6:

"For unto us a child is born, unto us a son is given: and the government shall be upon His shoulders: and His name shall be called Wonderful Counsellor, *The Mighty God, The Everlasting Father*, The Prince of Peace." [Emphasis added]

Since their Jesus was not God, he cannot qualify for two of the titles that this child is required to bear: the Mighty God, and the Everlasting Father. In the Jehovah's Witnesses' Theology, this prophecy remains unfulfilled. What is the danger of God not fulfilling every prophecy? The danger is that God's contract becomes invalid. If you invalidate God's contract, there is no alternative contract that we can appeal to or fall back on.

In Isaiah 7:14 the prophet notes that the title for the Messiah will be "*Immanuel.*" Matthew 1:23 tells us that Immanuel [Emmanuel] literally means that "*God is with us.*" God will physically be among us. If their Jesus is not God, then this prophecy remains unfulfilled.

Following this doctrine that their Jesus is not God, this leaves another prophecy unfulfilled. This prophecy was made by Abraham in Genesis 22:8:

270

"And Abraham said, 'My son, *God will provide Himself* [as] a lamb for a burnt offering:' so they went both of them together." [Emphasis added]

Since their Jesus is not God, then God did not provide Himself as the sacrifice. He provided another to die in His place. God lied when He revealed His Plan of Salvation to Abraham. Now consider Hebrews 6:18, which declares that "it is impossible for God to lie." How do you resolve this conflict? It can only be resolved if Jesus is God.

2. Because their Jesus was not God, but was the Archangel Michael, He did not exist forever. He had a beginning. This means that their Jesus did not fulfill the prophecy made in Micah 5:2:

"But you, Bethlehem Ephratah, though you are little among the thousands of Judah, yet out of you shall He come forth unto me who is to be ruler in Israel; whose goings forth have been *from of old, from everlasting.*" [Emphasis added]

This also creates a problem with John 1:3:

"All things were made by Him, and without Him was not anything made that was made."

If their Jesus is Michael, then their Jesus is a created being. Even if, as the Jehovah's Witnesses claim, Michael made everything after he was made, he did not make himself. This makes this statement by John false.

3. Because their Jesus is not God, but an angelic being, He lied when He declared that He was God. John 10:30:

"I and my Father are one."

John 10:31-33:

"And the Jews took up stones again to stone Him.

"Jesus answered them, 'Many good works I have shown you from My Father. For which of those works do you stone Me?'

"The Jews answered Him, saying, 'For good work we do not stone You, but for blasphemy, and because You, being a man, *make Yourself God.*'" [Emphasis added]

John 5:18

"Therefore the Jews sought all the more to kill Him, because He not only broke the Sabbath, but also said that God was His Father, *making Himself equal with God.*" [Emphasis added]

John 14:9:

"Jesus said unto him, 'Have I been so long time with you, and yet have you not known me, Philip? *He who has seen me has seen the Father*; and how [can you] say then, "Show us the Father?"'" [Emphasis added]

In this scenario, Jesus is declaring to Philip that He is God. If you have seen Jesus, then you have seen God. If you know Jesus, then you know God. They are the same. They are one. They are interchangeable. Jesus is God, and God is Jesus. Jesus even made belief in the teaching that He is God essential to our salvation. John 8:24:

"I said therefore unto you, 'that you shall die in your sins:' for if you believe not that I am *he*, you shall die in your sins."

I left this verse in its exact wording and font from the King James Bible. Notice that in the King James Bible version "*he*" is in italics. This was a code with the King James Bible translators to let the reader know that this word was not in the original Greek or Hebrew version of the verse. Someone added it to the verse thinking it would make the meaning of the verse clearer. In this case they were wrong.

Contrary to the teaching of the Jehovah's Witnesses' Theology, "*Jehovah*" is not the name God has chosen for Himself. That is what they teach, but that is not what God declares. "*Jehovah*" is not how He identified Himself to Moses. Exodus 3:13–14:

"And Moses said unto God, 'Behold, when I come unto the children of Israel, and shall say unto them, "The God of your fathers has sent me unto you;" and they shall say to me, "What is His name?" what shall I say unto them?'

"And God said unto Moses, '*I AM THAT I AM*:' and He said, 'Thus shall you say unto the children of Israel, "*I AM* has sent me unto you."'" [Emphasis added]

Now this was the perfect time and place for God to clarify forever how we should refer to Him. It was the perfect set up for God to reveal the name He wanted us to use when speaking of Him. But God did not use this opportunity to tell Moses, "*My name is Jehovah. Always refer to Me as Jehovah when you speak of Me.*" That is what Moses was looking for when he asked his question. If God is so adamant that His true name is Jehovah, and everyone should call Him "*Jehovah*" when they speak of Him; then this is where He should have said so. That was the information Moses was seeking. "*God, what is Your name?*"

No, God did not declare Himself to be Jehovah. He declared Himself to be I AM. "I AM THAT I AM." "Tell them I AM has sent you." The Jews recognize the use of the term "I AM" to be referring to God. Therefore, the proper translation of John 8:24 is:

"I said therefore unto you, 'that you shall die in your sins:' for if you believe not that I AM, you shall die in your sins."

The proper interpretation of this verse would then be: "Unless you believe that I AM [God], you shall not be saved." ["You shall die in your sins."] Now this is part of a lengthy debate with the Pharisees. They knew exactly what He was claiming. Notice John 8:58:

"Jesus said unto them, 'Verily, verily, I say unto you, "Before Abraham was, I AM.""'

Here the translators left the statement exactly as Jesus said it in the original language. Notice the reaction of the Pharisees to this statement. They knew exactly what He was saying. He was claiming to be God. John 8:59:

"Then took they up stones to cast at Him: but Jesus hid Himself, and went out of the temple, going through the midst of them, and so passed by."

They had threatened to stone Him in other places for claiming to be God and for being equal to God. They see these comments of Jesus using "I AM"—the title God revealed for Himself—as claiming to be God. Jesus noted that belief that He is God come in the flesh and dwelling among them was required for you to be saved. Therefore, if your Jesus is not God; then that Jesus cannot save you. If their Jesus is not God, he is an invalid Savior.

Now consider this, if Jesus lied about being God, then He is a liar. Lying is a sin. This means that He is no longer without sin. If He is no longer without sin, then He can no longer qualify as our sacrifice for sin because the sacrifice must be without sin.

4. If their Jesus is not God, then He has stolen from God. He has taken praise and worship that only belongs to God and accepted worship and praise from others. Matthew 9:18:

"While He spoke these things unto them, behold, there came a certain ruler, and *worshiped him*, saying, 'My daughter is even now dead: but come and lay your hand upon her, and she shall live.'" [Emphasis added]

Matthew 14:33:

"Then they who were in the ship came and *worshipped Him*, saying, 'Of a truth you are the Son of God.'" [Emphasis added]

It is forbidden for a man or even an angel to accept worship. An angel even told John not to worship him but to worship only God. Revelation 19:10

"And I fell at his feet to *worship him*; but he said to me, '*See that you do not do that!* I am your fellow servant and of your brethren who have the testimony of Jesus. *Worship God*! For the testimony of Jesus is the spirit of prophecy.'" [Emphasis added]

If their Jesus is not God, He has taken something that belonged only to God. If Jesus has stolen from God, then He is now a thief. If He has stolen, then He now has sin in His life, and can no longer qualify as the sacrifice for sin.

This is just a quick sample of the problems if Jesus is not God. I will conclude this point by noting that the Jesus they offer to us does not qualify as the sacrifice for sin. His death cannot save us because He, Himself, is a sinner.

5. The Jehovah's Witnesses' Theology does not offer salvation free and clear. It is a work program. We must work and earn our salvation. This clearly violates Ephesians 2:8–9:

"For by grace are you saved through faith; and that not of yourselves: it is the gift of God:

"Not of works, lest any man should boast."

Therefore, their Plan of Salvation does not comply with the Plan of Salvation God offers in the Bible. Any one of these differences listed above will invalidate God's contract. It will cause God's contract to become null and void. God does not offer any other contract. There is no backup to this Plan of Salvation. By invalidating the Plan of Salvation outlined in the Bible, they will "*die in their sins*"—as Jesus declared.

6. Their salvation can be lost. This challenges God's declaration that He will never change His mind about giving His gift [of salvation] or of calling us to follow Him. By teaching that salvation can be lost, they are calling God a liar. Romans 11:29:
"For the gifts and the calling of God are without repentance." [They are irrevocable.]

7. The Jehovah's Witnesses reject the physical and bodily resurrection of Jesus. This was the very proof that Jesus offered as a sign to prove to the Jews that He was who He claimed to be. John 2:18–21:
"Then answered the Jews and said unto Him, 'What sign [will you give] unto us, seeing that you do these things?'

"Jesus answered and said unto them, 'Destroy this temple, and in three days I will raise it up.'

"Then said the Jews, 'Forty-six years [has it taken] this Temple [to be built] and you will rear it up in three days?'

"But He spoke of the Temple of His body."

If Jesus did not resurrect from the grave in the same physical body He died in and through which He spoke and taught the Jews, then His sign is false. He did not offer the proof that He promised them. He was referring to "*this Temple.*" John notes that Jesus was speaking of the Temple of His body. Therefore, the body that stood before the Jews and made this promise must be the same body that comes out of the grave.

As I demonstrated earlier in this chapter, if you take the time to review the Bible and the account of the eyewitnesses, Jesus went to great lengths to present His body to those who knew Him for confirmation. Luke 24:39:

"'Behold my hands and my feet, that it is I myself: handle me, and see; for a spirit has not flesh and bones, as you see me have.'"

If you follow the accounts of His Resurrection and His appearance to His Disciples, He invited and submitted to every test that they had. He continued to offer proof until their doubts were gone. Jesus needed each Disciple and follower with Him to be 100% convinced that He had come back from the dead in the same physical body He had lived in and died it. It was the same flesh. It was the same bones. It was the same body, but it had been glorified. He needed to make sure that they were convinced, because so many of them would give their lives to prove that statement was true. If His followers—eyewitnesses— had doubts, then they would not die to prove it.

The Jehovah's Witnesses remove the very proof that Jesus offered that He was the Messiah. They also remove the one proof that the sacrifice of Jesus worked. How can they prove their claim that the death of Jesus resolved sin when in their own theology, the proof has been discredited and removed?

8. The Jehovah's Witnesses deny an actual resurrection of the body you are living in. They claim it will be a different body recreated for you. God's contract requires that the body you are living in must be resurrected and made whole and fully functioning. Job declared that in the latter day he would stand with his Redeemer upon the earth. He would see with his own eyes and not another's. [Job 19:27] This prophecy cannot be fulfilled because according to the Jehovah's Witnesses' Theology, your bodies shall decay. They will be replaced—not resurrected—in the Kingdom Age. The soul that is us will be annihilated. That, too, will have to be replaced.

If these differences were presented in a court of law, I do not believe that their teachings would hold up as being the same teachings that the Bible presents. It would be proven that they were offering an alternative contract—a fake Plan of Salvation—other than the one God has documented in His Bible.

The Jehovah's Witnesses have been deceived into believing another Gospel—a Gospel that was never offered by God. In their case, the fears that Paul voiced in II Corinthians 11:4 have come true:

"For if he who comes [after me] preaches another Jesus, whom we have not preached, or if you receive another spirit, which you have not received, or another gospel, which you have not accepted, [I am afraid that] you might [believe him]."

What did Paul say concerning those who present another Gospel? Galatians 1:8–9:

"But though we, or an angel from Heaven, preach any other gospel unto you than that which we have preached unto you, let him be accursed [damned].

"As we said before, so say I now again, 'If any preach any other gospel unto you than that you have received [from us], let him be accursed [damned].'"

This is why these deceptions are damned. Paul called for those who teach these deceptions to be damned. Those who believe them will believe a Jesus that Paul never taught. They will trust a Gospel that Paul never preached. The Jesus they believe in will not be the Jesus who is God among us. And, therefore, they will be deceived. And when they die, they will die in their sins. This is why this issue is so important.

But, would an angel ever give anyone false information about Jesus, the Bible, God or salvation? I'm glad you asked. Let's see what the *Church of Jesus Christ of Latter Day Saints* have to say about this…

CHAPTER THIRTEEN

THE LATTER DAY CHURCH'S PLAN OF SALVATION

So let's take a moment to discuss and summarize the Plan of Salvation presented by the Church of Jesus Christ of Latter Day Saints. To be honest, even though they put such emphasis on having the name *Jesus Christ* in their title, He plays a very small and insignificant role in their Church or salvation.

The death of Jesus upon the cross secures their resurrection into the next life. It secures everyone's resurrection into the next life: Mormon and Non-Mormon. What all the other worlds do to have resurrection is never discussed; but do they have someone dying on those worlds to be resurrected? Hasn't anyone on all those other worlds figured out a better plan for a resurrection?

The death of Jesus has no impact upon which kingdom they are resurrected into. Now keep in mind that this is not the first time that the Council of Gods have gotten together and created a new world. Earth is far from their first attempt. Yet according to their Prophets, Founding Fathers and leaders, when it came to the issue of salvation, those who were not yet Gods, and had never been mortal, were asked by these Gods to present their recommendations for what they called their Plan of Salvation. Why would you ask someone who has never done this before to address the most important part of creating a world? Especially when you have a Council of Gods there, and they would have experience as to what works and what doesn't work when it comes to creating worlds.

Per Mormon Theology, Jesus presented His plan to the Council of Gods. Also, per Mormon Theology, Lucifer had this plan where he would do everything, and everyone would be saved. Consider the Mormon Book of Moses 4:1:

"Lucifer, who was also a son of the Father, came forward with a counterproposal: "'Behold, send me, I will be thy Son, and I will redeem all mankind, that not one soul shall be lost and surely I will do it; wherefore, give me thine honor.'"

Notice the statement of Lucifer here. He was going to redeem all mankind. This is what Jesus did in the Biblical account. Does "*redeem*" have the same meaning here as it does in the Bible? He was going to ensure that not one soul would be lost. "*Lost*" is a Biblical term. We probably need the Latter Day Church definition for this word, as they seem to have given many different definitions to words we normally use. Is lost nothing more than ending up in the Telestial Kingdom? Do you atone for your own sins there and get out when you are done? Is Lucifer just bypassing this step in eternity? Or does "*lost*," in this case, suggest a non-Mormon doctrine of going to Hell? Was Lucifer's program actually going to save us from something bad? If it was going to save us from something bad, then by definition it was a Plan of Salvation.

For some reason, getting everyone saved was not the goal of this Council of Gods. Has this Council of Gods ever outlined their goals in creating a world? Are there any guidelines when doing this? Allowing everyone to get saved was the wrong goal here. It says that they rejected Lucifer's Plan because he had the wrong attitude. He was removing free will from man. But if his Plan achieved the right goal, why not adopt his Plan and have someone else implement it who had the right attitude? Why go with an inferior Plan over something as petty as the person's motivation? Lucifer's Plan saves everyone. Jesus' Plan in the Mormon Theology only saves a few—and only those who are worthy. Personally, I would have gone with Lucifer's Plan.

Let me make a suggestion. Why not implement Lucifer's Plan with a slight alteration? Why not make this Plan voluntary? Why not let mankind choose to accept it or choose to reject it? You know? The kind of Plan the Bible actually offers us. It wasn't that hard of a problem to fix. I fixed it and I'm not even a God.

Was this Plan for the good of creation, or was it for the glory of the one who would implement it? What really takes priority here? If you have two Plans before you, and they both have part of the solution in them; then why not learn to work together? Are these Gods that petty? Have they never learned how to compromise to achieve a common goal? They rejected Plan B submitted by Lucifer. So I have to ask why was it called a Plan of Salvation. If *"salvation"* was not the goal, then why do you create a Plan of Salvation? Needless to say, the Council of Gods rejected his plan. He was not happy, and according to their teachings, he did not *"keep his first estate."* Do they ever explain exactly what that means?

In Biblical terms, the angels not *keeping their first estate* suggests that they either moved out of Heaven, or that they became something other than angels to accomplish some task that they were trying to achieve. They may have became less than angels and assumed another form for their purposes. Did Lucifer and his followers move out of heaven? Did they stop being spirit beings or spirit sons? If not, then they did keep their first estate. They remained in Heaven, and they remained what they were when they had presented Plan B to the Council.

A lot of Biblical terms are being tossed around to make it sound like this is all Biblical. It is not. It really does not seem that anyone is taking the time to define these terms or understand what these expressions are actually saying. Someone is not asking the questions that need to be asked in order to get the information we need here. If I had conducted investigations where I never asked the hard questions, a lot of scam artists would be very rich today.

According to Latter Day Church resources, not keeping his first estate means that Lucifer led a great rebellion. If he did not stop being a spirit being; then why not just say, *"He led a rebellion."* He enlisted one-third of the other spirit-beings to his cause. He was fighting for his plan. Stop and think about that. He was fighting to ensure that everyone would be saved—

everyone would make it. That *everyone* would be us. If we were to put this into modern-day terms, Lucifer was a freedom fighter. He was fighting for our right to become a God. He led a rebellion to set us all free and to ensure that we would all attain Godhood. If this is the case, shouldn't I and the rest of humanity be joining him? Shouldn't we all be cheering him on? He was fighting to give us what we all wanted: Godhood.

If we support him, then the Council of Gods would punish us. Doesn't that begin to sound like a dictatorship or tyranny on some level? Are the Council of Gods tyrants who force their will on us and withhold from us what they, themselves, have already achieved?

In other words, are they not guilty of the very thing that they accused Lucifer of? Are they not guilty of denying us free will and a choice in our destiny? Why can't we select which Plan of Salvation we want? After all, their Plan of Salvation is not the subject of a written contract. There were multiple options.

Doesn't morality demand that we rise up against such tyranny and fight for our rights to become Gods like them? If a Plan B was available, and it would work to provide Godhood to all, and Lucifer was willing to pay the price to obtain Godhood for all; then why can't we reject Plan A, and fight the Council of Gods to make them give us Plan B? Wouldn't that put free choice back into the equation?

Instead, the Council of Gods went with Plan A. They went with the plan that would restrict most of us from Godhood, and award Godhood to only a small percentage. This would be the plan submitted by their Jesus—not our Jesus of the Bible. His plan was to restrict Godhood to just those who were able to prove themselves worthy. His plan did not secure salvation for the world. His plan secured nothing for anyone. His plan permitted salvation [exaltation] for a limited number based upon their actions and not His. His plan would exclude more than it would include. His plan was not as effective as Lucifer's...unless the Council of Gods does not really want us to become Gods.

The Council of Gods went with Plan A. They liked the fact that not everyone could make it to Godhood. They liked the idea that you had to prove yourself worthy. Therefore, they went with Plan A offered by their Jesus—not our Jesus. As far as Plan B was concerned, they defeated Lucifer and his rebellion. And then to punish them for questioning their decision, they banned him and all of his followers from ever getting born into a physical body. By doing this, they prevented Lucifer and his followers from ever attaining Godhood.

The Mormon Lucifer and his followers all sacrificed their chance to become Gods in an effort to secure each of us the right to be a God. [That is, if this account is true.] I would think that if this were true, then we should all flock to his side and to his defense and demand that he be forgiven.

Did not Brigham Young note that souls have always existed? Did he not claim that souls were sinless when they were born into the world? If Lucifer were barred from birth, would that not be a sin upon him? Is there no way in the Pre-Mortal Estate to remove sins? I'll discuss this in more detail later on.

***

So what does Jesus do to secure Godhood for this planet? Actually, according to Latter Day Church Theology He does nothing to secure Godhood for anyone. He does not even get Godhood. He still has to work for it and to prove Himself worthy of it. But His willingness to be the *"Savior"* of this world does get Him points in His efforts.

Here is the most disgusting lie concerning the Jesus that Mormon Theology suggests. They do not come out and say this, but their doctrines and structure suggests this. Their theology attacks the very motivation of Jesus. It degrades His motivation, and it degrades Him. He is not doing this because He is God, and because He loves us. He is doing this in order to become God. His motivation is not love. His motivation is 100% purely personal. They have reduced Jesus to a mercenary who is only in this for His own personal benefit.

In the Biblical account, Jesus does not receive anything out of His death on the cross—nothing for Himself personally.

He already was God. He set aside His divinity. He became one of us, and He was returning to Heaven to resume His divinity. However, He would remain human throughout all eternity. He can never stop being human because human is what He became to save us. That pre-Incarnation Jesus ceased to exist when He was born into our world. It was a price—like the death on the cross—that He paid for us.

In the Biblical account, Jesus sacrificed. He gave up so much for us. The only benefit Jesus received for these sacrifices made on our behalf is that we are able to be with Him in eternity. He did this for love. Love was His only motivation. He loved us, and He gave Himself for us.

In the Latter Day Church Theology, those who obtain "*salvation*," do so based upon their own merits. They are not going for "*salvation*." They are going for something called being *exalted*, not being *saved*.

The Latter Day Church has redefined the word, "*salvation*." In Mormon Theology, "*salvation*" has been redefined as "*exaltation*." Consider this quote from Bruce McConkie:

"…[S]alvation in its true and full meaning is synonymous with exaltation or eternal life and consists in gaining an inheritance in the highest of the three heavens within the celestial kingdom…

"This full salvation is obtained in and through the continuation of the family unit in eternity, and those who obtain it are gods." [Bruce McConkie, Mormon Doctrine page 670]

Notice that Bruce McConkie did not say that this exaltation or "full salvation" was obtained through the death of Jesus. Jesus is strangely missing from this discussion of "salvation."

I would have to challenge their use of the word "*salvation*" just from a grammatical point of view. Unless I am wrong, "*exaltation*" is a positive thing. How can we be "*saved*" from something that is positive, and which does not pose any danger for us? Has Mr. McConkie ever considered the basic definition in the English Dictionary for "*saved*" or "*salvation*"?

So if "*salvation*" in its ultimate Mormon state is "*exaltation*" and Godhood, what is "*salvation*" for the rest of us? It is resurrection. We are resurrected in the afterlife.

We all are resurrected no matter how good or bad we are. We are not being saved from anything. There is nothing to save us from. If our actions send us to the Telestial Kingdom, it will be our actions that deliver us from the Telestial Kingdom. Jesus' death has nothing to do with that. If we become *"exalted,"* it will be due solely to what we do or do not do. Jesus had nothing to do with our becoming *"exalted."*

What did Jesus do for the world? What does His death provide for us? According to Latter Day Church Theology, His death does nothing more than to ensure that we are going to be resurrected. I have to ask, if Jesus had not died on the cross, then when we died in our physical bodies, would we have died and ceased to exist? Let me continue that train of thought. If this spirit world is all about proving yourself worthy or ending up in the Telestial Kingdom to pay for our sins; aren't there a lot of people who do not see this as a good thing? Aren't there many who would be only too happy to be done with all of this, and to never have to worry about it ever again? Resurrection is not a positive thing for everyone.

By comparison, according to the Bible, the death of Jesus secured our salvation. This means that Jesus paid the price for original sins in our lives—the sin nature we inherited from Adam; and His death paid for each of our personal sins—those sins that we personally committed. That is what the death of Jesus on the cross did for us. Without the removal of sin from our lives, when we died, we would go to Hell, and there would be no escape. So the death of Jesus—according to the Bible—saved us from something. That is why it is called the Plan of Salvation. The Mormon Plan of Salvation saves us from nothing.

In addition to this, the death of Jesus made it possible for each one of us who accepts His forgiveness to move into Heaven, and live in Heaven for all eternity. Add to this that the death of Jesus, and our acceptance of His forgiveness, ensures that we will make it, and that we will live in Heaven. It will keep us secure in this life, and in the next life. God will never change His mind. We will never be cast out. We will never go back to the fate that we had without Jesus. We will make it—guaranteed!

In this scenario, there is more than enough reason to worship Jesus, praise Jesus, thank Jesus, and to honor and love Him for all eternity. There is every reason for us to call out to Jesus, and pray to Him because He is willing to help us. He wants us to succeed. The Jesus of the Bible accomplished a lot for me personally, and for each and every believer personally. He saved us. He continues to work with us and help us. He wants to be part of our lives every day.

The Jesus of the Latter Day Church has done nothing worthy of praise or worship. Perhaps this is why the Latter Day Church discourages the worship of Jesus. I can see why there would be no reason to pray to Him since it's all on you. If you ask for His help, then He will not help you. Further, if you have to ask for help; then, obviously, you are not worthy. If you have to ask for help, then you did not make it on your own. I repeat, in the Latter Day Church Theology, Jesus really has not done anything worthy of worship or praise. So why did they name their Church after Him? Since they prove themselves worthy, are they not lifting themselves up? Shouldn't a more accurate name for their Church be the *Church of Me, A Latter Day Saint*? After all, it is all about them, isn't it?

***

The Jesus of the Bible died to pay for both original sin, and for personal sin in each person's life. He died to remove sin, so that a personal relationship with God the Father is possible. How does this compare to the theology of the Latter Day Church? First of all, the Latter Day Church does not recognize original sin. They teach that Adam was given two conflicting orders. I have to ask, "Who gave him his orders?" It seems to have been the Council of Gods, because the Book of Abraham keeps mentioning "Gods" each time actions are taken or decisions are made concerning the creation of the world and of Adam and Eve. Who gave the order? Why did they set Adam up to fail?

Do we even know who the God of this world truly is? Do the Mormons even know the name of the God of this world if that is who they are to worship?

It all depends on whom you ask. Brigham Young taught that Joseph Smith, himself, revealed to him that Adam was the God of this World. This created a doctrine taught by Brigham Young called the Adam-God Doctrine. The Latter Day Church has since rejected this teaching, and claims that what Brigham Young said was misquoted or taken out of context—but they are the ones who quoted him and kept his records. They will not admit that Brigham Young and Joseph Smith might have been wrong. Yet there are still Latter Day Saints today who hold to this theory, and support it. If Adam is the God of this world, then is he the one who gave himself conflicting orders?

It is important to identify who—at this Council of Gods—made all of these decisions. As we saw in the King James Bible, God establishes His jurisdiction over His Creation by documenting that He is the sole Creator, and He does not share that jurisdiction. With the introduction of the word "*Gods*" in the Book of Abraham, we now have documentation that the ownership—and therefore the jurisdiction over Creation—is still opened to debate. It must be a shared jurisdiction.

As I mentioned previously in this book, per Mormon Theology, earth is only one of a very long list of planets that various Gods have created. If it is one of ten thousand—which would be a very low number since there are more than ten thousand Latter Saints who have probably made it to Godhood since our world was created—then is there a record of any world [other than Kolob] not falling? Have other Gods gotten it right the first time and created a world that did not fall? Since there is a teaching in the Mormon Theology that there are other worlds still close to Kolob, then other Gods must have gotten it right. Their worlds did not fall.

So I have to ask, if there are Gods on the Council of Gods who got it right, why don't they oversee all the new Gods doing this to ensure that none of these new worlds fall? Wouldn't that be the goal of each Council of God? Or do they let other worlds fall just to prove if they are worthy of Godhood? Have any of the other thousands of planets needed a Plan of Salvation for them? Haven't any of the meetings of Councils of God finally figured out what they are trying to achieve with these world creations, and what is the best way to do it? Obviously, not everyone was convinced the Plan A of Jesus was the best plan. One-third of the spirit beings at that time rebelled trying to stop that plan from being put into effect. It was a majority rules structure. If these Gods are so enlightened, then why can't they sit down and discuss this and convince everyone which plan is best. Why resort to force when you cannot convince everyone?

So if there is no original sin, and you must atone for your own personal sin; then when the Latter Day Church speaks about salvation, "What is being saved?" And "What are we being saved from?" And why is it that women do not seem to need this same salvation? The Plan of Salvation is offered only to men.

The Latter Day Church, for lack of a better explanation, is a Males-Only Club. Let's be honest, it's all about the males. It is the males who will work their way to Godhood. It is males who will chose to resurrect their wives in the afterlife. It is the males who will create their own world. The women will be there for the sole purpose of producing spirit children. How is that for a career path?

There is no structure in place for a woman to ensure her own salvation. There is no program for a woman to earn her own salvation. If she dies without a husband, and no husband is provided for her by the Latter Day Church, then it's all over for her, and she will sleep forever.

Now, is your sex in the world pre-determined by your sex in your Pre-Mortal Estate? Does a Pre-Mortal female have any chance of being born into a male mortal body? Is their fate determined back in the Pre-Mortal world and they have no choice? Didn't the Council of Gods take issue with Lucifer for not giving mortals free choice? If a Pre-Mortal female has no choice of being a male and being able to work toward Godhood;

have they not done the very thing they punished Lucifer for; of removing free choice from females?

Does anyone else get the feeling that this system was designed by and for males only? Is this a system that only secures free will for males? It's a pretty exclusive club.

***

So, if Jesus has to die in order for all males in the world to resurrect, what is it about His death that makes resurrection possible? A lot of people were crucified. For that matter, a lot of holy and religious men were martyred for their faith. Couldn't one of their deaths have done the same thing as the death of Jesus? What is missing in this system that only the death of Jesus in such a horrible way could fix? In the Biblical account of the death of Jesus, His death removes sin from the equation. He is the sin sacrifice. Sin is removed so that we can have a relationship with God the Father. What does the death of Jesus in the Latter Day Theology add or remove from the men of this world so that they can resurrect? What is it about the death of Jesus that makes Him different from thousands of holy and righteous men who were martyred for their faith? Why couldn't one of them accomplish the same thing?

If salvation is resurrection, what is it about the men in this world that keeps them from resurrecting? If their souls have always existed, and will always exist as Mormon leaders claim, then if the soul exists forever; it should resurrect and exist after death in this world no matter what Jesus did. Obviously, it has nothing to do with women and their souls. They end up in the afterlife waiting to be resurrected by their husbands—I guess Jesus was unable to resurrect them. The death of Jesus does nothing for them. Their resurrection is dependent on their husband, not Jesus. The only thing keeping them from resurrecting is their husband.

Now here is one of the bigger questions: "If the death of Jesus makes resurrection possible for men in this world, what happened to all the men and their souls who died before Jesus died?"

If men's souls survived death before Jesus died; then was His death even necessary to the program? If they survived death before Jesus died, where were they kept? If the Council of Gods were able to fix all these problems, then couldn't they fix the resurrection problem without having Jesus to die?

He was not paying for original sin when He died. Per Mormon Theology, there was no original sin. Obviously, whoever gave Adam his conflicting commands wasn't paying attention, or was it a test that was designed to be a no win scenario? Without knowing which God gave Adam that command, do we even know if this God has legal authority to give such a command?

If there was no original sin, and each man has to atone for his own sins; then I have to ask, "Who atones for the sins of women?" Is that their husband? If the sins of the wife can keep the husband from attaining exalted status; then wives are more of a liability to his exaltation than a benefit. But if he does not atone for his wives' sins, does that mean that Latter Day women never sin? Are they somehow exempt?

I keep coming back to the question of: "Why did Jesus have to die to ensure our resurrection?" What sin did He pay for with His death? There was no original sin to atone for. His program requires everyone else to pay for their own sins. To be more than blunt, why do we need Him? According to Mormon Theology, Jesus is on His way to Godhood. Do we know if He ever made it? Did He come back, and tell us He made it? Has anyone received a card, a letter, an e-mail from Him other than Joseph Smith? What if He ended up resurrecting in the Telestial Kingdom, and is still stuck there? In short, what proof do we have that this system presented by Joseph Smith works?

We need this kind of information to make an informed decision about this Plan of Salvation if we are going to buy into it. All we have is Joseph Smith telling us that this is how it worked. No one has offered any kind of proof to support the Latter Day Church. As Joseph Fielding Smith noted:

"Mormonism, as it is called, must stand or fall on the story of Joseph Smith. He was either a prophet of God, divinely called, properly appointed and commissioned, or he was one of the biggest frauds this world has ever seen. *There is no middle ground.* [Emphasis added]

"If Joseph Smith was a deceiver, who willfully attempted to mislead people, then he should be exposed; his claims should be refuted, and his doctrines shown to be false, for the doctrines of an imposter cannot be made to harmonize in all particulars with divine truth." [Joseph Fielding Smith, *Doctrines of Salvation* (1954) 1:188.

Brigham Young also gave this challenge:

"Take up the Bible, compare the religion of the Latter-Day Saints, and see if it will stand the test." [Brigham Young, Journal of Discourses (London: Latter-Day Saints Book Deposit 1854- 1856) 16:46]

Both leaders of the Latter Day Church have mandated that the only way to see if what Joseph Smith has told us is the truth is to compare his teachings with the Bible—not with any Mormon Publications or documents.

So let's take a quick comparison of the Latter Day Church Plan of Salvation in light of what the Bible tells us…

***

According to Latter Day Theology, your exaltation begins long before you are born into this world. The God of this world will have sexual relations with one of his celestial wives. You will be born as a spirit baby. Now your actions and attitudes from that moment on are held against you. From the moment of your spirit birth, you must prove yourself worthy. I wonder if anyone in the Latter Day Church has realized that this means that they can never declare themselves "*saved.*" The best they can declare is "*I'm trying.*"

In the Pre-Mortal Estate, their actions and decisions will determine how favorable their birth into this world might be. If they do everything right, they will be born into a devout Mormon family, who will teach them the truth from the beginning and get them started on the road to exaltation. If they do something wrong, then they might be born in China, India or Africa. They might be born into poverty. They might end up being born to an atheist, and have no clue of how to be exalted. Consider this statement of one of the former Apostles of the Mormon Church, Mark E. Peters when he wrote:

"Is there reason then why the type of birth we receive in this life is not a reflection of our worthiness or lack of it in the pre-existent life? . . .

"Can we account in any other way for the birth of some of the children of God in darkest Africa, or in flood-ridden China, or among the starving hordes of India, while some of the rest of us are born here in the United States?"

Notice what Brigham Young had to say concerning this:

"Our spirits were pure and holy when they entered our tabernacles;" [Brigham Young, Journal of Discourse 8:138]

I have to disagree with Brigham Young at this point. If Lucifer and his followers were barred from being born into the human race, then there appears to be some issue of sin in effect in the Pre-Mortal Estate world. As Mark Peters noted, our performance in our Pre-Mortal Estates can benefit us or hinder us; then obviously there is some issue of sin in the Pre-Mortal Estate world. Who is judging us in our Pre-Mortal Estate? Who is determining that our actions or attitudes will have a positive or adverse effect on us when we are born?

How can our souls be pure and holy when they enter our "tabernacles" if our placement in this world is based upon our performance or attitudes before we are born? These two teaching contradict each other. So which is correct?

If our actions and attitudes in our Pre-Mortal Estate affect how we will be born, is there anything we can do in our Pre-Mortal Estate to increase our odds of being born into the right environment? If not, then the soul would not be pure and holy when it is born into the world.

"We understand, for it has long been told us, that we had an existence before we came into the world...Our religion teaches us that there was never a time when they were not, and there will never be a time when they cease to be…" [Brigham Young, Journal of Discourse 3:367]

Now this is not quite true. According to Latter Day Theology, each soul had a beginning. It began in the Pre-Mortal Estate. With this statement, Brigham Young is attributing a truth about God who has no beginning and no end to Mormon souls. The Latter Day Church Theology does not bear this out or support it.

***

I want to discuss the Latter Day Church's concept of salvation. There is a general salvation "which comes by grace alone without obedience to gospel laws… [It] consists of the mere fact of being resurrected." [Bruce McConkie—Mormon Doctrine]

"Then there is individual salvation and is 'that which man merits through his own acts through life and by obedience of the Gospel.'" [Joseph Fielding Smith, Doctrines of Salvation, 1:134]

I have to ask if "*being saved*" is even in the Latter Day Church vocabulary. From the moment of their spirit birth and long past their physical death, they are still trying to prove that they are worthy. We would have no way of knowing. I wonder if anyone who achieved this Exalted Status and attained Godhood ever had it revoked and they had to start over again? That is what the structure of the Latter Day Saint afterlife suggests.

I read a statement from a Latter Day Church website just this evening in which the writer stated that the afterlife is according to Bible teachings, but there are some differences. I would have to ask if this author had ever read the Bible if he believes the afterlife of Mormon Theology is close to the afterlife described in the Bible.

In the Latter Day Church Theology, there are three kingdoms. There is the Celestial Kingdom for Gods and wives. Did you notice that? It is Gods and their wives. Not Gods and Goddesses. Do women ever attain a Goddess status? There is the Terrestrial

Kingdom for the rest of us, the non-Latter Day Saints. And then, there is the Telestial Kingdom, which is where you go to work off your sins. Some sources even suggest that this is a kind of *"Prison World."*

In Latter Day Church Theology, you can transfer between these kingdoms, and going to the Telestial Kingdom is not a permanent change of address. You go, you get rid of sins, and then you come back out. With such a system in place, it strongly suggests that those in the Celestial Kingdom, may, from time to time, blow it and need to get rid of sins so that they can go back into the Celestial Kingdom.

The Latter Day Church has created a list of what you must do to be saved. There are seven elements dealing with salvation for those men in the Mormon faith:

1. Repentance,
2. Baptism,
3. Membership in the LDS church,
4. Innumerable good works,
5. Abiding by the Mormon "Word of Wisdom"
6. Marriage and other temple rituals
7. Keeping all the Lord's commandments

If we compare these steps to salvation to the steps of salvation in the Bible, there is only one point that is the same: *repentance*. Looking at this list, I have to ask where Jesus comes into play. There is nothing about accepting Jesus as your Savior. There is nothing about praying to Jesus. There is nothing in here about trusting Jesus. Remember Ephesians 2:8–9?

"For by grace are you saved through faith, and not of yourselves, it is the gift of God.

"Not of works lest any man should boast."

Where is faith [trust] in this list of items required by the Latter Day Church? Ephesians 2:9 specifically notes that salvation is not by works. Yet how many of the items on the list involve work or actions? The Latter Day Church Plan of Salvation does not conform to the Biblical Plan of Salvation. Only one point mentioned in this list is found in the Bible. All the other items are not listed in the Bible, or they contradict what the Bible clearly states.

So where did this list of items come from? They came from Joseph Smith. They came from leaders of the Latter Day Church who quoted Joseph Smith. Where did Joseph Smith get his information? He claims an angel named Moroni revealed it to him. He claims to be a prophet, and God told him.

We need to keep in mind several points the Bible makes. First, we test the spirits that are revealing things to us by what they say about Jesus Christ. Did this source claim that Jesus Christ was God before He was born, and that He was God while He was among us? It does not. Therefore, our conclusion is that whatever source Joseph Smith received his information from, it was not from God.

Keep in mind that God does not lie, and God does not change. So we are required to take any new information someone offers about God, Jesus and the Plan of Salvation, and test it against the information we know came from God. These new teachings do not agree with what God has revealed about Himself. Many of these new teachings contradict what God has said about Himself, His Son and the Plan of Salvation. Therefore, we must reject these revelations. They may be spiritual revelations. Joseph Smith may have actually heard these things. But they did not come from God. That much is clear.

What did Paul warn us about in Galatians 1:8?

"But though we, or an angel from Heaven, preach any other gospel unto you than that which we have preached unto you, let him be accursed."

Did Joseph Smith claim that it was an angel that spoke to Him? Yes, he did. What did the Golden Plates that he claimed to have translated call what he translated? It is called another "*Testament*" of Jesus Christ. That is another term for "*Gospel*." This is clearly intended to be another Gospel. Is it the same Gospel that Paul and Silas preached to those at Galatia? It's not even close. This is why this deception should be called a damned deception. It is cursed by the Apostle Paul.

294

Now take a look at the proof that Joseph Smith presents. His account is designed to present important information without being able to confirm or document that information. He claims that the angel came to him when he was alone. [I will discuss his witnesses below.] So all we have is Joseph Smith alone with the angel. He claims he was shown the Golden Plates, but then not allowed to retrieve them. When he was allowed to retrieve them, no one was allowed to see them or look at them except for himself. [I will discuss his witnesses below.] When he was given the priesthood, Oliver Cowdery was with him and no one else. We will look at Oliver Cowdery in a few minutes.

However, in the Book of Mormon, there is a document signed by three witnesses. These would be Oliver Cowdery, David Whitmer and Martin Harris. The statement they signed at the beginning of the Book of Mormon states:

"Be it known to all nations, kindreds, tongues and people, unto whom this work shall come, that we through the grace of God the Father, And our Lord Jesus Christ, have seen the plates which contain this record, which is a record of the people Nephi, and also the Lamanites, his brethren, and also of the people of Jared, which came from the tower of which hath been spoken; and we also know that they have been translated by the gift and power of God for his voice hath declared it unto us, wherefore we know of a surety that the work is true. And we also testify that we have seen the engravings which are upon the plates; and they have been shewn unto to us by the power of God, and not of man. And we declare with words of soberness, that an Angel of God came down from heaven, and he brought and laid before our eyes, that we beheld and saw the plates, and the engravings thereon; and we know that it is by the grace of God the Father, and our Lord Jesus Christ, that we beheld and bear record that these things are true; and it is marvelous in our eyes: Nevertheless, the voice of the Lord commanded us that we should bear record of it; wherefore, to be obedient unto the commandments of God, we bear testimony of these this.— And we know that if we are faithful in Christ, we shall rid our garments of the blood of all men, and be found spotless before the judgment seat of Christ, and shall dwell with him eternally in the heavens. And the honor be to the father, and to the Son, and to the Holy Ghost, which is one god. Amen."

A type set of their names is affixed to this page. It is in the order of Oliver Cowdery, David Whitmer, and the third name is David Harris.

Now I do not know of, nor have I seen the original document, which should contain the actual signatures of these three men. You cannot accept a signature as proof of a statement, if someone else could have made the statement and signed on their behalf.

During my times as a Special Investigation Unit member, numerous documents were presented to me that came from medical providers. These statements required that a signature under penalty of perjury had to be affixed to the documents and bills. Each time either a name stamp was used or an electronic signature was used. Anyone in the office could have done this. These do not qualify as a valid certification. Neither do the names of these three men printed on a page.

Now I will accept that printing technology at that time may have made printing their actual signatures on copies of their statement difficult if not unlikely. Has the Latter Day Church, since that time, reproduced facsimiles of the document so that we can compare signatures of these three men with the signatures on the statement. If not, then this amounts to nothing more than an unsigned document and would not stand in a court of law. This statement would not be admissible in a court of law. These men have not certified their statements.

Let me point out another important piece of information. The closing statement in this declaration contradicts the theology of the Church of Latter Day Saints. As the document closes out, these three witnesses, if they did testify to these statements, noted that "the Father, and to the Son and to the Holy Ghost which is one God."

Now the Latter Day Church claims that there is no Trinity. They see these as three separate Gods. Jesus, who is the Son, was not a God when He was in His Pre-mortal Estate. He was not a God while He was on this earth. And if He attained exalted status in the afterlife, it was as His own and separate God.

Here is something else to consider…The witnesses noted twice in their declaration that Jesus was their "*Lord*." According to Mormon Theology, this would not be possible. "*Lord*" has authority over you. "*Lord*" is deserving of worship and praise. Latter Day Theology discourages worship or praise for Jesus. Latter Day Theology teaches that Jesus was not God before He was born into this world. Latter Day Theology teaches that He was not God while He was on this earth. Latter Day Theology teaches that He did not become God—if He did become a God—until after He died. Latter Day Theology teaches that when/if He did become a God, it was not a God of this world, and, therefore, He would have nothing to do with this world any more than any other good Mormon male who attains exalted status and becomes a God.

They also equate the Holy Ghost as being God, but in Mormon Theology, the Holy Ghost is not a person. It is an impersonal energy like electricity. Their concluding declaration contradicts Mormon teaching.

Mormon teaching that suggests that Jesus came back to this world, and began to preach in America must be highly suspect. Teachings that Jesus returned to this world and started another Church would also have to be suspect. Under what authority did Jesus return to this world? It was not His world. According to Mormon Theology, He did not create it. He was not responsible for it. He had done all that He could do for it by His death. Everything else fell on believers to prove themselves worthy.

These returns of Jesus cited by Joseph Smith raises a serious legal question. Jesus is supposed to be off creating His own world. He would have authority over that world as its Creator. Under what authority does Jesus come into someone else's jurisdiction, and give orders? Shouldn't this be the task of the God of this world, and not the God of another world?

If Jesus became a God, He would be focusing on creating His own world. He would not have jurisdiction to come into this world and interfere in any way with the plans or actions of the God of this world. The problems of this world would be the responsibility of the God of this world—not Jesus. The Mormon Jesus would not have any authority over this world any more than other Mormon males who attained their exalted status would have here. Otherwise, we would have thousands of new Gods running around and getting involved in the day-to-day activities in our world.

Why are they declaring Jesus to be Lord and placing themselves under Jesus' authority contrary to Mormon Theology? Do these Witnesses even know what theology they are endorsing with their statements?

This declaration contradicts the information that is central to the Latter Day Theology. If these men signed this statement using a theology that was not Latter Day Saint Theology, did they see the same thing that Joseph Smith claimed to have seen and translated, or were they shown a counterfeit? Obviously the theology in whatever documents they saw did not contradict the theology under which they signed their names—if they did, in fact, sign their names.

Another conflicting doctrinal statement is made in this declaration. It speaks of these three witnesses standing before the judgment seat of Jesus. Jesus, according to Latter Day Theology, is not the God of this world. It is not Jesus who will judge these three in the afterlife, if Mormon Theology is true. Again, we have to ask if these three men even knew what the documents they were testifying of were about. If they did not know what these documents purported to say, and which they claim were true; then why are they quoting and relying upon doctrines that contradict the doctrines they are testifying to?

Now notice what they did testify to in their declaration:
1. They have actually seen the plates, which contain the record of the Book of Mormon.
2. That they know that these plates have been translated by the power of God.
3. That they knew for a surety that the work is true.
4. That they have seen the engravings upon these plates.

5. That these have been shown to them by the power of God, and not man.
6. That an Angel of God came down from Heaven and showed them these plates.
7. When this Angel of God showed them the plates, they also saw the engravings that were on the plates.
8. They are testifying that each of these statements is true.
9. They testify that the voice of the Lord commanded them to bear witness of these things.

Now as a claim adjuster, and working for Special Investigation Units, it was important that we tested the credibility of the evidence and the witnesses submitted for a claim. Let me take a moment to do this here.

Their first statement is that they have actually seen the plates. This would be referring to the Golden Plates that Joseph Smith said came from an older civilization and which an angel led him to dig up. My first question to them would be to ask them to describe the details of the plates. What was the height and width of the Golden Plate? How many Golden Plates were there? How thick was each Gold Plate? Were these plates stiff and fixed, or flexible? I would need to know that the plates they saw were the same plates that Joseph Smith claims he translated. Their statement claims that they saw these plates when an Angel brought them to them to see. They did not see them when Joseph Smith translated them. How do they know that these are the same plates? They are claiming that they are, but if they did not examine the plates when Joseph Smith translated them, how can they know that they are the same plates?

Given these doctrinal conflicts between the Bible and the Latter Day Theology demonstrated by their statements when they signed this declaration—if they signed this declaration—one of three things happened.

The first would be that they did not write or read the declaration before they signed it. The second would be that they read the declaration, but did not know that these doctrinal conflicts existed. This may be because they did not know what the Mormon Theology would be or they did not comprehend the Golden Plates they claim to have seen. The third would be that someone wrote this declaration and affixed their names to it without their knowledge.

What this would mean in an investigation is that these witnesses lacked credibility. They would not be allowed to testify in a court of law. Their declaration would be suspect and barred as evidence.

Their second testimony is that they know the plates were translated by the power of God. According to accounts, Joseph Smith was to have used the Urim and Thummim to translate each plate. This has been described by the Latter Day Church as a form of eyeglasses, or "stones set in bows" through which he could look at these plates and translate their etchings.

The Urim and Thummim described by Joseph Smith are not the traditional Urim and Thummim of the Jewish High Priests. These were believed to have been two identical stones of different colors. One would signify "yes" to a question, the other would signify "no" to a question. They were in a pouch on the High Priest's ephod, and when asked a yes/no question, the High Priest would reach into the pouch and pull out one of the stones. This is how God was supposed to guide the High Priest.

Apparently, several people were present when this translating took place. I have to ask, did any of these other people who were part of the translating have the opportunity to put on these glasses and read the plates to confirm that Joseph Smith was correct in the translation? If it were the eyeglasses that gave Joseph Smith the ability to translate, then anyone would have been able to put on these eyeglasses, and receive the same translation as Joseph Smith. Was this ever tested, or did those present only take Joseph Smith's word for the translation?

Given the differences between the Jewish Urim and Thummim, and the one used by Joseph Smith, do any of these witnesses confirm that Joseph Smith's version of the Urim and Thummim was correct? Did any of them actually see this device in person, or did they take the word of Joseph Smith?

If there is a process that the witnesses say produces the information of one witness, then that process should be tested and collaborated by more than one person. This is why you have witnesses. You have witnesses who can confirm that what is being said is true. If no one tests the evidence, then the testimony of the witness is lacking in credibility. Here the witnesses say that they *"know."* To *"know"* means that you have personally tested the process and know that it works, and that the information is true. They are attributing the translation to the *"power of God,"* but all they saw were the actions of Joseph Smith. They were taking Joseph Smith at his word. This invalidates their declaration.

Their third testimony is that they *"know for a surety"* that the work is true. Again, for their testimony to have any credibility with a court of law, they would have had to have tested the eyeglasses and the process, and seen for themselves how the translating process worked, not to have taken the word of someone who claims that this is how it works.

Their fourth testimony is that they, personally, have seen the engravings on these plates. I would ask them to give me a drawing of what these engravings looked like. I would have placed each witness in a separate room without knowing what I was going to ask them. I would have each one of them pick the first page that they saw—or the first Golden Plate, and to draw what they saw. Without such drawings, there would be no way to confirm the witnesses.

In the first place, if all three saw the same page and all three drew what they saw, then we can conclude that they all saw the same things. Even if we did not believe them for other reasons, we would know that there was something tangible there, and that all three of these men saw the same thing. No such drawings by these witnesses have ever been rendered. There is no way to test these Reformed Egyptian texts. All physical proof has been removed so that nothing can be tested, confirmed or verified. This would not hold up in a court of law.

The fifth testimony of these men is that they have been shown this by the power of God and not man. I would need them to clarify what they are saying here. Are they saying that it was the power of God that showed them the plates and engravings? Were the plates and the engravings actually there? Were they allowed to touch them? When looking upon these plates, did the power of God allow them to read and understand the engravings? Or is their testimony only that an angel showed them the plates, and they made the assumption that this angel was from God?

Their sixth statement is that an Angel of God came down from Heaven and showed them these plates. My question is how do they know that this was an Angel from God? How do they know that this Angel came down from Heaven? For anyone who has ever been involved in an exorcism or had to deal with supernatural manifestations, you know that just because it is a supernatural manifestation does not ensure that it is of God. There are tests that must be made. There are statements that have to be tested. John gave us just such a test in I John 4:1–3:

"Beloved, believe not every spirit, but [test] the spirits whether they are of God: because many false prophets are gone out into the world.

[This is how you can know] the Spirit of God: Every spirit that confesses that Jesus Christ is [God] come in the flesh is of God:

And every spirit that does not confess that Jesus Christ is [God] come in the flesh is not of God: and this is that spirit of antichrist, whereof you have heard that it should come; and even now already is it in the world."

John accepted the manifestation of the spirit world. He believed that we could receive messages from the spirit world. He had been with Jesus when Jesus cast out demons. On the Isle of Patmos, John would be given a message from the spirit realm. He would know how to test these messages, and to tell truth from deception.

Do not forget the warning of Paul in Galatians 1:8:

"But though we, *or an angel from heaven*, preach any other gospel unto you [other] than that which we have preached unto you, let him be accursed [damned]." [Emphasis added]

Through this warning Paul gave two thousand years ago, he warned us that it is possible for an angelic being to appear and to teach false doctrines. With such a warning clearly documented in the Bible, this puts a great burden on Joseph Smith and his Witnesses to test the angelic being, and to ensure that it is sent by God. Without such testings and proof, what we have is a fulfillment of a prophecy Paul wrote two thousand years ago. As a fulfillment of a prophecy by Paul, there is greater conviction to reject the angel and his message than to accept it. A message coming from an angel is not confirmation that it is true and can be trusted. These Witnesses have just made that mistake in their judgment.

I will give these Witnesses the benefit of the doubt, and accept their testimony that something of a supernatural nature appeared to them. I will accept that something of a supernatural nature communicated with them. But I would also have to ask if they tested this angel to see whom it served. Without this testing, we must reject any message given from the supernatural.

Given the fact that Latter Day Theology claims Jesus was not God—the God—before His birth, then Latter Day Theology does not pass this test given by John. They do not teach that Jesus was God who was incarnated into our world. He was not God among us. If this is their teaching, and this teaching came from this angel; then this was not an Angel of God. This was not an Angel who came down from Heaven.

As a result, these Witnesses would lack credibility. They did not test the source of their information. They accepted information without verifying that it is true. From the evidence and the later teachings from this source, they were deceived into thinking a supernatural manifestation was of God when it was not. Their testimony is false.

Their seventh testimony is that this Angel showed them the plates and the engravings on the plates. I will repeat my comments above. I will accept that they may have seen something. But again, I would want details. I would want descriptions. I would want drawings to make sure that all three saw the same thing.

Their eighth testimony is that everything they saw was true. I will have to stop at this point and challenge this statement.

These three may believe that what they have seen is true, but as I pointed out, did they test the evidence? Did each of them put on the eyeglasses and read the same passage on the plate as Joseph Smith, and get the same translation? Did they test the source? Did they compare notes to make sure that they were seeing and hearing the same thing? They cannot testify as to the truth. When a person is put under oath at trial, they must testify as to the truth, the whole truth and nothing but the truth. Speculations, conjectures and surmise are not accepted as being the truth. Speculations, conjectures and surmise cannot be admitted into evidence. The court would never accept such statements.

If I had these men under oath in a deposition, I would be challenging them. If they did not personally test the eyeglasses and the source of the Angel, then they are not qualified to testify as to it being true. They can only testify to what they saw and heard. But unless they tested these resources for themselves, they could have been deceived. As such, they cannot testify as to the truth—only to the events.

Their ninth and final testimony is that they heard the voice of the Lord command them to testify. Now I would want to know if this was an audible voice that they personally heard. I would ask about the sound of the voice and the words that were spoken. I would ask this with the witnesses separated from each other and then compare their descriptions. Or, could it be that they heard the voice of God in their mind? This would be different for each one. Or, could it be that Joseph Smith, claiming to be a Prophet of God, is the one who told them what God was saying to them?

You may gather from the above that I do not trust that many people. I probably don't. I tend to be more on the antisocial side of society. My wife is the people person, I am not.

But in the course of conducting an investigation, you must consider all sources and the investigation is on-going as long as evidence and information is still forth coming. Let's look at these three witnesses aside from this document.

With regards to Martin Harris, he later testified that they never saw the actual plates. What they were shown was an object that might be the plates, but it was covered with a cloth. From his statement, it seems that it was Joseph Smith who showed them the object covered by a cloth, and not an Angel. According to Martin Harris, Joseph Smith told them that if they saw the plates they would be struck dead. Martin Harris later left the Mormon faith.

We have just had one of the three witnesses recant his testimony. His testimony does not confirm what was said in the document.

David Whitmer did not collaborate the account of Martin Harris, but his testimony does not collaborate the declaration. He claimed that they saw the Golden Plates in their mind. Of interest, David Whitmer also left the Mormon Church.

Oliver Cowdery never made any public statement concerning the document. However, it was reported that he told his law partner that it was all a hoax. Oliver Cowdery also left the Mormon Church.

One would have to ask that if all Churches were corrupt, and this was God restoring the True Church, and these three men were close to Joseph Smith and part of the birth of this Church, then why did all three of them walk away from the Mormon faith. I would be surprised to find all three of them walking away from the Mormon faith if all three knew that it was through membership in the Mormon Church that they could attain Godhood. If they were not members of the Mormon Church, they could never attain Godhood. If all three believed this; then not one of them would walk away. For a witness to walk away from this opportunity, strongly suggests that not one of them actually believed Godhood was possible.

For these three witnesses to walk away from the chance of Godhood, you have to ask if they ever believed that the offer of Godhood was real. If they did not believe that membership in the Mormon Church was necessary to attain Godhood, or that Godhood was not real; then what does that say about their signed testimony?

All three of the witnesses who testified as to the authenticity of the Golden Plates, the Angel, the engravings; and Joseph

Smith ability to translate them were excommunicated from the Latter Day Church. Joseph Smith is quoted as having said of them and others:

"Such characters…as John Whitmer, David Whitmer, Oliver Cowdery and Martin Harris are too mean to mention, and we had liked to have forgotten them."

The conclusion of my investigation based on the above information would have to be that not one of these three witnesses believed the teachings of the Latter Day Church.

Joseph Fielding Smith had noted that the Mormon faith must stand or fall based upon Joseph Smith. Either he was a Prophet and man of God, or he was a deceiver. We have just considered the evidence he submitted for the authenticity of the Book of Mormon, and both the documents, the statements and the character of the witnesses have all be discredited. Is there any other evidence available?

***

For those who have read any of the Book of Mormon, you know that in addition to the Three Witnesses, Joseph Smith also provided a declaration signed by eight others. These would be: Christian Whitmer, Peter Whitmer, Jr., Jacob Whitmer, John Whitmer, Hiram Page, Joseph Smith, Sr., Hyrum Smith; and Samuel Smith

Now before I even get to the declaration, I need to note that three of these Eight Witnesses are biased. They are not impartial. Joseph Smith, Sr., is the father of Joseph Smith; and Hyrum Smith and Samuel Smith are Joseph Smith, Jr.'s brothers. As such, their testimony would be called into question by a court of law. So let's examine the second declaration and these other witnesses.

In addition to the Declaration of the Three Witnesses, there is a second Declaration "*signed*" by Eight Witnesses:

"And Also The Testimony Of Eight Witnesses

"Be it known unto all nations, kindreds, tongues and people, unto whom this work shall come that Joseph Smith, Jr., the Author and Proprietor of this work, has shewn unto us the plates of which hath been spoken, which have the appearance of gold; and as many leaves as said Smith has translated, we did handle with our hands, we also saw the engravings thereon, all of which have the appearance of ancient work, and of curious workmanship. And this we bear record, with words of soberness, that the said Smith has shewn unto us, for we have seen and hefted, and know of a surety, that the said Smith has got the plates of which we have spoken. And we give our names unto the world, to witness unto the world to witness that which we have seen: and we lie not, God bearing witness of it."

Now this declaration has the same problem as the first declaration in that the names of these Witnesses is nothing more than their names typeset on the page. There is no signature that will confirm that they had read this document, agreed to it and signed it. Again, given the lack of printing technology, I would overlook this. But I would also expect the Latter Day Church to have the original document with their signatures on file somewhere. And that with our current technology, facsimiles of this document can be made available, and we can test the signatures on that document with other signatures, which have been certified to be their true signatures.

I have a question concerning the titles given to Joseph Smith, Jr. by these Witnesses. They note that Joseph Smith, Jr. is *"the Author and Proprietor of this work."* The title of *"Author"* is someone who wrote the work, not the person who translated the work. Someone performing the work that Joseph Smith, Jr. claims to have done would be either the *"translator"* or *"editor."* As such, the Declaration should note Joseph Smith, Jr. as either *"Translator"* or *"Editor."* He did not write the Golden Plates. He took a work written by someone else and prepared it for publishing. In addition, is Joseph Smith, Jr. the *"Proprietor"* of the work? Is this his personal property? Does he own it? How did he obtain ownership of what would otherwise be public domain material? Did he own the Golden Plates, which are alleged to be the basis for the printed book?

Now I will be the first to admit that this declaration is a better declaration than the first. There are fewer problems with the wording. There is nothing citing non-Mormon Theology in it. There are no statements of Angels or "power of God" taking place around these Witnesses. I also note that there is no date on this document or the prior declaration of the Three Witnesses, and so I would want to know when they were signed, and when this event actually took place. The date and location of this presentation of these Golden Plates is missing from this document and the prior declaration of the Three Witnesses. Whenever you present a statement under penalty of perjury, you need to identify that date, the location and the actually written signature. This way you can confirm the document and test the information in it. Also, if these statements prove to be false, it establishes the jurisdiction of the court to prosecute for perjury.

We do not know from these eight men when they saw these plates, or where they were when they saw these plates. Based on a painting, these eight men were back in the woods with Joseph Smith. It seems that everything happened in these woods.

The witnesses were called upon to certify the authenticity of the Golden Plates and to give a sworn statement to what they saw. That information about the date and location should have been added. Without this information and the handwritten signatures of the Witnesses attached to the declaration, it is nothing more than a piece of paper as far as the courts would be concerned.

Now in this document, there is less information, and the witnesses are certifying to fewer statement. They note that they saw the Golden Plates. They testify that they saw the engravings. They even "*hefted*" the Golden Plates. That would mean someone would have had to have touched these Golden Plates and lifted them in order to know what they weighed. I do not see where any of the Witnesses gave any description of the number of plates, the weight of the plates or book, or the dimensions of each page. They note that these appear to be "*ancient work*" but none of the Witnesses has introduced his credentials as to how he or they could know that it was ancient.

I would have to challenge this portion of that statement without such credentials.

They tell us that Joseph Smith translated these Golden Plates. But they do not give us any information as to how he did so. They cannot certify that he did, in fact, translate these plates because they were not present—according to this declaration –when this was done. What we have are eight men certifying that Joseph Smith claimed to have translated these Golden Plates. They can testify as to what Joseph Smith told them. They cannot certify the authenticity or accuracy of the statement.

But I have a problem here. We have the statement of Martin Harris when questioned later and in person about his statement. He noted that they did not see the actual plates and that they saw something that was covered with a cloth and "*could have been*" the plates. But his other statement raises all kinds of issues with the declaration of the Eight Witnesses. Martin Harris says that Joseph Smith told him that if they saw the Golden Plates, they would be struck dead. And yet, in this statement, these eight men not only see the Golden Plates, they touched the Golden Plates and lifted the Golden Plates. I have to ask why none of them were struck dead. Did something happen to remove this curse from the Golden Plates? If not, then I would have to ask if these were the same Golden Plates that had that curse placed upon them.

It would be nice if I could post a kind of family tree for the court at this point, but let me describe the relationships at this point. It seems that the Three Witnesses for the first document were not as unbiased or impartial as we were led to believe. It turns out that Oliver Cowdery was a cousin of Joseph Smith, Jr. They were related. This is the same person whom Joseph Smith claims was present when they were given the Aaronic and Melchizedek priesthoods in the woods. It seems that the second Witness, David Whitmer was a close friend of Oliver Cowdery. The third Witness, Martin Harris, was a wealthy neighbor of Joseph Smith. It seems that he was financing the publication of the Book of Mormon.

With regards to the Eight Witnesses, I have already noted that Joseph Smith, Sr., was the father of Joseph Smith, Jr., and that Hyrum Smith and Samuel Smith were brothers of Joseph Smith, Jr.

With regards to John Whitmer, Jacob Whitmer, Christian Whitmer, and Peter Whitmer, Jr., these were all brothers of one of the Three Witnesses, David Whitmer, who was a close friend to Joseph Smith, Jr.'s cousin, Oliver Cowdery. The Eighth Witness was Hyrum Page. It seems that he is the brother-in-law of David Whitmer.

To be honest, there is not an unbiased or impartial witness in the entire lot. They are all connected to Joseph Smith, Jr. in some way, and they had had something to gain from the success of the Book of Mormon being published.

Let's look at those remaining witnesses that were not directly related to Joseph Smith Jr. Jacob Whitmer left the "*church*" in 1838. John Whitmer was excommunicated in 1838. Hiram Page left the "*church*" in 1838. Christian Whitmer died 1835—three years later his family left or were excommunicated. Peter Whitmer, Jr. died 1836 two years before his family left or were excommunicated.

Joseph Smith has denounced David Whitmer and it seems his family either left the "*church*" or were excommunicated from the "*church*." The exception were two of the Witnesses who died before their families left or were excommunicate. As witnesses go for a court of law, none of these would hold up.

***

Now some of you will comment that there is an actual reproduction of the Reformed Egyptian Characters found on the Golden Plates. You would be referring to the *Anton Transcript*. The account, as related by Joseph Smith, is that he wrote down Reformed Egyptian characters in 1828, and gave them to Martin Harris to take to Charles Anton of Columbia University. Charles Anton was reported to be a noted classical scholar.

According to Joseph Smith, Charles Anton gave Martin Harris a glowing recommendation of the Reformed Egyptian.

Then when he discovered it was connected to a religion and an angel, he took back his recommendation and tore it up.

Joseph Smith was kind enough to write a statement on behalf of Martin Harris and wrote it as if he were Martin Harris. Again, it was Joseph Smith who denounced Martin Harris, and so any statements made by or on behalf of Martin Harris must be called into question.

It should be noted that this meeting between Harris and Anton took place in 1828. The Egyptian hieroglyphics were not first deciphered until the early part of the 1820's by Jean-François Champollion using the Rosetta Stone. This is less than ten years later. The Rosetta Stone, itself, was not discovered until 1799.

We would have to question if Professor Anton would have been able to decipher regular Egyptian hieroglyphics within ten years of the code being cracked. Then we would have to know the relationship of Egyptian hieroglyphics in relation to Reformed Egyptian to determine if Professor Anton could be considered an expert on the language. So far, there have been no samples of Reformed Egyptian discovered in any archeological dig anywhere in the world. How could Professor Anton know, identify or translate a language for which there is no known key, code or sample?

There is no discussion as to the alphabet or pictographs used in Reformed Egyptian as compared to the Egyptian hieroglyphics and the Rosetta Stone. These are all recent developments in the world at that time. Professor Anton did, however, claim that the Anton Transcript appeared to be characters from other sources available at that time.

According to a statement from Charles Anton, he claims he told Martin Harris it was a hoax. He has stated publicly that he never made any such endorsement. According to Martin Harris' statement written by Joseph Smith, Jr., Martin Harris then took the characters to a physician in New York who claims to have authenticated the Reformed Egyptian and the translations. How a medical physician could be an expert in an unknown language called Reformed Egyptian still needs to be settled.

The archeological community does not accept the concept of a language called Reformed Egyptian unless the community is directly connected to the Latter Day Church.

***

So what about the Urim and Thummim Joseph Smith used to translate the Golden Plates? Well, there is a problem with this as well. Mormon artists show Joseph Smith wearing a breastplate with these eyeglasses connected and he could look through them. However, a person who was present at the time the Golden Plates were being "*translated*" was Martin Harris. He gave this description of the process:

"Joseph Smith would put the seer stone into a hat, and put his face in the hat, drawing it closely around his face to exclude the light; and in the darkness spiritual light would shine. A piece of something resembling parchment would appear, and on that appeared the writing. One character at a time would appear, and under it was the interpretation in English. Brother Joseph would read off the English to Oliver Cowdery, who was his principle scribe, and when it was written down and repeated to Brother Joseph to see if it was correct, then it would disappear, and another character with the interpretation would appear. Thus the Book of Mormon was translated by the gift and power of God, and not by any power of man."

Now given this description, it is clear that the Urim and Thummim were never even used to look upon the Golden Plates. A "*parchment*" would appear inside the hat where the "*seer stone*" was placed. In other words, the translation of the Golden Plates were made without the use of the Golden Plates. Would this even qualify as a translation if the original document was not involved?

It sounds as if Joseph Smith, Jr. dismantled the Urim and Thummim in order to obtain a single lens [*seer stone*] and place it in the bottom of a hat. Now please note that I am making a presumption here. I am presuming that the seer stone was part of the Urim and Thummim. If my presumption is incorrect, then the translation of the plates took place without the Urim and Thummim, and without the Golden Plates.

Now I have to ask, how do we know that the message given by one lens of the Urim and Thummim would be the same as a message involving both lenses? If that were the case, then only one lens would have been needed, why have two, and if the lens had to be closed off from all light for it to work, why mount them in frames like eyeglasses? Obviously, the design of the Urim and Thummim was deceptive in its design to mislead a person how to read the Golden Plates.

The above information is according to Dave Whitmer [Dave Whitmer, *An Address to All Believers in Christ*, Concord, CA; Pacific Publishing Company, 1887, page 12]. I would note that this is the same Dave Whitmer who later left the Mormon faith and was denounced by Joseph Smith.

But the eyewitness description of the use of the Urim and Thummim contradicts how the translation is reported to have taken place. These were not stones set in bows, but was a single stone, Joseph Smith put into a hat and blocked out all the light to see the stone.

Unfortunately, the Urim and Thummim were taken by the angel when he took the Golden Plates.

So it boils down to the fact that we have the word of Joseph Smith, and only the word of Joseph Smith that all of this is true. His Witnesses were not unbiased. His Witnesses were not impartial. Most left the Church or were excommunicated, and the physical evidence of his claim was taken away by an angel. There is no evidence to collaborate his statements. Therefore, we have to ask: "Where is the proof?" We are called to have faith in God, but the Latter Day Church is calling for us to have faith in Joseph Smith, even though everything about his claims and teachings contradict the Bible, and would not hold up in a court of law.

The Bible calls for us to have faith, but there is evidence. We have manuscripts. We have witnesses who were not excommunicated, but who chose to die to prove that their testimony was true. It is faith to believe in Jesus, but it is not a blind faith. God has provided evidence for us to trust when we believe. This is not the case with Joseph Smith, Jr. and the Latter Day Church.

CHAPTER FOURTEEN

CLOSING THOUGHTS

I wanted to wrap this book up with a quick overview and the key points I want the reader to take away with him or her.

The first point is that Christianity is not just a religion, meaning it is not a collection of beliefs. If it were only a collection of beliefs, then there would be no way to test to see if those beliefs are true. I would point out that Christianity is a collection of truths, and being truths there is evidence and documentation to prove that truth.

The second is that the Bible is not written just by man, but there is ample evidence of *something* outside of our time line sending us messages. These messages are prophecies. When we look at predictions of events written in the Bible, in many cases the details as so precise that those coming afterwards accuse the writers of writing these things after-the-fact. Evidence continues to show that this is not the case.

The number of prophecies written in the Bible, and the number of prophecies that have come true exactly as predicted tells us that there is *something* out there telling us what is going to happen. *Something* knows what is going to happen centuries before it happens, and is passing that information on to us. The Bible identifies this *something* as God. He has chosen to reveal Himself to us. We are not trying to figure out who or what He is. We are not making Him up or creating Him. He is telling us what He wants us to know about Himself.

Fulfilled prophecies prove three things. The first is that God exists. The second is that God is in charge and controlling events to bring these prophecies true. The third is that the

Bible is influenced and probably written by Him through mere mortals.

As such, the Bible becomes God's revelation of who He is, what He is, and what He is doing. He uses the Bible to establish His jurisdiction over us—His Creation. He has the right to set standards for us and to hold us accountable.

God does not want us to die and be lost, and so beginning with Adam and Eve, God created a contract between Himself and His Creation. This contract is how He is going to save us from our fate—a fate created for us by sin.

God gives three historical events that we can now point to and say, this is from God. This is from God. And this is from God. God told us that as part of this contract to save His Creation from sin, God would set aside His divinity, and be physically born into the human race, and become one of us. This action gives God the legal standing and the price needed to save us from our sins.

This birth would be through a Virgin Birth where the fetus would be created by the female without the aid or use of any male genetic material. This would insure a sinless child when He was born.

God then gives us detailed information on the way He will die in order to become a sacrifice for our sins. There are over three hundred prophecies relating to this first coming of God into our world. This death is how He will save us.

The third event is the proof that the power of sin and death has been broken. God will return from the grave three days after He has given His life for us.

You may have noted that I chose not to mention God by name in these three events. The Bible identifies God in His human form as Jesus. This contract is a written agreement by God to save us from our sins, and to give us everlasting life in Heaven forever. The Bible is the contract God is offering all of mankind. No one is excluded from this offer.

Each of the details of this contract is listed throughout the Old Testament. Job—the oldest book in the Old Testament outlines how we can enter into this contract with God. We must confess our sins and agree that we need to be saved. We must repent of our sins and want to change. Then Job outlines how God will make this salvation possible. God will arrange for someone to appear before Him with us. This will be Jesus. There is a price that must be paid to satisfy the legal hold sin has upon us. Jesus will pay that price and we will be free. We will be redeemed.

The New Testament is the documentation of these three historical events. Ten men spent three-and-a-half years as personal witnesses to these events. They chose to die a violent death rather than change a single word of their testimony. An eleventh man was also a witness. He was tortured and survived, but he did not change his testimony, either. This is how we can know two thousand years later that they were convinced of what they saw and heard. They were convinced enough to die to prove it is true.

There is only one Plan of Salvation. It has not changed since God has offered it to man. There is only one who is our Savior and our Redeemer. That is Jesus. There is no other way to be saved other than to confess our sins, repent of our sins, and trust Jesus to save us.

This is why this book has been written. The above is God's Plan of Salvation. This is what it is. This is how it works. We can go through history and see the birth of Jesus, the death of Jesus and the Resurrection of Jesus. All these were intentional on the part of God. Each was essential to the salvation of each one of us. This is what God promised through His contract to us. We can test each event to prove that it is true and actually happened. This is how salvation works. Ephesians 2:8–9:

"For by grace are you saved through faith; and not of yourselves; it is the gift of God. Not of works lest any man should boast."

It is that simple. We do not work for it. We do not earn it. We do not deserve it. God's grace offers it to us, and we receive it through faith as a free gift from God.

This is what God has done. This is what God has been doing. The Father of All Lies—Satan—has created deceptions.

And he has used his deceptions—his counterfeits—to distract us, and keep us from seeing or hearing the true message.

So here is my research, my investigation, and my conclusion into these deceptions that can keep us from being saved, and which will result in our being damned. God does not want any one to be lost. He offers His salvation free of charge to anyone who wants it. All you need to do is ask. It really is that easy.

Let me wrap up this book with the statement of the Apostle John when he wrote to one of the early Churches. I John 5:13:

"These things have I written unto you that believe on the name of the Son of God; *that you may know that you have eternal life*, and that you may believe on the name of the Son of God." [Emphasis added]

It is possible to know that you are saved. You do not have to hope that you are saved. You do not have to guess that you are saved. You can know—really know that you are saved. It is possible to know in this life that you have eternal life. It is a simple legal argument. God promised it. I have entered into His contract and am now guaranteed salvation. Here is what the contract says. Here is what God has done. These are real events. They are not beliefs. They are historical events, a legal document and contract law that ensures God will do what He has promised to do.

Here is my investigation report. Take it. Read it. Decide for yourself. If however, you reject my investigation and my conclusions, you have the right to do so. But I would strongly urge you, if you reject my investigation and my conclusion, please, please, please conduct your own investigation. Do not settle for what someone tells you, but test the evidence. Demand proof. Ask the hard questions. We are talking about your eternal destiny here. Make sure, very sure, before you commit to any Plan of Salvation you are offered…because if you are deceived; then you will be damned.

APPENDIX

APPENDIX ONE

PROPHETS AND PROPHECY

This is a topic that applies to both the Jehovah's Witnesses and the Latter Day Church organizations. In fact, it is a topic that comes up in many Cults, as those behind the Cults want to force others to obey them, and what better way to make people obey than to tell them God is speaking through you. I had wanted to discuss this in the body of the book, but I came to realize it would be too much of a distraction, and so I needed to deal with it as a completely separate issue. So here it is, in the Appendix.

Those who want to manipulate and frighten people into obeying them will quote Deuteronomy 13:1–10:

"I will raise them up a Prophet from among their brethren, like unto you [Moses], and will put my words in his mouth; and he shall speak unto them all that I shall command him.

"And it shall come to pass, that whosoever will not [listen] unto my words which he shall speak in my name, I will require it of him."

This can make a lot of people afraid to challenge a prophet. God does not look kindly upon those who challenge or ignore a prophet of God. So we need to ask some serious questions. We need to ask the questions and we need answers. How can you tell when someone is speaking for God? How can we test if the message they are sharing with us is from God or some other source? When should we be listening, and when should we be rejecting and ignoring the message and messenger? Deuteronomy 13:1–10:

"If there arise among you a prophet, or a dreamer of dreams, and gives you a sign or a wonder,

"And the sign or the wonder come to pass, whereof he spoke unto you, saying, 'Let us go after other gods, which you have not known, and let us serve them;'

"You shall not [pay attention] unto the words of that prophet, or that dreamer of dreams: for the Lord your God [is testing] you, to know whether you love the Lord your God with all your heart and with all your soul.

"You shall walk after the Lord your God, and fear Him, and keep His commandments, and obey His voice, and you shall serve Him, and [cling] unto Him.

"And that prophet, or that dreamer of dreams, shall be put to death; because he has spoken to turn you away from the Lord your God, who brought you out of the land of Egypt, and redeemed you out of the house of bondage, to thrust you out of the way which the Lord your God commanded you to walk in. So shall you put the evil away from the midst of you.

"If your brother, the son of your mother, or your son, or your daughter, or the wife of your bosom, or your friend, which is as your own soul, entices you secretly, saying, 'Let us go and serve other gods,' which you have not known, you, nor your fathers;

'Namely, of the gods of the people which are round about you, near unto you, or far off from you, from the one end of the earth even unto the other end of the earth;

"You shall not consent unto him, nor [pay attention] unto him; neither shall your eye pity him, neither shall you spare, neither shall you conceal him:

"But you shall surely kill him; your hand shall be first upon him to put him to death, and afterwards the hand of all the people.

"And you shall stone him with stones, that he die; because he has sought to thrust you away from the Lord your God, which brought you out of the land of Egypt, from the house of bondage."

This is pretty harsh treatment, but speaking in the name of the Lord when He is not speaking through you is a serious crime as far as God is concerned.

Notice that there is more than one way to be a false prophet. Moses was discussing a specific kind of false prophet in this passage. He noted that the person did make a prediction, and that prediction came true. That, as we shall see in a few minutes, is one of the tests for a prophet of God. But the second part of the test is even more important. Does this person lead you away from the God of the Bible? As we have seen in the body of this book, that is exactly what Joseph Smith and the leaders of the Latter Day Church have done. They have introduced a pre-existent world that does not exist. They have introduced a creation that is not the Creation God has revealed through Moses. They have introduced other Gods that are not the God of the Bible. It does not matter if they suggested that you follow them or not. They have presented false information. They are leading you away from God the Father, and they are leading you away from God the Son. THAT makes them false prophets.

Now the second test to see if a person is a prophet of God is listed in Deuteronomy 18:20–22:

"But the prophet, who shall presume to speak a word in my name, which I have not commanded him to speak, or that shall speak in the name of other gods, even that prophet shall die.

"And if you say in your heart, 'How shall we know the word which the Lord has not spoken?'

"When a prophet speaks in the name of the Lord, if the thing follow not, nor comes to pass, that is the thing which the Lord has not spoken, but the prophet has spoken it presumptuously: you shall not be afraid of him."

How does all of this boil down? When a prophet is a prophet of God, that prophet will be correct 100% of the time. If a prophet even makes a single prophecy and it does not come true; then that prophet is not a prophet of God. We should not listen to that person nor believe anything that person has to say.

Now Joseph Smith claimed to be a prophet. He claims that God appointed him to be His prophet. He wrote his documents many times as if God were speaking through him to the believers the way a prophet would speak for God:

"Verily, thus saith the Lord unto you who have assembled yourselves together to receive his will concerning you:" [Doctrine and Covenants 88:1]

This was a "Revelation" described in the opening introduction of Doctrine and Covenants #88 as: "Revelation given through Joseph Smith the Prophet at Kirtland, Ohio, December 27 and 28, 1832 and January 3, 1833…"

Joseph Smith made the claim that he was given this and other titles by God. At the initial meeting of the One Truth Church on April 6, 1830, Joseph Smith received a revelation from God that he would be "a seer, a translator, a prophet and apostle." [*History of the Church of Jesus Christ Latter-Day Saints* (Salt Lake City, UT, Deseret 1978) pages 1:40–42]

Now as we look at whom this God is that Joseph Smith claims he is speaking for, this "*God*" does not line up with the God of the Bible. Joseph Smith is speaking on behalf of a different God. This makes him a false prophet per this definition in the Bible. As each leader of the Latter Day Church claims that this same God speaks through them, this makes each and every one of them a false prophet. They may be a prophet of "a God," but they are not prophets of the God of the Bible.

Now Joseph Smith and the Latter Day Church are not the only Cults who use prophecy to manipulate and deceive their followers. The Jehovah's Witnesses have a long history of setting dates for the return of Jesus and the beginning of the Kingdom Age. I will provide a list of some of these prophecies later in this Appendix. Now the more recent leaders of the Jehovah's Witnesses have learned not to set dates when so many failed to materialize; but it only takes one false prophecy to classify a person or organization as a false prophet.

Cults will try to convince people that they are speaking for God or that God is speaking through them. They try different things to make it look like there is a rubber stamp reading: "God-Approved" on their movement. One of the techniques used by Joseph Smith was to quote passages from the Bible with slight changes so it sounded like the Bible. When writing the publications for the Latter Day publication he wrote as if he were using the King James English—even though the documents he claimed to have been translating were either much earlier than King James [the Book of Abraham] or much later [the Book of Mormon] when He wrote his own doctrines and teachings. Joseph Smith also used many Biblical terms and references to make it appear that God was speaking through Him. Here is a third proof that this was not the God of the Bible speaking through him. God does not speak in King James English. A lot of people try to talk like that thinking it makes them sound more religious and closer to God, but God speaks to us in our language today. God spoke to His prophets in the language of their day.

So we have Joseph Smith qualifying as a false prophet in that He sought to lead people away from God. He was a false prophet because he was not speaking for the God of the Bible, but the God he describes is a different God. He also qualifies as a false prophet because he predicted events, and those events did not come to pass. I know people try to explain these mistakes away and not make it his fault the prophecy failed; but a prophet of God never fails—ever!

These are very clear instructions from God. Again, we do not pay attention to the appearance of the speaker. It does not matter if the speaker looks like a wolf or a sheep. It does not matter if the speaker can perform signs and wonders, or if the speaker can perform miracles. We pay attention to what the speaker is saying. We test the message of the messenger. It must line up with the message of God.

The Latter Day Church founders and leaders will tell us that the God of this world they are telling us to follow is the God of the Bible. He is not. When we peel away all the deceptions, lies and misrepresentations, the God of the Latter Day Church is NOT the God of the Bible. He is not even close. We are not to listen to them. We are not to believe them. We are not to follow them. God is testing us.

Joseph Smith made a prophecy concerning the Temple.

"Hearken, O ye elders of my church, saith the Lord your God, who have assembled yourselves together, according to my commandments, in this land, which is the land of Missouri, which is the land I have appointed and consecrated for the gathering of the saints.

"Wherefore, this is the land of promise, and the place for the city of Zion.

"And thus saith the Lord your God, if you will receive wisdom here is wisdom. Behold, the place which is now called Independence is the center place; and a spot for the temple is lying westward, upon a lot which is not far from the court-house." *Doctrine and Covenants*, Section 57:1-3. This Revelation was given through Joseph Smith the Prophet, in Zion, Jackson County, Missouri, July, 1831. Notice that he spoke as if God were speaking through him. Notice he spoke in King James English.

Did the Temple get built in Independence, Missouri? No. It was not built there. Joseph Smith claimed that he spoke as a prophet of God, and that this was the message God had given him. Did Joseph Smith repeat this prophecy another time? Yes, in 1832 Joseph Smith had this to say:

"1. A revelation of Jesus Christ unto his servant Joseph Smith, Jun., and six elders, as they united their hearts and lifted their voices on high.

"2. Yea, the word of the Lord concerning his church, established in the last days for the restoration of his people, as he has spoken by the mouth of his prophets, and for the gathering of his saints to stand upon Mount Zion, which shall be the city of New Jerusalem.

"3. Which city shall be built, beginning at the temple lot, which is appointed by the finger of the Lord in the western boundaries of the State of Missouri, and dedicated by the hand of Joseph Smith, Jun., and others with whom the Lord was well pleased.

"4. Verily this is the word of the Lord, that the city New Jerusalem shall be built by the gathering of the saints, beginning at this place, even the place of the temple, which temple, shall be reared in this generation.

"5. For verily, this generation shall not all pass away until an house shall be built unto the Lord, and a cloud shall rest upon it, which cloud shall be even the glory of The Lord, which shall fill the house." [*Doctrine and Covenants*, Section 97:19, Revelation given through Joseph Smith, the Prophet, at Kirkland, Ohio, September 23, 1832.]

Again, did the Temple get built in Missouri the way that Joseph Smith described? No, the Temple did not get built in Missouri. Did Joseph Smith repeat this prophecy again? Yes, in 1833:

"And the nations of the earth shall honor her, and shall say: Surely Zion is the city of our God, and surely Zion cannot fall, neither be moved out of her place, for God is there, and the hand of the Lord is there." [*Doctrine and Covenants*, Section 84:1-5, Revelation given through Joseph Smith, the Prophet, at Kirkland, Ohio, August 2, 1833.]

Was this prophecy repeated again? Yes. Joseph Smith repeated it a second time in 1833:

"A revelation given to Joseph Smith the Prophet at Kirkland, Ohio, December 16, 1833. Doctrine and Covenants, Section 101:17-21:

"17. Zion shall not be moved out of her place, not withstanding her children are scattered.

"18. They that remain, and are pure in heart, shall return, and come to their inheritances, they and their children, with songs of everlasting joy, to build up the waste places of Zion-

"19. And, all these things that the prophets might be fulfilled.

"20. And, behold, there is none other place appointed than that which I have appointed; neither shall there be any other place appointed than that which I have appointed, for the work of the gathering of my saints." [*Doctrine and Covenants*, Section 107:17-20, 12:16, 1833, p. 172.]

I won't belabor the point. As I said, it only takes one prophecy not coming true to prove that a person is not a prophet of God. Joseph Smith gave his prophecy. He continued to repeat this prophecy. This prophecy did not come true. The logical conclusion is that Joseph Smith is a false prophet and should not be listened to. He should not be trusted. He should not be believed. He should not be followed.

Now some will suggest that the Temple—or a Temple was built; but the Latter Day Church set a time frame for the return and the building of the Temple in Missouri:

"God promised in the year 1832 that we should, before this generation then living had passed away, return and build up the City of Zion in Jackson County; that we should return and build up the temple of the Most High where we formerly laid the corner stone. He promised us that He would manifest Himself on that temple, that the glory of God should be upon it; and not only upon the temple, but within it, even a cloud by day and a flaming fire by night.

"We believe in these promises as much as we believe in any promise ever uttered by the mouth of Jehovah. The Latter-day Saints just as much expect to receive a fulfillment of that promise during the generation that was in existence in 1832 as they expect that the sun will rise and set to-morrow. Why? Because God cannot lie. He will fulfill all His promises. He has spoken, it must come to pass. This is our faith." [*Journal of Discourses*, Vol. 13, p. 362, Discourse by Elder Orson Pratt, May 5, 1870.]

Elder Orson Pratt continued to believe in this prophecy issued by Joseph Smith even thirty-nine years after they had left Missouri.

"... [A]ll the people that were living thirty-nine years ago have not passed away; but before they do pass away this will be fulfilled."

"We just as much expect that a city will be built, called Zion, in the place and on the land which has been appointed by the Lord our God, and that a temple will be reared on the spot that has been selected, and the corner-stone of which has been laid, in the generation when this revelation was given; we just as much expect this as we expect the sun to rise in the morning and set in the evening; or as much as we expect to see the fulfillment of any of the purposes of the Lord our God, pertaining to the works of his hands. But say the objector, "thirty nine years have passed away." What of that? The generation has not passed away; all the people that were living thirty-nine years ago have not passed away; but before they do pass away this will be fulfilled." [*Journal of Discourses*, Vol. 14, p. 275. Discourse by Elder Orson Pratt, delivered in the New Tabernacle, Salt Lake City, April 9, 1871.]

The prophecy was not fulfilled. A time limit was placed on the prophecy, and that time limit came and went. It does not matter if the Latter Day Church moved to Jackson County, Missouri today and built the Temple of promise. The prophecy has been proven false. Joseph Smith has been proven to be a false prophet.

As mentioned above, the Jehovah's Witnesses also have a problem with prophecies that do not come true. There is a book entitled, *"Why We Left Jehovah's Witnesses—A Non-Prophet Organization"* by Bill Cetner. Bill Cetner and his wife, Joan, ran a ministry dealing with the Jehovah's Witnesses. Unfortunately, the book is out of print at this time. Here is a listing of the prophecies made by the Watchtower Society regarding the Second Coming of Jesus and the Coming Kingdom Age. You should note that it is the Watchtower Society that presents the prophecy, and then begins to down play—and later disavow—the prophecy as the date approaches. This was a handout during one of our Cult Classes; the original source is unknown.

***

ONE HUNDRED YEARS OF DIVINE DIRECTION

1972—IDENTIFYING THE "PROPHET"—"So, does Jehovah have a prophet to help them, to warn them of dangers and to declare things to come? These questions can be answered in the affirmative. Who is this prophet. . . This "prophet" was not one man, but was a body of men and women. It was the small group of footstep followers of Jesus Christ, known at that time as International Bible Students. Today they are known as Jehovah's Christian Witnesses...Of course, it is easy to say that this group acts as a "prophet" of God. It is another thing to prove it." THE WATCHTOWER 4/1/72 (see Deut. 18:21)

1889—"The 'battle of the great day of God Almighty' (Rev. 16:14), which will end in A.D., 1914 with the complete overthrow of earth's present rulership is already commenced." THE TIME IS AT HAND p 101 (1908 edition)

1897—"Our Lord, the appointed King, is now present, since October 1874," STUDIES IN THE SCRIPTURES, VOL. 4 p. 621

1916—"The Bible chronology herein presented shows that the six great 1000 year days beginning with Adam are ended, and that the great 7th Day, the 1000 years of Christ's Reign, began in 1873" THE TIME IS AT HAND p. 2 (forward)

1918—"Therefore we may confidently expect that 1925 will mark the return of Abraham, Isaac, Jacob and the faithful prophets of old, particularly those named by the Apostle in Hebrews 11, to the condition of human perfection." MILLIONS NOW LIVING WILL NEVER DIE p. 89

1922—"The date 1925 is even more distinctly indicated by the Scriptures than 1914" WATCHTOWER 9/1/22 p. 262

1923—"Our thought is, that 1925 is definitely settled by the Scriptures. As to Noah, the Christian now has much more upon which to base his faith than Noah had upon which to base his faith in a coming deluge." WATCHTOWER p. 106 4/1/23

1925—"The year 1925 is here. With great expectation Christians have looked forward to this year. Many have confidently expected that all members of the body of Christ will be changed to heavenly glory during this year. This may be accomplished. It may not be. In his own due time God will accomplish his purposes concerning his people. Christians should not be so deeply concerned about what may transpire this year." WATCHTOWER 1/1/25 p. 3

Sept.—"It is to be expected that Satan will try to inject into the minds of the consecrated the thought that 1925 should see an end to the work." WATCHTOWER p. 262

1926—"Some anticipated that the work would end in 1925, but the Lord did not state so. The difficulty was that the friends inflated their imaginations beyond reason; and that when their imaginations burst asunder, they were inclined to throw away everything." THE WATCHTOWER p. 232

1931—"There was a measure of disappointment on the part of Jehovah's faithful ones on earth concerning the years 1914, 1918, & 1925, which disappointment lasted for a time...and they also learned to quit fixing dates." VINDICATION p.338

1941—"Receiving the gift, the marching children clasped it to them, not a toy or plaything for idle pleasure, but the Lord's provided instrument for most effective work in the remaining months before Armageddon." WATCHTOWER 9/15/41 p. 288

1968—"True, there have been those in times past who predicted an 'end' to the world, even announcing a specific date. Yet nothing happened. The 'end' did not come. They were guilty of false prophesying. Why? What was missing? Missing from such people were God's truths and the evidence that he was using and guiding them." AWAKE 10/8/68 (See Luke 21:8)

1968—"WHY ARE YOU LOOKING FORWARD TO 1975?" THE WATCHTOWER 8/15/68 p. 494

Prophecy is the evidence God offers that He does exist, and that He is in control of everything so that He can make each prophecy come true exactly as predicted and, if a date is given, when predicted. Consider Isaiah 46:9–10:

"Remember the former things of old: for I am God, and there is none else; I am God, and there is no one like me,

"Declaring the end from the beginning, and from ancient times the things that are not yet done, saying, My counsel shall stand, and I will do all my pleasure:"

In Isaiah 44:28, Isaiah identifies that a man named Cyrus—who was not even born at the time of the prophecy would be the one to send the Jews home from captivity and rebuild the Temple:

"Who says of Cyrus, 'He is my shepherd, and shall perform all my pleasure: even saying to Jerusalem, "You shall be built;" and to the temple, "Your foundation shall be laid."'"

In Jeremiah 29:10, we see that this will be fulfilled in seventy years:

"For thus says the Lord, 'That after seventy years be accomplished at Babylon I will visit you, and perform my good word toward you, in causing you to return to this place.'"

These are examples of God's true prophecies. They give details. They tell us of events before they happen. They give information a normal person could not know at the time. God makes the prediction, and then God controls events to ensure the prediction comes true. This is why a prophet speaking for God can/will never make a prophecy that does not come true. A prophet of God will be correct 100% of the time. A single prophecy that does not come true will invalidate that person as a prophet of God.

We do not stone false prophets today, but the message to not listen to them or pay any attention to them is still in place, and we should not consider the things that they are telling us.

So when Joseph Smith or other founder fathers or leaders of the Latter Day Church, the Jehovah's Witnesses—or any institution—claims to be a prophet; they are subject to God's Law concerning prophets. For this reason, I would be very careful, and not lay any claim to being a prophet of God.

APPENDIX TWO

WHO WROTE THE BOOK OF MORMON?

The material in this Appendix was part of a presentation made in our School of Ministry class. The original research came from a book entitled, "*So Who Really Wrote The Book of Mormon?*" Dr. Walter Martin had heard comments that the Book of Mormon was not actually written by the ancient races in America, and that the story was not preserved on Golden Plates the way Joseph Smith claimed. Two men undertook the challenge to do the research and test the evidence. This section represents their work and effort, and all credit should go to them. Their book is not currently in print, and some sources for used books set the price at over $100. Some used book sites do provide a copy at a reasonable price. You can check ABE books.com, which is a collection of used books stores to see it they have a copy available for a reasonable price. If you can access this book, I strongly suggest that you read it for yourself.

I would caution that if you do obtain a copy so you can do your own research, be careful not to loan the book out—especially to a member of the Latter Day Church. Such books have a habit of not being returned.

It was Joseph Fielding Smith who noted that the Latter Day Church would stand or fall based upon Joseph Smith. Either he was a prophet of God and his teachings would be vindicated, or he was a deceiver and he should be exposed and rejected.

Let me expand on this. What was the one thing that Joseph Smith pointed to as proof that God had called him? It was the

Book of Mormon. Joseph Smith claimed that he was called by an angel to found the Latter Day Church. He was called to restore the Church that had been lost. All of this came together in the physical plates of gold that had been buried, and which the angel led him to uncover.

The Book of Mormon was Joseph Smith's proof to the world that he had been called, and that he had been given the truth by God. So if the Book of Mormon were to fall and be proven to not being of God, then, so too, would the proof of Joseph Smith that he had been called of God.

***

If we accept the claims of Joseph Smith, the Book of Mormon is the vehicle through which the true Gospel and the lost history of America were preserved and transported into our Modern Age. Without the Book of Mormon, no one would ever know the truth. The importance of the Book of Mormon to the Latter-Day Saints cannot be underestimated.

Being given these plates by the Angel Moroni established that Joseph Smith was the Prophet chosen to reestablish the Church. His Pearl of Great Price, and Doctrine and Covenants grow from this claim to be chosen of God. If the Book of Mormon does not prove itself to be credible; then the entire Mormon Church is in danger of crumbling.

So what does Joseph Smith say about the Book of Mormon? On September 21, 1823, the Angel Moroni appeared to Joseph Smith and told him of Golden Plates buried under a hill called Cumorah—which (conveniently) was located near Joseph's home. Smith went to Cumorah every year until September 22, 1827, when he was allowed to dig up the plates and take physical possession of them.

Joseph Smith claimed that he translated these Golden Plates into the Book of Mormon between 1828 through 1829 using the Urim and Thummim—which had been buried with the Golden Plates. So, what information is believed to have been recorded on the Golden Plates and translated by Joseph Smith?

The Book of Mormon claims to be an account of two great migrations to North and South America by Semites [Semitic races (Jews)]. The first is the account of the Jaredites and took place around 2250 B.C.—just after the Tower of Babel. The second is an account of Lehi who traveled to America in 600 B.C.

The Jaredites lived near the Tower of Babel and left to cross the ocean in 2250 B.C. aboard eight barges. They settled in Central America and after some time, began to fight among themselves. In one battle, one million men plus their families were slain.

Finally, only Coriantumr, Shiz and Ether were left of their entire race. Ether was a prophet, and he witnessed the final battle between Coriantumr and Shiz. Shiz was killed, and Coriantumr lasted nine moons before dying from his wounds. Ether recorded their history on 24 plates.

A second group of Semites came to America led by Lehi. Lehi was of the Tribe of Manasseh. He had been persecuted because of his prophecies, and so he, his wife and four sons left Jerusalem in 600 B.C. Lehi's other two sons remained faithful. Lehi's son, Nephi, became the leader. Nephi is reported to have given a prophecy of Jesus coming to America in 34 AD. Jesus is reported to have taught baptism and communion to the Nephites, and repeated most of His Sermon on the Mount.

Over the years, the Nephites and the Lamanites fought. In 385 AD, the two groups fought for a final time. All the Nephites were killed with the exception of Mormon's son, Moroni. Mormon had been recording the history of his people on Golden Plates. Mormon hid them in the ground

After the death of Mormon, Moroni added to these records and in 421 A.D., he buried all of these under the hill Cumorah. Moroni returned as an angel in 1823–1827 and gave the Golden Plates to Joseph Smith. [This Synopsis of the Book of Mormon was taken from *Who Really Wrote The Book of Mormon?* by Wayne Cowdrey, Howard Davis, Donald Scales. (Note: Wayne Cowdrey is not related to Oliver Cowdery.) Vision House 1977 pages 24–26]

It turns out that several sources have done extensive investigation into the Book of Mormon So let's see what these researchers have to say about this book that the entire Mormon faith is based upon...

We discussed this in more detail in the body of this book, but this is just a quick summary. There are Three Witness who confirmed the Book of Mormon and noted that they saw the Golden Plates: Oliver Cowdery, Martin Harris and David Whitmer.

Martin Harris testified that they did not actually see the plates, but an object that looked like plates covered with a cloth. They were told that if they saw the actual plates, they would be struck dead. Martin Harris later left the "*Church*."

David Whitmer testified that he did not see the plates with his natural eyes, but by "the eyes of faith." Later, David Whitmer left the "*Church*."

Oliver Cowdery never public changed his testimony, but it is reported that he confided with his law partner, Judge Lang, and former apostle, William McClellan that the Book of Mormon was a hoax. Oliver Cowdery later left the "*Church*."

All three were excommunicated from the "*Church*." Joseph Smith was quoted as saying: "Such characters...as John Whitmer, David Whitmer, Oliver Cowdery and Martin Harris are too mean to mention, and we had liked to have forgotten them."

So...When you call upon three people to testify that what you are saying is true, and then you publicly discredit all three sources; what does that do for the credibility of you own testimony?

There are similar problems with the Eight Witnesses listed in the Book of Mormon. Each was either related to Joseph Smith Jr. or were related to a close friend of Joseph Smith. None would qualify as unbiased or impartial witnesses. His brothers and father were the only ones who did not leave or get excommunicated from the Church. The exceptions were those who died before their families left the Church. All the Whitmer Witnesses or their relatives left and/or were excommunicated from the "*Church*." In short, all physical evidence of the Golden Plates is gone. All witnesses to the Golden Plates have been discredited. There is no evidence to prove that the Golden Plates ever existed, or that Joseph Smith was given them.

So the question is raised, "Where did the story of the Nephites and the Lamanites come from?" That was the basis for the book, "*Who Really Wrote The Book of Mormon?*" by Wayne Cowdrey, Howard Davis, Donald Scales. (Note: Wayne Cowdrey is not related to Oliver Cowdery.) Vision House 1977.

To follow this story, we need to focus on another associated of Joseph Smith, Jr. who was not listed as a witness: Sidney Rigdon. We need to look at his connection with a publishing company called Patterson and Lambdin Printing Office. The last person we need to consider is a former minister by the name of Solomon Spalding.

There are allegations that Sidney Rigdon either worked for or was connected to the Patterson and Lambdin Printing Office. Solomon Spalding was a retired minister—he was disabled and in poor health—who had submitted a manuscript to the Patterson and Lambdin Printing Office for publication.

The Spalding–Rigdon Theory of Book of Mormon authorship is the story that the Book of Mormon was plagiarized in part from an unpublished manuscript written by Solomon Spalding. The theory first appeared in print in the book *Mormonism Unvailed*, published in 1834 by E. D. Howe. This was close enough to the publication of the Book of Mormon and Solomon Spalding that the author could obtain actual statements and test the evidence. The story is that a Spalding manuscript was stolen by Sidney Rigdon, who used it in collusion with Joseph Smith and Oliver Cowdery to produce the Book of Mormon.

Although Rigdon claimed that he was converted to the Latter Day Saint movement through reading the Book of Mormon, Howe argued that the story was a later invention to cover the book's true origins. There is documentation that Sidney Rigdon was preaching doctrines found in the Book of Mormon two years before the book was produced. And though he claims to have converted after the Book of Mormon was published, there are witnesses that testified that he was a regular visitor with Joseph Smith while the book was being '*translated*.'"

Around 1812, Spalding completed a historical romance entitled *Manuscript, Found* which "purported to have been a record found buried in the earth." There is a website that discusses this: [http://www.solomonspalding.com/docs/1834howf.htm].

Spalding moved to Pittsburgh and reportedly took *Manuscript, Found* to the publisher Patterson & Lambdin. The publishers agreed to print the book if he could fund the printing. Spalding had written the book originally to explain why strange mounds were found near their first home. He later sought to use the manuscript to pay for his family's support when he could no longer support them. Throughout the writing of the book and afterwards while trying to raise money to publish the book, Spalding would read it to family, neighbors and clients. In the book by E. D. Howe, several statements were taken from these friends, family members and clients who testified that the names of the ancient races and the details of their battles were the subject of Spalding's book.

These accusations were made while the witnesses were still alive and their testimonies were still available.

During the time Spalding was working to raise money to publish the book, the manuscript remained at the Patterson and Lambdin Printing Office. Sidney Rigdon was a frequent visitor to the Printing Office and after several years, the manuscript was lost. Spalding died in 1816, without *Manuscript, Found* being published.

An unfinished manuscript copy of a historical fiction by Spalding, written from 1809 to 1812, about a Roman discovery of the Americas exists, called the "*Oberlin Manuscript*" or "*Honolulu Manuscript*." It is an historical romance "purporting to have been translated from the Latin, found on 24 rolls of parchment in a cave, on the banks of the Conneaut Creek".

It tells of a Roman ship, which discovers America. In 1884, this manuscript, known as *Manuscript Story—Conneaut Creek*, was discovered and published, and the manuscript now resides at Oberlin College in Ohio. Some authors claim it contains parallels in theme and narrative.

This Spalding Manuscript is a fictional story about a group of Romans who, while sailing to England early in the fourth century A.D., were blown off course and landed in eastern North America. One of them kept a record of their experiences among Eastern and Midwestern American Indian tribes.

In 1833, Spalding's brother John and seven other residents of Conneaut signed affidavits stating that Spalding had written a manuscript, portions of which were identical to the Book of Mormon. Spalding's widow told a similar story, and stated that "the names of Nephi and Lehi are yet fresh in my memory, as being the principal heroes of his tale." [Howe 1834, p. 279]

Although Sidney Rigdon denied the allegations, this refuting of the statement was little more than an attack on an excommunicated Mormon who broke the story, and Rigdon performed character assassination [which was untrue] on those involved.

Rigdon also denied living in Pittsburgh at the time Spalding was there or of knowing the Patterson and Lambdin Printing House. While it may be true he did not live there until 1822, he did visit frequently as was noted by a worker of the post office. [*Who Really Wrote The Book of Mormon?* Wayne Cowdrey, Howard Davis, Donald Scales, Vision House 1977 pages 95 - 96]

There were also some statements obtained confirming the theft and plagiarism of the manuscript. J. C. Bennett, a former Mormon made this statement:

"I will remark here…that the Book of Mormon was originally written by the Rev. Solomon Spalding…as a romance, and entitled the '*Manuscript Found*,' and placed by him in the printing office of Patterson and Lambdin in the city of Pittsburgh from whence it was taken by a conspicuous Mormon divine, and re-modeled, by adding the religious portion, placed by him in Smith's possession, and then published to the world as the testimony exemplifies.

"This I have from the Confederation [Smith's inner circle of friends] and of its perfect correctness there is not a shadow of doubt. There never were any plates of the Book of Mormon, excepting what was seen by the spiritual, and not the natural eyes of the witnesses. The story of the plates is all chimerical [the product of unchecked imagination]." [Ellen E Dickerson, New Light on Mormonism, New York, Funk & Wagnall's, 1885, page 23]

The Mormons reject his statement as being that of a disgruntled ex-Mormon. However, Susan M. Pratt, the wife of an early Mormon leader provided a statement that the information relayed by J. C Bennett was correct. [*Who Really Wrote The Book of Mormon?* Wayne Cowdrey, Howard Davis, Donald Scales Vision House 1977 page 103]

Other statements have come forth:

In 1884, James Jeffries related information he had obtained directly from Sidney Rigdon:

"...He told me several times that there was in the printing office with which he was connected...a manuscript of the Rev. Spalding tracing the origin of the Indians from the lost tribes of Israel. The M.S. was in the office several years. He was familiar with it. Spalding wanted it published, but had not the means to pay for the printing. He [Rigdon] and Joe Smith used to look over the M.S. and read it on Sundays. Rigdon said Smith took the M.S. and said, 'I'll print it.' and went off to Palmyra, New York." [W. Wyl, Mormon Portraits or the Truth About Mormon Leaders—From 1830–1886, Salt Lake City Tribune Printing & Publishing Co. 1886, page 241]

In 1852, Martin Harris—after leaving the Mormon Church—revealed the true source of the Book of Mormon to R. W. Alderman:

"Rigdon had stolen the manuscript from a printing office in Pittsburgh, Pa, which Spalding, who had written it in the early part of the century had left it to be printed, but the printer refused to print it, but Jo [Smith] and Rigdon did, as the Book of Mormon." [Ellen E Dickerson, New Light on Mormonism, New York, Funk & Wagnall's, 1885, page 12]

The Mormon Church has challenged these allegations. The Mormon Church has attacked the characters of those involved. But the Mormon Church has never actually disproved or refuted these allegations. The allegations still remain.

Despite these denials, there are several statements of those who attended Rigdon's Church and listened to his sermons. Rigdon began to profess Mormon doctrines two years before the Book of Mormon was released. [*Who Really Wrote The Book of Mormon?* Wayne Cowdrey, Howard Davis, Donald Scales Vision House 1977 pages 109–112]

Rigdon's wife's niece remembers him pulling a manuscript out of a locked trunk and making notes and writing on it. [*Who Really Wrote The Book of Mormon?* Wayne Cowdrey, Howard Davis, Donald Scales Vision House 1977 page 107]

In conclusion, there is ample evidence to show:

1. That Rigdon was familiar with Spalding's book
2. That Rigdon had access to Spalding's book
3. That Rigdon was familiar with the teaching of the Book of Mormon two years before it was released and before he had converted to Mormonism; and
4. That the account of Golden Plates discovery with strange writings must now be called into question.

The authors of "*Who Really Wrote the Book of Mormon?*" did some additional research. When the courthouse was being built in Jackson County, Joseph Smith produced a metal box from his home that he personally placed within the cornerstone. In later years, this metal box was retrieved and in it was found what some claim to be the first hand-written version of the Book of Mormon. The authors of "*Who Really Wrote the Book of Mormon?*" requested facsimiles of several pages from the Latter Day Church. They took these facsimiles, and through the use of the manuscript *Manuscript Story—Conneaut Creek*, housed at Oberlin College in Ohio and submitted these documents to handwriting experts without revealing the sources. The handwriting experts confirmed that these were written by the same person. That would be Solomon Spalding. This raised the question of how Joseph Smith obtained hand-written pages containing the Book of Mormon written by Solomon Spalding. The Mormon Church had identified these pages as the translation of the Golden Plates by an *"unknown scribe."*

When the connection between the facsimiles and Spalding's other manuscript were identified, the handwriting experts suddenly could no longer be sure of their findings.

Just as a closing on this discussion of the origin of the Book of Mormon, it should be noted that Joseph Smith claimed the writing on the plates was something called Reformed Egyptian and was used because it allowed the writer to compress more information in a smaller area. However, to date, there has been no evidence of Reformed Egyptians from any other source, and no documents using this language has been found.

APPENDIX THREE

THE BOOK OF ABRAHAM

Joseph Smith's book, Pearl of Great Price, has already been delivered a serious blow. According to the Latter Day Saints website, eleven mummies and several papyri were discovered in Thebes during excavations between 1818 and 1822. These artifacts were sent to New York in 1830, where they were sold to Michael Chandler. These were put on display through a traveling exposition, and this presentation was held in Kirtland Ohio on June 30, 1835. At this time, Joseph Smith and the Latter Day Saints resided in Kirtland, Ohio.

Smith, making claim to having translated the Book of Mormon from Reformed Egyptian claimed that upon review, these parchments were the writings of Abraham and Joseph. Joseph Smith purchased two of the mummies and at least five of the papyri. He paid $2,400 for the objects.

Now Joseph Smith is the person who is reported to have translated these parchments for the Book of Abraham. This is after the Urim and Thummim were returned to the angel along with the Golden Plates. There is no record of Joseph Smith becoming an expert in translating Egyptian languages without the use of the Urim and Thummim. So we need to ask how he was able to translate the parchments.

Smith never shared how he was able to translate the parchments, but he produced his translation of the papyri between 1835 and 1842. It was canonized by the Mormon Church in 1880 and entitled The Book of Abraham. The mummies were lost, and the papyri were believed to have been lost in the Chicago fire, but fragments were found in the Metropolitan Museum in New York in 1966.

In 1967, the Metropolitan Museum of Art in New York City gave a collection of papyrus manuscripts to the Mormon Church. The translation of these documents was assigned to Dee Jay Nelson, a recognized Egyptologist, and a member of the Mormon Church. Nelson, however, discovered the documents were part of an Egyptian book called, *The Book of Breathing*—a collection of prayers buried in tombs.

The Mormon Church denounced Nelson, and he left the Church, taking his wife and daughter with him. They now denounce Joseph Smith's Book of Abraham. [*"Who Really Wrote the Book of Mormon?"* Wayne L. Cowdrey, Howard A. Davis & Donald R. Scales pages 4–5]

***

I want to close out this part of the Appendix with an observation, more as a writer, and looking at the writing style—not so much as to what the writings say. Notice how the Book of Abraham reads so similar to the King James Bible in its writing style.

The King James Bible reads this way because it was translated by a committee who checked and double-checked the translations and published it in what was considered an upper-class version of the English language at the time. In other words, it was produced in their own language with a touch of prose. The Bible had been written by over 40 authors, covering thousands of years, and written from various times and cultures. The common translating team is what makes the Bible read as if written by a single person. It was not, but the translation was written by a single source.

If we were to look at original documents, we would find those written in Hebrew. Some may have even been written in Paleo-Hebrew. Some were written in Aramaic. Some were written in Greek. Parts of Job were written in Syrian. If we had the ability to read these original languages, we could tell that they were different books—sixty-six of them. We could tell that each was different. We accept the King James Version or the modern versions as the committees' translations into the language of their time, and this is why the Bible feels like a single book, when in reality, it is a collection of books—a portable library, if you will.

So I have to ask, given the time of the translations, and the time and locations of the writings, why do Mormon publications read like a continuation of the King James Bible with doctrines that contradict the King James Bible. With this level of contradicting doctrines, these were not inspired by the same God—a God who does not lie and does not change. Why does it read like King James?

This would be highly unlikely as Abraham was about 2,000 B.C. and the reason the King James reads the way it does is that English scholars at the time of King James used a sophisticated variation of the English language to make it more poetic. If the Book of Abraham was written at the time of Abraham, and translated by Joseph Smith, then we have to ask where this form of English prose was slipped into the manuscript. The people in America at the time of Joseph Smith did not speak King James English. As the Golden Plates that make up the Book of Mormon were written over a thousand years ago by people who did not speak English, and whose culture was never touched by the King James culture, and the translation was through supernatural means; why is the Book of Mormon and other manuscripts translated/written by Joseph Smith so rich with the King James prose. If he was, in fact, translating these original documents, they should have grammar and sentence structure similar to the culture in which it was written; or Joseph Smith should have translated it into the vernacular of the people at the time he translated it. At the time of the translation, people did not walk around speaking King James English—especially here in America.

Therefore, as mentioned previously, it is obvious that Joseph Smith or someone close to him during the translation process was very well versed on the King James Bible. Whole sections, terminology, sentence structure and grammar from the King James Bible is spread throughout all of the documents as if they had been written or translated at the time King James English was in use.

APPENDIX FOUR

THE CROSS VERSUS
THE TORTURE STAKE

The Jehovah's Witnesses make a major point of rejecting the cross. New converts to the Kingdom Hall are encouraged to destroy any crosses that they have—not just get rid of them. We can trace this hatred of the cross to Satan, himself.

When I began to teach my classes on the Cults, I told myself to stick to the key issues: "*Was Jesus God?*" However, along the way there were so many other issues that needed to be addressed before I could make my argument as to the Jesus of the Bible versus the Jesus of each of the Cults. I told myself that the issue the Jehovah's Witnesses raise about Jesus being killed on a torture stick versus a cross were not important enough to refute.

Apparently, I was wrong. During the class, I found myself doing research on how important it was for Jesus to die on a cross versus dying on a torture stick. Was it all that important? Wasn't this all just semantics? But then several verses came to my attention, and I found that the issue of whether Jesus died on a torture stick or a cross did make a difference. It made a serious difference. It was the difference of whether the sacrifice of Jesus qualified under the Laws of Moses as a valid sacrifice for sin or not. Did His death on the cross fulfill all the prophecies concerning His death?

One of the things I have done over the last several years is to return to the Law of Moses and to the Crucifixion to unravel as many details as possible. These three events determine if Jesus fulfills the Law of Moses: the Virgin Birth, the Crucifixion; and the Resurrection. These became the three physical, historical proofs in our world that God's contract was valid, and that God had fulfilled His part of the contract.

The Passover Meal is a picture of what the Messiah will be and do for us. The Jews perform this meal in millions of homes each year, and their spiritual blindness keeps them from seeing the pictures of their Messiah. I could go into all the pictures, but for this topic, I need to focus on just one picture.

There are four cups of wine in the meal. Each cup represents one of the Four "I Wills" promised by God. These are found in Exodus 6:6:

"Wherefore say unto the Children of Israel, 'I am the Lord, and *I will bring you out from under the burdens of the Egyptians*, and *I will rid you of their bondage*, and *I will redeem you with a stretched out arm*, and with great judgments;

And *I will take you to me for a people*, and I will be to you a God, and you shall know that I am the Lord your God, which brings you out from under the burden of the Egyptians." [Emphasis added]

I want to focus on the third, "I Will." "I will redeem you with a stretched out arm." This description caught my eye. This is the third cup of wine for the Passover Meal. It was this cup of wine that Jesus used for His Lord's Supper. It is called the Cup of Redemption.

I always thought that the outstretched arm would be God raising His arm as if holding a sword and fighting to deliver Israel. But this is not deliverance. This is redemption. Pastor Robert Probert showed me the difference. "This is how God will redeem us." And as he spoke, Pastor Probert spread both his arms out as if he were on a cross.

The description requires that the arms be stretched in an outward motion—out away from the body, not stretched up as if hanging on a torture stick that is straight up and down.

Now the bronze altar used for the sacrifices was built with four horns upon it—one on each corner. I thought that these horns were ceremonial until I read Exodus 29:12:

"And you shall take of the blood of the bullock, and put it upon the horns of the altar with your finger, and pour all the blood beside the bottom of the altar."

I wondered why it was important to put the blood on the horns of the altar, and why do you pour the blood out at the base of the altar. I discovered that the requirement to place the blood on the horns of the altar was repeated several times in the Law of Moses.

The blood is required to be placed upon the horns of the altar in: Exodus 29:12, Leviticus 4:7, Leviticus 4:18, Leviticus 4:25, Leviticus 4:30, Leviticus 4:34, Leviticus 8:15, Leviticus 9:9; and in Leviticus 16:18. Obviously, with this many references, there is a reason why you anoint the horns of the altar with the blood of the sacrifice.

As I went to each of these passages looking for the reason, I found it in Leviticus 8:15:

"And he slew it; and Moses took the blood, and put it upon the horns of the altar round about with his finger, and purified the altar, and poured the blood at the bottom of the altar, and sanctified it, to make reconciliation upon it."

The priest is required to purify the altar before offering the sacrifice. The priest is required to sanctify the altar so that it has the authority to make reconciliation for sin upon it.

Obviously, the torture stick does not have horns upon it. It cannot be purified or sanctified. But the more I studied the cross, the more I realized the fulfillment of several pictures.

On the Day of Atonement, the priest was required to change his garments before performing the sacrifices. He was wearing the garments of the High Priest, which included the ephod, the breastplate, the miter and other items. God instructed Moses to make these garments for the High Priest so that they would be "for glory and for beauty" for the High Priest. Exodus 28:2:

"And you shall make holy garments for Aaron your brother for glory and for beauty."

For the Day of Atonement, the High Priest must remove the garments—the glory and the beauty. Leviticus 16:4:

"[The High Priest] shall put on the holy linen coat, and he shall have the linen breeches upon his flesh, and shall be girded with a linen girdle, and with the linen miter shall he be attired: these are holy garments; therefore shall he wash his flesh in water, and so put them on."

This is a picture of Jesus. When Jesus left Heaven and was born into the human race, He set aside both His beauty and His glory. In fact, Isaiah Chapter Fifty-Three specifically notes that He has no beauty that we should desire Him.

Linen is a picture of righteousness. The white linen is the righteousness of the saints. Revelation 19:8:

"And to her [the Church] was granted that she should be arrayed in fine linen, clean and white: for the fine linen is the righteousness of saints."

Jesus set aside His glory and His beauty when He came to the earth. He hung on the cross in the one thing He had retained from Heaven—His righteousness. He hung there in only His righteousness. When it came time to bury the body of Jesus, His body was washed just like the High Priest's body was washed, and it was wrapped in linen while the High Priest was dressed in linen to perform his sacrifice.

Then I realized that in this position, nailed to the cross, there were four horns that made up the cross. The cross was His altar. He had spread Himself out upon it. He had stretched out His arms as God had promised Moses.

While on the cross, the nails in His hands anointed the two horns of the crossbeam with His blood—the blood of the offering. The nail through His feet anointed the base—the third horn of the altar was anointed with His blood. His head was cut from the crown of thorns and so this blood anointed the fourth horn of the altar, the top of the cross. Jesus anointed all four horns of His altar with His own blood because He was to be the sacrifice. He sanctified the wood of the cross and He purified the cross with His own blood exactly as required by the Law of Moses. The cross was now empowered to act as an altar capable of offering sacrifices to redeem us from our sins.

After His death, the Romans pierced His side and all of His blood drained out and was poured out at the base of His altar— the cross. This was the final requirement of a sacrifice per the Law of Moses.

Therefore, it does make a difference if Jesus died on a torture stake, or if He died upon a cross. The torture stake could not qualify as an altar under the Laws of Moses. The cross can. So it makes the difference of whether or not the sacrifice of Jesus was performed exactly as required of the Law of Moses and was acceptable; or it was not performed as required by Law and the sacrifice would not have been accepted by God. If the sacrifice had not been accepted by God, then all of this would have been for nothing, and we would still be lost in our sins.

Now let me point out one last point about the Crucifixion of Jesus. He became the Curse for us. When God judged Adam, Adam deserved to be cursed. But if God had cursed Adam, then Adam could not have been redeemed. So God cursed the ground for Adam's sake. Genesis 3:17:

"And unto Adam [God] said, 'Because you have listened unto the voice of your wife, and have eaten of the tree, of which I commanded you, saying, "You shall not eat of it:" cursed is the ground for your sake; in sorrow shall you eat of it all the days of your life;'"

God transferred the cursed that should have been placed upon Adam to the ground. [Remember, Adam came from the dust of the ground.] Now notice the result of this curse. Genesis 3:18:

"Thorns also and thistles shall it bring forth to you…"

The physical representation of the curse that should have been placed upon Adam is thorns and thistles. When Jesus was prepared for Crucifixion, the Romans created and placed on Him a crown of thorns. He was crowned with the curse that rightfully belonged to Adam. Jesus wore this symbol to the cross and He bore the curse that God should have placed upon Adam as He hung upon the cross.

APPENDIX FIVE

JESUS IS GOD

These verses have been collected by my wife, Bev Knotts. I am using them with her permission. Emphasis has been added to call attention to the important portion of each passage.]

Isaiah 7:14

Therefore the Lord Himself will give you a sign; Behold, the virgin shall conceive and bear a Son, and shall call His name Immanuel.

Matthew 1:23

"Behold the virgin shall be with child, and bear a Son, and they shall call His name Immanuel," which is translated, "God with us."

Isaiah 9:6

And His name shall be called Wonderful Counselor, Mighty God, Everlasting Father, Prince of Peace.

John 1:1-5; 14

In the beginning was the Word and the Word was with God and the Word was God. He was in the beginning with God. All things were made through Him and without Him nothing was made that was made... And the Word became flesh and dwelt among us, and we beheld His glory, the glory as of the only begotten of the Father, full of grace and truth.

Philippians 2:5-11

Let this mind be in you which was also in Christ Jesus, who being in the form of God did not consider it robbery to be equal with God. But made Himself of no reputation, taking the form of a bondservant and coming in the likeness of men. And being found in appearance as a man, He humbled Himself and became obedient to the point of death, even the death of the cross. Therefore God also has highly exalted Him and given Him the name which is above every name, that at the name of Jesus every knee should bow, of those in heaven, and of those on earth, and of those under the earth, and that every tongue should confess that Jesus Christ is Lord, to the glory of God the Father.

Isaiah 45:23

I have sworn by Myself; The word has gone out of My mouth in righteousness, And shall not return, That to Me every knee shall bow, Every tongue shall take an oath. *(This is God speaking.)*

John 10:31-33

And the Jews took up stones again to stone Him. Jesus answered them, "Many good works I have shown you from My Father. For which of those works do you stone Me?" The Jews answered Him, saying, "For good work we do not stone You, but for blasphemy, and because You, being a man, make Yourself God."

John 5:18

Therefore the Jews sought all the more to kill Him, because He not only broke the Sabbath, but also said that God was His Father, making Himself equal with God.

John 20:28

And Thomas answered and said to Him, "My Lord and my God." *(A Rabbi's duty is to rebuke blasphemy. What was Jesus" response?)*

Jesus said to him, "Thomas because you have seen Me, you have believed. Blessed are those who have not seen and yet have believed."

Colossians 2:9

For in Him dwells all the fullness of the Godhead bodily; and you are complete in Him who is the head of all principality and power.

Hebrews 1:8-9

But to the Son He says:

Your throne, O God, is forever and ever. *(God is speaking.)*

Matthew 26:63-66

And the high priest answered and said to Him, "I put You under oath by the living God: Tell us if You are the Christ, the Son of God!" Jesus said to him, "It is as you said. Nevertheless, I say to you, hereafter you will see the Son of Man sitting at the right hand of the Power, and coming on the clouds of heaven."

Hebrews: 1-6

But when He *(God)* again brings the firstborn into the world, He says:

Let all the angels of God Worship Him.

Revelation 19:10

And I fell at his feet to worship him; but he said to me, "See that you do not do that! I am your fellow servant and of your brethren who have the testimony of Jesus. Worship God! For the testimony of Jesus is the spirit of prophecy."

Matthew 4:10

Then Jesus said to him, "Away with you, Satan! For it is written, you shall worship the Lord your God, and Him only you shall serve."

1 Timothy 3:16

And without controversy great is the mystery of godliness:

God was manifested in the flesh, Justified in the Spirit, Seen by angels, Preached among the Gentiles, Believed on in the world, Received up in glory.

Exodus 3:14

And God said to Moses, "I AM WHO I AM." And He said, "Thus you shall say to the children of Israel. 'I AM has sent me to you.' "

John 18:4-6

Jesus therefore, knowing all things that would come upon Him went forward and said to them, "Whom are you seeking?" They answered him, "Jesus of Nazareth." Jesus said to them "I AM" And Judas, who betrayed Him also stood with them. Now when He said to them, "I AM," they drew back and fell to the ground.

John 8: 24, 28, 58

"Therefore, I said to you that you will die in you sins; for if you do not believe that I AM, you will die in your sins."

Then Jesus said to them, "When you lift up the Son of Man, then you will know that <u>I AM</u>, and that I do nothing of Myself; but as My Father taught Me, I speak these things."

Jesus said to them, "Most assuredly I say to you, before Abraham was <u>I AM</u>.

Zechariah 12:10

And I will pour on the house of David and on the inhabitants of Jerusalem the Spirit of grace and supplication; Then <u>they will look on ME whom they pierced.</u> Yes, <u>they will mourn for HIM</u> as one mourns for his only son, <u>and grieve for Him</u> as one grieves for a firstborn.

Revelation 1: 7-8

Behold, He is coming with clouds and every eye will see Him, even they who pierced Him. And all the tribes of the earth will mourn because of Him. Even so. Amen. "I am <u>the Alpha and the Omega, the Beginning and the End</u>," says the Lord, "<u>who is and who was and who is to</u> <u>come, the Almighty</u>."

Revelation 11: 16-17

And the twenty-four elders who sat before God on their thrones fell on their faces and worshiped God, saying:

We give You thanks, O Lord God Almighty, <u>The One who is and who was and who is to come,</u> Because You have taken Your great power and reigned.

Revelation 1:17-18

And when I saw Him, I fell at His feet as dead. But He laid His right hand on me, saying to me, "Do not be afraid; I am <u>the First and the Last. I am He who lives, and was dead and behold, I am</u> <u>alive forevermore.</u> Amen. And I have the keys of Hades and of Death.

Revelation 21:6

And He said to me, "It is done! I am the <u>Alpha and the Omega, the Beginning and the end</u>. I will give of the fountain of the water of life freely to him who thirsts.

Revelation 22:16

"I Jesus, have sent My angel to testify to you these things in the churches. <u>I AM</u> the Root and the Offspring of David, the Bright and Morning Star."

ALSO BY THIS AUTHOR

**Live the Fantasy Adventure
with the DULAN ARCHIVES**

THE SEARCH FOR LOGOS
Book One of the Dulan Archives

THE BATTLE OF ES-SOH-EN
Book Two of the Dulan Archives

THE SONG OF ES-SOH-EN
Book Three of the Dulan Archives

THE BALLAD OF PENTRA
Book Four of the Dulan Archives

THE SILENCE OF THE SWORD
Book Five of the Dulan Archives

THE RETURN OF THE ADONI
The Final Book of the Dulan Archives

**Experience the End Times Battles
with the AFIKOMEN SERIES**

THE RAPTURE SYNDROME
Book One of the Afikomen Series

THE 144,000
Book Two of the Afikomen Series

THE LIONS OF JUDAH
Book Three of the Afikomen Series

AFIKOMEN: I AM COME!
The Final Book of the Afikomen Series

THE GHOST OF BEECHNUT HOLLOW
by Moody Knotts

CPSIA information can be obtained
at www.ICGtesting.com
Printed in the USA
LVHW051913020320
648718LV00002B/124